Bat, Ball and Field

The Elements of Cricket

JON HOTTEN

WILLIAM
COLLINS

William Collins
An imprint of HarperCollins*Publishers*
1 London Bridge Street
London SE1 9GF

WilliamCollinsBooks.com

HarperCollins*Publishers*
Macken House, 39/40 Mayor Street Upper
Dublin 1, D01 C9W8, Ireland

First published in Great Britain in 2022 by William Collins
This William Collins paperback edition published in 2023

1

'The Myth of the Nightwatchman' on pages 110–2 has previously been published in
the essay 'Don't Think of an Elephant – The Nightwatchman's Lot', by Jon Hotten,
which appeared in the first issue of *The Nightwatchman* in 2013.

Original illustrations by Owen Gatley, Tom Jay and Tavan Maneetapho

Additional illustrations: page 11, Patrick Guenette / Alamy Stock Vector; page 13,
Bettmann / Contributor / Getty Images; page 16, agefotostock / Alamy Stock Photo;
page 27 © Look and Learn / Bridgeman Images; page 57, World History Archive /
Alamy Stock Photo; pages 123, 135 and 191, Patrick Guenette / Alamy Stock Vector;
page 175, NSA Digital Archive / Getty Images; page 204, Garth Willey collection

A catalogue record for this book is available from the British Library

ISBN 978-0-00-832836-8

Typeset in Austin News Text and Mrs Eaves Sans by
White Label Production

Printed and bound by CPI Group (UK) Ltd, Croydon

To Yasmin

'It's great. What time does it start?'
— Groucho Marx, after watching an hour's play at Lord's

'Let me bring you love from the fields ...'
— Ian Anderson

CONTENTS

A Map of Cricket 10

Introduction: Ben Stokes Connects 12

The Chain and the Notch 17

—▬

BAT

28

The Batsman as Hero 30

99.94 39

The Wood that Makes the Bats 53

Phillip Hughes and Youthful Promise 63

Brian Lara and the Urge for Beauty 74

Interlude: Bat Names 88

The 3-2-1 of the Universe Boss 92

Interlude: The Myth of the
    Nightwatchman 110

Chris Martin's Bike 113

Virat Kohli, Steve Smith
    and the Unknowable Future 124

●

BALL

144

At Stonyhurst   148
The Over: Holding to Boycott   160
Interlude: What Was it Like to
    See Overarm Bowling for the
    First Time?   176
Warnie: The Magician's Fingers   178
Spedegue and the Quest for Novelty   202
Cricket and Sadness: Sylvers
    and Maco   216
WG Grace: Bowler   230

❧

FIELD

238

On Hating Fielding   241
Endless Summer   247

Postscript: Cricket as Metaphor   251
A Note on Women's Cricket   258
Acknowledgements   259
Index   261

A MAP OF CRICKET

FULL MEMBERS

Afghanistan
Australia
Bangladesh
England
India
Ireland
New Zealand
Pakistan
South Africa
Sri Lanka
West Indies
Zimbabwe

ASSOCIATE MEMBERS

Asia

Bahrain
Bhutan
China
Hong Kong
Iran
Kuwait
Malaysia
Maldives
Myanmar
Nepal
Oman
Qatar
Saudi Arabia
Singapore
Thailand
UAE

Africa

Botswana
Cameroon
Gambia
Ghana
Kenya
Lesotho
Malawi
Mali
Morocco
Mozambique
Namibia
Nigeria
Rwanda
Saint Helena
Seychelles
Sierra Leone
Swaziland
Tanzania
Uganda
Zambia

Americas

Argentina
Bahamas
Belize
Bermuda
Brazil
Canada
Cayman Islands
Chile
Costa Rica
Falkland
  Islands
Mexico
Panama
Peru
Surinam
Turks & Caicos
  Islands
USA

East Asia Pacific

Cook Islands
Fiji
Indonesia
Japan
Papua New
  Guinea
Philippines
Samoa
South Korea

Europe

Austria
Belgium
Bulgaria
Croatia
Cyprus
Czech Republic
Denmark
Estonia
Finland
France
Germany
Gibraltar
Greece
Guernsey
Hungary
Ireland
Isle of Man
Israel
Italy
Jersey
Luxembourg
Malta
Netherlands
Norway
Portugal
Romania
Russia
Scotland
Serbia
Slovenia
Spain
Sweden
Turkey

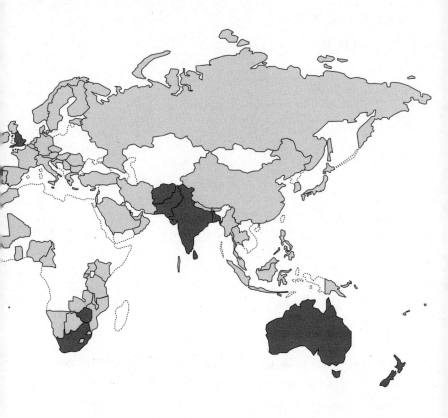

KEY

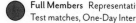

Introduction
Ben Stokes Connects

Cricket lasts a long time. It's a big ship on a wide sea. Even its shortest form takes twice as long as a football match, and at any one moment almost half of the players spend that time sitting in the pavilion and watching. It's a game of eleven versus two, rather than eleven versus eleven, and the length of any single cricketer's involvement comes down to a combination of performance and luck that can go one way or the other. In ninety minutes of football, an outfield player can expect to have between sixty and ninety seconds actually kicking the ball, whatever their position. A round of golf takes four hours and – for a pro at least – about seventy shots, give or take the odd putt. That's one shot every three and a half minutes or so. A tennis player contests hundreds of points, runners run. Perhaps only bad snooker players spend more of their time sitting around. They all have more certainty than the waiting cricketer. The game's endless languor, its long and quiet rhythms, heighten its fleeting moments of contact.

LONGEST TEST MATCH:
10 days

South Africa versus
England
Durban
3–14 March 1939
Match drawn.
The 5th and 12th of
March were rest days.
The eighth day of play was
abandoned due to rain.

SHORTEST TEST MATCH:
50 minutes

West Indies versus
England
North Sound, Antigua
13 February 2009
Match abandoned as
a draw due to an
unfit outfield.

Someone once asked the great Australian wicketkeeper-batsman Adam Gilchrist about his favourite moment on a cricket field. He had plenty to choose from, but he didn't pick landmark innings or Test match victories. Instead he described something far more intimate. His favourite moment, he said, was the fraction of a second when the ball made contact with the middle of his bat, and he and only he, out of all of the people in the ground and all of the viewers watching on television, knew that the connection was sweet and perfect.

In the summer of 2019, Ben Stokes was batting in the Third Test against Australia at Headingley. England had lost the first match, drawn the second and were about to lose this one, too, and with it any chance of winning back the Ashes. The penultimate wicket had fallen with England still 73 runs short of their target of 359, which was more than the entire team had made in the first innings, when they'd been skittled for 67. With Stokes was Jack Leach, a left-arm spinner from

Somerset playing his seventh Test, who'd become a cult hero at Lord's earlier in the summer when he'd gone in against Ireland as night-watchman and made 92.

They were an odd couple. Like many true athletes there was something machine-like about Stokes, a sense of singular purpose. Already that summer he'd held a miraculous boundary catch at the Oval against South Africa in the first game of the World Cup, and then, in the final, had played the match-winning innings in 'Boy's Own' circumstances. Stokes somehow finding a way to win this Test was not entirely improbable, but Jack Leach doing it with him was.

Leach looked like what he sometimes was, a club cricketer who'd turn out anywhere for the love of it. His first match after the Ireland Test was a league game for his childhood side, Taunton Deane. He batted in glasses, and as his partnership with Stokes grew, he began removing his helmet at the end of each over and cleaning the lenses. It was like the Terminator batting with Philip Larkin. Stokes aimed to face the first four or five deliveries of each over, belting and carving as many as he could before taking a single and allowing Leach to keep out the remaining one or two. At first it was freeing, euphoric, defiant, as such partnerships sometimes are, but as the target grew closer the pressure changed sides, from Australia onto England.

Stokes barely acknowledged the runs that took him to a hundred. Leach held on for an hour, scoreless. Then Stokes hit a six that just cleared the rope to bring the match to the brink, England one run behind now, and somehow survived a close leg before shout and a botched run-out in successive balls. It left Leach exposed to the fast and deadly bowling of Pat Cummins, but he cleaned his glasses one last time and nudged one off his hip for a single that meant the scores were level. The stage was clear for Ben Stokes.

The side-on slow-mo replay caught what happened next, the sequence slow enough to track: Cummins bowled short and wide, the ball slammed into the middle of Stokes' bat and held there for a fraction. He alone knew he'd done it as he felt the impact in his hands and arms. The ball was through the field and almost to the boundary before the crowd behind him knew it too, standing, jumping, screaming, jaws flapping open at thirty frames per second.

There it was, between contact and realisation: Gilchrist's moment.

It's a profound thing in cricket, the point at which bat, ball and field come together. In a game that has been able to reinvent itself again and again across centuries, these elements have been unchanging, central to its genius. They formed the basis of the sport when Elizabeth I was on the throne and Shakespeare was alive, and they have spread across the world. Cricket's abiding, romantic image has been one of permanence, of an idyllic refuge during uncertain days. In reality it has responded to the urges of time unlike almost any other sport, yet in its modernity it remains instantly recognisable.

'The best way to love cricket,' Neville Cardus wrote, 'is to see it against the background of the years.' The game is in love with its past, and the past only ever gets bigger. The past and time are its two great subjects, its two measures, and the past is constantly referenced: like Gatsby's final lines, we are forever being drawn back towards it.

For almost as long as the game has been played it has been written about. There's something about its timescales that allows gaps for rumination, for mulling, and its symbolism is obvious. It has a moral element imposed on it, and it has the rhythm and structure of a story. And it's inexhaustible. Every new match and each new series contextualises the last, subtly adjusts its meaning. Cricket struggles to engage the casual watcher, partly because it demands something deeper from them, and not everyone can feel the pull of it.

As a subject it's too big for any one writer, any one book. The idea I had was to take the fundamentals of the game – bat, ball and field, and its internal terrain – and find a way to tell their stories, or some of them at least. *Bat, Ball and Field* aims to be more of a companion than a history, just one of many possible pathways through this strange place.

My first two cricketing heroes were a writer, John Arlott, and a player, Barry Richards, and I didn't see them as different. Arlott, with his typewriter and his voice, and Richards, with his ghostly, easily spent talent, walked me to the foothills and pointed the way. We can each only take one journey here, and we will never see it all, only these elements, only these fleeting moments of connection.

The Chain
and the Notch

The first thing is the birdsong.

England in 1677 has six million humans and maybe half a billion birds. In great tracts of countryside, the birdsong to our ear is deafening. Wild flowers and plants grow knee-deep in unenclosed fields and meadows. With a small population and no traffic, the Downs feel eerie and abandoned. You might walk for fifty miles and see no-one. When night falls, the darkness is complete and enveloping. To our contemporary eye, life is rough. Rich or poor, you need physical resilience to prosper. The rich are beginning to enjoy themselves again in the Restoration, the Puritan mind slipping away; the professional classes are rising; the 'Merrie Monarch', Charles II, is holding hedonistic court. Leisure time stretches out across days and weeks, and across their lands. And the rich man revels in strength and power, in the old sports of bull-baiting and cock-fighting, dog-tossing, bear pits and hunting with hounds; events the puritans had hated not for their cruelty but for the gambling and dissolution they encouraged. They were being enjoyed again at full-throttle and would be for another fifty years. A gentleman should be able to scrap, too, with swords, cudgels and particularly his fists. Some take lessons in London, where brawling in the street is an entertainment for combatants and spectators alike. More genteel sports – horse racing, lawn bowls, tennis – exist around gambling, and the parliament, stuffed full of self-interested Tories and Whigs, regulates this by legislating a maximum wager of £100, more than the annual salary of ninety-nine per cent of the population. Even so, the Great Plague and the Great Fire are thought to be divine retribution for such sins.

The physical hardship and the roughness, the long hours of work and travel, the scarcity of food, the untreated water, the sewage, the absence of pain relief, the lowered horizons and the lack of possibility, the relentlessness, the sheer not-knowing-anything of what the world is and how it works, the fear of all those unknowns rolled up into religion and superstition, the glacial pace of life, the lack of communication and stimulation, the unbridgeable physical distance from almost everything and everyone on the planet ... Any and all of these things frighten and disturb the twenty-first-century traveller to this distant place.

But there is cricket.

Herstmonceux Castle is an architectural wonder, one of the first brick structures in England, rising powerfully above the Pevensey Levels. Its owner is Thomas Lennard, the new Earl of Sussex since his marriage to Lady Anne Fitzroy, the illegitimate daughter of the King and one of his favourite mistresses, Barbara Villiers. Lennard's bride is fourteen years old and already so wild the pair have retreated from court to Herstmonceux (and before the year is out, she will leave the isolation of the castle and its fusty earl to join her mother in Paris, where she will begin an affair with the Duke of Montague). One June afternoon, Lennard withdraws £3 from the family accounts 'to go to the crekkit at ye Dicker'.

The Dicker is a tranche of common ground not far from Herstmonceux. What the earl has planned with his £3 is lost to history, but with that single line in his ledger, he leaves his mark in time and gives us a thread to pull on.

Like much of the rest of the world of 1677, what he sees at Dicker that June day has an alien strangeness: a game played with curved bats and two stumps, no boundaries and variable laws, but already within it are the two fundamentals that somehow contain its genius. It, and we, are alive.

Cricket was a rural game. No-one can find a record of it being played in London before 1700. Its stronghold was the weald of Kent and the downs of Sussex, places like the Dicker. In March 1706, a schoolteacher called William Goldwin published a book of his verse, most of which he'd written as a student at Eton College and King's Cambridge. Its callow nature was acknowledged in its title, Musea Juveniles. Inside, ninety-five lines of Latin hexameters titled *In Certamen Pilae* (On a Ball Game) describe a cricket match. It is the sport's first work of literature.

The poem is light-hearted, a comedy of recognition in which the players compete with deathly seriousness but suffer the humiliations of the game: dropped catches, run-outs, outrageous turns of luck. The real riches are in the detail: finding a place to play ('Happy chance! A meadow yields a smooth expanse'); the umpires leaning on sticks

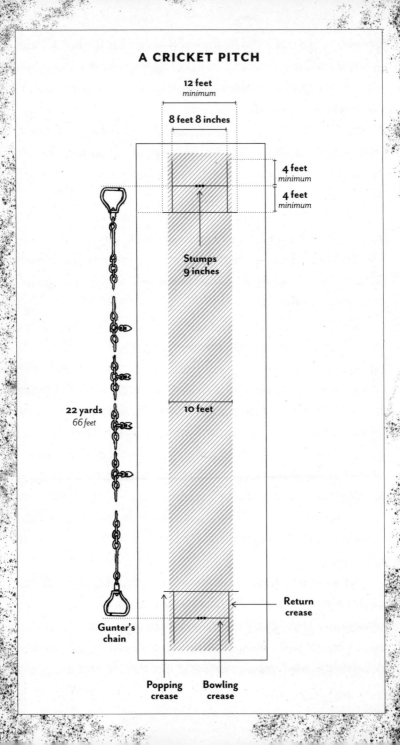

A CRICKET PITCH

12 feet
minimum

8 feet 8 inches

4 feet
minimum

4 feet
minimum

Stumps
9 inches

10 feet

22 yards
66 feet

Return
crease

Gunter's
chain

Popping
crease

Bowling
crease

that the batsmen touch to complete a run; the scorers sitting on a mound and notching marks into sticks of their own; the 'leathern orb' of a ball; the overs made up of four deliveries; the teams consisting of grey-headed veterans and impetuous kids.

What's astonishing about *In Certamen Pilae* is not how little of modern cricket is contained within it, but how much.

Having found a little familiarity, we enter the deep mysteries of the game's creation. Land across Britain, America and the territories was being measured out and parcelled up, and the measure that they used was Edmund Gunter's chain. A 'chain' was sixty-six feet long and divided into one hundred links. Ten chains made a furlong, and eighty chains a mile. An acre was ten square chains, or 100,000 links. The genius of Gunter's system was that it reconciled traditional land measurements, which used a base of four, with a decimal system. It allowed linear measurements to be taken of topographical features and their area calculated. The system was so mathematically pure that the chain and its subdivisions, the link and the rod, were the statutory measure for two centuries, and the chain was not removed from British law until 1985.

And a single chain – sixty-six feet, or twenty-two yards – became the length of a cricket pitch. It was a chain in 1677 and it is a chain now, a distance with magic in it, somehow right for underarm, round-arm and overarm bowling at anything from 30 to 100 mph, the perfect scale to survive across the centuries and across continents, used in Northern Europe and at the southern tip of New Zealand, on the islands of Sri Lanka and the Caribbean, with all their variations in terrain and surface.

One chain makes all players equal, where six feet ten can compete with five feet four,* where a sixteen-year-old can make a 37 ball hundred† and WG Grace can play for forty-four seasons; a strip of land that bowlers cover thousands of miles running up to and batsmen further thousands running up and down on; a distance upon which every single recorded run and wicket has been made and taken. The chain remains a kind of golden ratio, the equivalent of the Vitruvian Man, a divine proportion that has never needed to change, despite the changes in strength and style and playing conditions and equipment. It copes with the natural severity of the professional game, and is forgiving enough for the gentlest of amateurs.

For all of the chain's lifespan, the size and weight of the ball and the natural material of the bat have remained the same. In this, cricket is unlike other sports. Tennis has adjusted the weight and speed of the ball to limit the effectiveness of the serve, and now has matches that last as long as a day's cricket. Golf courses have been extended by hundreds of yards to cope with advances in equipment and a fetishisation

---

* For obvious reasons, bowlers, especially fast bowlers, tend to be taller than batsmen. And for many years, being shorter, with a lower centre of gravity, was considered a boon for batsmen. Bradman was five feet seven. Cricket's greatest international run-scorer Sachin Tendulkar is five feet five. Of the top ten all-time run-makers in Test cricket, only one, Alastair Cook, stands at six feet or above. But as power has increased in currency in white ball cricket – and as human beings become generationally bigger and stronger – so has size increased. Two of the architects of modern batting, Kevin Pietersen and Chris Gayle, stand at six feet four and six feet two respectively (and have played between them some of the great Test innings too).

† Shahid Afridi, playing for Pakistan against Sri Lanka in Nairobi in 1996. Afridi's official date of birth, 1 March 1980, was often remarked upon with a wry eye, and when Afridi published his autobiography in 2019, he wrote: 'I was born in 1975. So yes, the authorities stated my age incorrectly.' If true, then his 1996 record is perhaps less impressive, but his appearance in the 2016 T20 World Cup, at the age of – at least – forty becomes more admirable.

THE DINKY DYNAMOS

Are most great batsmen under six feet tall?

Sachin Tendulkar	Don Bradman	Brian Lara	Rohit Sharma
5' 5"	5' 7"	5' 7"	5' 6"
Most international runs in all formats: 34, 357	*Highest test average: 99.94*	*Highest individual Test and first class innings: 400 and 501*	*Highest individual ODI innings: 264*

of power.‡ Javelins were made heavier to stop them being hurled out of athletics stadiums. Footballs and rugby balls are smaller and lighter, and so on. Cricket still exists within the chain's length. Did it emerge as

---

‡ Making golf courses longer became known as 'Tigerproofing', a way of defending them against the new style of game that Tiger Woods began playing in the late 1990s. Woods' late father Earl said that the best way to Tigerproof was to make the courses shorter rather than longer. Only that would nullify the advantage in distance that he had.

its own universe in a weird kind of big bang, with all of its potential already there waiting to be discovered? Or did the game evolve to fit it, placing all of its varieties and inventions on it?

Was it nature or was it nurture, or is it both?

Neville Cardus, *The Manchester Guardian*'s star cricket correspondent and its music critic too, once wrote: 'I studied Wally Hammond in the same way that I listened to the Jupiter symphony of Mozart.' There are twelve notes in Western music, and they are enough for everything ever written.

Cricket has the chain, where everyone plays.

Decades after *In Certamen Pilae*, London felt almost medieval. As Peter Ackroyd describes it: 'The heads of the executed still rotted on Temple Bar. Stocks were a great public spectacle. Disobedient soldiers and charity boys were lashed on the streets. Oxford Street was "a deep hollow road ... full of sloughs". Side-lanes were full of ordure, offal and thugs.'

Yet even as this went on, the Laws of cricket were being written down, encoded for the first time in 1744 by the Cricket Club that played at the Artillery Ground in Finsbury. London had cricket now, in the fields of Islington and Marylebone. The keeper of the inn at Angel hosted games on the open land behind his pub. Cricket began at White Conduit Fields in 1718, and would birth a short-lived but influential club whose members included the Earl of Winchilsea George Finch, and the Duke of Richmond Charles Lennox, important early patrons and mad-keen players who would employ some of the great professionals of the era: Lumpy Stevens, 'Silver' Billy Beldham and Thomas Lord, the latter commissioned by Lennox and Finch to find the club a new ground. The field Lord staked out was in what is now Dorset Square a few miles to the west, and became the first of three locations for Lord's, a stone's throw from the modern ground. These villages on London's rural outskirts, kept neat by grazing animals, became new cradles for the game as it moved from country to city, places where stumps could be pitched and a fancy crowd accommodated.

The game itself was still odd, still emerging. The first Laws specified stumps twenty-two inches high, with a bail across them of six inches.* It was a small target for the ball to be rolled at, yet as Derek Birley points out in *A Social History of English Cricket*, in those days a team score of 40 was a high one. The popping crease replaced the umpire's stick as the marker for the batsman to run to, three-feet-ten inches from the stumps. The umpire was declared sole arbiter – 'his judgement shall be absolute' – and the wicketkeeper commanded to 'be still and quiet until the ball is bowled'. The new Laws on 'Hitting the Ball Twice' and 'Obstructing the Field',† were back then vital. Cricket's earliest fatalities came in collisions between fielders and batsmen as batsmen tried to strike the ball again to prevent a catch:

---

* The modern three-stump wicket is twenty-eight inches high and nine inches wide.

† 'Handled the Ball' is now incorporated into the Law of 'Obstructing the Field'. The last batsman to be dismissed 'handled the ball' in international cricket was Chamu Chibhabha of Zimbabwe in an ODI against Afghanistan in 2015. Although the batsman can be dismissed for touching the ball at any point (hence the custom of asking a fielder before picking it up), being dismissed handled the ball was generally only given if the batsman stopped the ball from hitting the stumps or a catch going to a fielder. The most (in)famous modern example came at Lord's in 1993 during the first Ashes Test of the summer. Graham Gooch deflected a Merv Hughes delivery down into the ground and then spun around in horror as it bounced backwards towards the stumps. Just as the ball was about to descend on the bails, Gooch swatted it away with the back of his free hand and umpire Dickie Bird sent him on his way.

Jasper Vinall and Henry Brand lost their lives that way. A toss was established as the way to begin a game, and in the years when matches were played on open ground, the winning captain was granted choice of where the stumps would be pitched.

Central to it all, the other seed in cricket's expanding universe was the 'notch', which evolved into the run. The game's scoring system, like the length of the chain, held wonders within it. It had a vivid simplicity that became with time an even more vivid complexity, a numerical language that can describe long-dead matches, that can illuminate the games of long-dead players. The run and the way that is recorded are the atoms that allow the whole to exist.

So much of cricket and how it is framed is statistical. Down the centuries a notch is a notch, a run is a run, a wicket a wicket, their values permanent. It's a bridge across time and the one immutable thing. And in the game's new age, analysts are digging into the numbers in the way that physicists dig into their sub-atomic universe, to understand what exists there, the hidden patterns and shapes made by players that only the numbers can light up.

And it all exists in the single act of the run. The ball is bowled and then struck – or strikes the batsman, or eludes him and the wicket-keeper – and the run happens. Once the scoring system moved from the notched stick of *In Certamen Pilae* onto paper, its genius was realised. A run went to the batsman, and later against the bowler, a single entity both scored and conceded. The contest was enjoined. At first wickets from catches were credited, or at least listed, to the fielder, but then they went to the bowler too, and the game's uniquely individual aspect became immortalised. Every match had an overall score, and within that, many individual ones, both batting and bowling. Great performances and great players became empirically great, as well as anecdotally so.

It took a while. The game's early works of literature, John Nyren's *The Cricketers of My Time*, James Pycroft's *The Cricket Field* and on through Ranjitsinhji's *Jubilee Book of Cricket*, made little play of stats as a way of interpreting performance. Even as late as 1948, when Bradman made his last appearance at the Oval, the fact he needed to score four runs for a career average of 100 was not widely known or publicised. The book that blazed the way, that turned stats into something integral to the game, was John Wisden's *Cricketers' Almanack*, first published in 1864. Yet its stats, however eagerly awaited, came just once per year and were already history. Only with live cricket on radio, where they employed their own scorer and gave them a microphone, and on television, did the notion of numbers as language become implanted. Cricinfo was one of the first truly global websites, ushering in an age of numbers updating in real time and millions following as they do.

The simple notch is at its heart; alongside the chain, cricket's first and most essential measures, the seeds of a universe that can only ever expand.

BAT

The Batsman
as Hero

Mike Brearley introduces his book *On Cricket* with an anecdote about opening the batting with Geoffrey Boycott in Harare in 1964. Boycott played out the last delivery before tea and took off for the pavilion without waiting for his partner. Brearley caught up with him and said, 'cheerfully, I think, but perhaps also sarcastically, "Are we going to the same place?" He turned on me, snapping, "None of your egghead intellectual stuff..."'

Boycott, undeniably great but famously self-absorbed, realised perhaps that Brearley's question was open to interpretation. Boycott and Brearley were both going to the same place, the pavilion, but their destinations in cricket and in life would be quite different. Brearley's question could also be read a third way: were these two opening batsmen having the same experience while batting? Were they going to the same place, the strange hinterland where cricket exists in the mind?

The psychology of batting is vast but it has a fulcrum, a central tenet. One mistake excludes a batsman from the game, a threat that hangs over every innings, every ball, every moment of existence on the field. This single fact has made players compulsive, ritualistic, obsessive, depressed, inhibited, cautious, scared. It has built and destroyed egos, attacked the sense of self. It has forced them to formulate defences both physical and psychological. It is the tyranny of a professional batsman's daily life, when a run of low scores can destroy a career.

Brearley, who became a psychoanalyst once his playing days were done, compared being dismissed to a series of little deaths: 'Cricket more than any other sport helps a person work through the experience of loss by virtue of forcing its participants to come to terms with symbolic deaths on a daily basis', he wrote. And as a batsman, Brearley was intimate with failure. He was by his own admission disappointed with a Test career of thirty-nine matches in which he averaged 22.88 and didn't make a hundred. His outstanding value was as a captain, where his understanding of the game and its players turned him into cricket's *éminence grise*: a man who so bewildered Australia and Australians that one of their defeated skippers, Kim Hughes, moaned, 'He had nothing going for him except that he was intelligent.' In particular, Brearley's role in the resurrection of Ian Botham during the mythical – for England at least – 1981 Ashes gave rise to his legend.* He was deeply scholarly, holding a first in classics and a 2:1 in moral sciences from Cambridge, but wore it lightly, as easy in his friendship with the straightforward, quixotic Botham as he was in working with

---

* Brearley understood not just what he did for Botham, but what Botham did for him: 'He takes the piss out of me and I take it out of him, but he was good for me because he wouldn't let me get too serious and kept me human.'

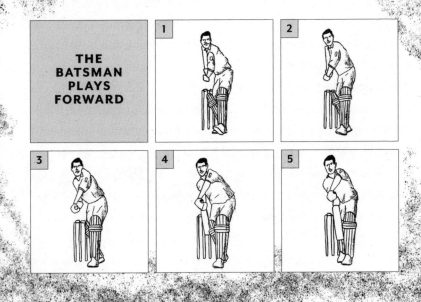

THE BATSMAN PLAYS FORWARD

the complex and insular Boycott or the highly strung and quirky fast bowler Bob Willis. All three would play major roles for England under Brearley. In all of cricket history, perhaps only Douglas Jardine was remembered in the way that Brearley was, firstly as a captain, and then as a player.*

---

* Brearley said this of being remembered for his captaincy: 'I suppose it's a bit like you might be a very good teacher of English literature but actually you really wish you'd written the novels.' Jardine, the captain at the heart of the Bodyline series of 1932–33, did make a Test hundred, and averaged 48.00 in his 22 Tests. It's worth saying, too, that Brearley was a highly capable batsman at first-class level, making more than 25,000 runs in his career, and skippering Middlesex to four Championship titles.

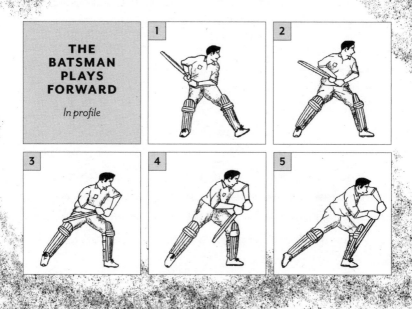

THE BATSMAN PLAYS FORWARD

In profile

1 2 3 4 5

Yet in 2013, more than three decades after he played his final Test match, Brearley admitted that he still reflected on his failings. 'I wake up thinking about ways I got out in Test matches, in stupid ways, when I probably wouldn't have got out to the same ball bowled by the same person in a different match.'

Mike Brearley was at least superficially serene. Cricket made up just one strand of who he was. Geoffrey Boycott was quite different, a man whose identity was so bound up in his success as a batsman that he once said he would give up the rest of his life for five more years of playing at his best,[†] and who admitted that

---

† Boycott revised this opinion later in life, after he had overcome throat cancer.

it was too painful for him to touch a cricket bat once he had retired as the old emotions would flood through him. He could be scathing, capricious, self-serving, yet he was also brave, driven and unbreakable: a player who evoked a sliding scale from frustration to loathing in some, but also deep admiration and unshakeable loyalty in others.

At his peak, he occupied a place in the national psyche that went beyond cricket. In the winter of 1983, his supporters at Yorkshire, his county team, rose up and overthrew the committee who had voted not to extend Boycott's contract, beginning a civil war that raged for months. It was a polarising argument that began over a single innings played the previous August, in which Boycott was accused of batting too slowly.

There were few batsmen as singular as Boycott; and yet all batsmen, ultimately, stood alone. From the moment that 'Silver Billy' Beldham, 'a beau idyll of grace, animation and concentrated energy' in the Regency era, stepped out to the crease and made batting beautiful, it became the aesthetic and psychological heart of the game. And the game itself demanded that the batsman be subject to its existential forces, that he become the hero of his own story. It was this state most of all that Geoffrey Boycott understood and embodied. A batsman was a self-reliant entity in a hostile universe. His problems could be solved by him alone, but he was subject not just to his eleven opponents, but the fates of luck, both good and bad. He had one chance. He hung by that single thread, the destiny of the team bound up with his own.

The great batsmen across history embraced this. They did it in their own way, with their own style. Boycott's mastery was based on his technical skill and endurance. Viv Richards oozed a primal, alpha power that enabled him to dominate opponents from the minute he stepped onto the field.* WG Grace had cowed bowlers in a similar way, by force of personality. Brian Lara was like a great duellist, quicker than anyone else; Ricky Ponting an Australian gunslinger as implacable as Clint Eastwood in a spaghetti western. Don Bradman, the greatest of all, simply destroyed all hope with his weight of scoring.

What they had was a way of imposing themselves on the game that went beyond simply their skill with the bat. Like boxers, they constructed a personality that acted as a force field around them, protection from the endless little deaths they all faced.

It was a necessary thing. Boycott took each dismissal deeply personally, and he could brood for days over one. He once said, 'For a long time I found it very difficult to discuss getting out with anybody. Basically it was because I felt shame ... I cannot bear failure.' Everything he did was designed to avoid it, and he was, and is, far from alone in that quest.

All batsmen journeyed to the place that Mike Brearley's anecdote suggested, a hinterland where they came to terms with what the game asked of them. Each took that journey in a different way. Statistics showed that even the best failed to make their average score in two out of every three innings. It meant that success, when it came, could be overwhelming, an adrenaline surge that nothing outside of cricket could replace.

---

* Viv Richards' walk out to bat was a piece of theatre in itself. He would wait for the stage to clear and the dismissed batsman to vanish before making his entrance with a slow cowboy swagger, hips moving as if he was wearing a gun belt. He chewed gum and occasionally windmilled an arm. His head, with its great Roman nose, was usually tilted slightly upwards, an emperor surveying his lands. For a final flourish, he would sometimes smash the heel of his right hand into the top of the bat handle just before he took guard.

A CRICKET SCORE CARD

BATSMEN

AT AUSTRALIA
WOOLLOONGABBA

V
INNINGS OF

1	MJ SLATER	④ ∙∙ 4
2	MA TAYLOR	⊙̇ 1
3	DC BOON	
4	ME WAUGH	
5	MG BEVAN	
6	SR WAUGH	
7	IA HEALY	
8	SK WARNE	
9	CJ McDERMOTT	
10	TBA MAY	
11	GD McGRATH	

Slater hit the first ball of Australia's innings to the boundary for four. The shot appears in the batsman's 'runs' column and also in the bowler's analysis below.* The runs count for Slater and against DeFreitas, the central battle between bowler and batter.

A delivery from which no run is scored is recorded as a dot ∙. Hence the phrase, 'dot ball', used regularly in commentary.

The batting team (Australia) in the order they will bat appears here.

UMPIRES:- RANDALL/MITCHLEY
SCORERS:-
PLAY COMMENCED 11-00 STUMPS DRAWN 6-00
RESULT:-

WIDES	
BYES	←
LEG BYES	
NO BALLS	
FALL OF WICKETS	①

At this moment in this scorecard, 9 runs have been recorded.

THE "AUTOADD" SCORER

DRAW A CONTINUOUS LINE THROUGH THE SQUARES AS RUNS ARE SCORED OR EXTRAS GAINED.
WHEN A WICKET FALLS NOTE THE NUMBER OF IT IN LAST SQUARE MARKED.

DON'T MARK THESE FIGURES	1 2 3 4 5 6 7 8 9 10 11 12 13 14 15 16 17 18 19 20 21 22 23 24 25
1 - 100	
101 - 200	
201 - 300	
301 - 400	
401 - 500	

BOWLERS

RUNS SCORED EACH OVER

BOWLERS	1	2	3	4	5	6	7	8	9	10	11	12
DeFREITAS	④ ∙ ∙ 4											
McCAGUE	∙ 1											
→ GOUGH												
TUFNELL												
HICK												

*Bowler's analysis as mentioned above.

England's bowlers are listed here.

This sample scorecard is of a real match, the first Test between Australia and England in the 1994/5 Ashes series. This card shows Australia's first innings, after two overs have been bowled.

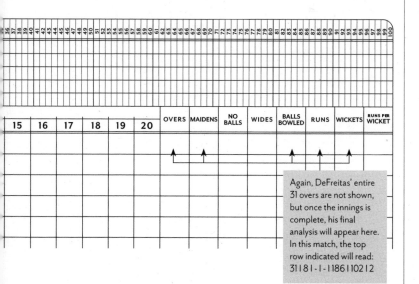

| ENGLAND | | | | |
| AUSTRALIA **DATE** 25/11/1994 | **HOW OUT** | **BOWLER** | **Total** | |

Slater's long innings is not fully shown here, but once dismissed, the way he was out, the bowler that dismissed him, and his final tally of runs are recorded here. In this match, the final text to go in this row will be:
CT Gatting I Gooch I 176

Extras are entered in this section.

Again, DeFreitas' entire 31 overs are not shown, but once the innings is complete, his final analysis will appear here. In this match, the top row indicated will read:
31 I 8 I – I – I 186 I 102 I 2

Like all sport, cricket demanded authenticity. Nothing could be faked, and the results, good or bad, were obvious. Without a hiding place and alone on the stage, those who could somehow command that space had the game and those watching it in their grasp.

Geoffrey Boycott
1962–1986
48,426 runs; 151 hundreds

99.94

He had batted in front of vast crowds all his life, and he had shown them things that no-one else had ever been able to do. Now he was sixty-nine years old and hadn't played in decades, standing at the end of a grass net in a backyard in Adelaide one Sunday afternoon in January 1978. He wore glasses and had no gloves, pads or box. The backyard belonged to Dr Donald Beard, who had been the South Australia Cricket Association medic and a prodigious bowler in Grade cricket. Beard had the net laid by Les Burdett, the curator at the Adelaide Oval, but even so, it was a backyard strip not a Test match pitch. The other players were Beard's teenage sons Matthew and Alistair, and one of the lunch guests, Jeff Thomson, Australia's opening bowler.

HOW TO CALCULATE BATTING AND BOWLING AVERAGE

BATTING	BOWLING
A batting average is calculated by dividing the number of runs scored by a player over a particular period (a tournament, a series, a season, a year, a career) by the number of times they have been dismissed. Career average is the standard measure of a player's value.	Bowling average follows the same principle, with the average arrived at by dividing the number of runs conceded by the number of wickets taken.

CALCULATING BRADMAN'S TEST MATCH AVERAGE				CALCULATING SHANE WARNE'S TEST MATCH AVERAGE			
MATCHES	**INNINGS**	**NOT OUTS**	**RUNS**	**MATCHES**	**INNINGS**	**RUNS (CONCEDED)**	**WICKETS**
52	80	10	6,966	145	273	17,995	708

Bradman batted 80 times, but the not out innings are deducted from the number used to divide the number of runs scored. So Bradman's average is 6,996 ÷ 70 = 99.94	17,995 ÷ 708 = 25.41 Warne conceded 25 runs for each wicket he took, the standard measure of a bowler's value.

In the stats-driven modern game, an average, whether batting or bowling, has become a blunt tool. While it's a strong indication over a Test or first-class career of where a player stands in relation to their contemporaries and to history, it doesn't drill far enough down into performance. In the shorter formats of the game, the ability to measure ball-by-ball outcomes and break them down into a variety of conditions and circumstances has become more valuable analytically. Effectiveness for batters can be measured in strike rate, which can be used to reflect not just performance in a single innings, but analysed in detailed sub-categories against different forms of bowling. For bowlers, economy rate can be key indicator of value at various points of the T20 game.

STRIKE RATES

BATTING

A batting strike rate expresses the number of runs scored per 100 balls faced. Like average, it can be used over a season, tournaments or a career, but also a single innings. It's calculated by dividing the number of runs scored by the number of balls faced and then multiplying by 100.

BOWLING

A bowling strike rate expresses the average number of deliveries a bowler needs to take a wicket. It's calculated similarly to average, by dividing the number of balls delivered by the number of wickets taken, and can be used over any scale from a single innings to a career.

CHRIS GAYLE IN T20 CRICKET

MATCHES	INNINGS	BALLS FACED	RUNS
400	392	13,152	8,944

RASHID KHAN IN ONE-DAY INTERNATIONALS

MATCHES	DELIVERIES	RUNS	WICKETS
71	3,558	2,467	133

$13,152 ÷ 8,944 = 1.4704$
$× 100 = 147.04$

Gayle will score 147 runs per every 100 deliveries he faces in T20 cricket.

$3,558 ÷ 133 = 26.7$

Khan will take a wicket once every 27 deliveries, or every 4.3 overs he bowls.

ECONOMY RATE

A bowler's economy rate is taken alongside their strike rate for an overall measure of their effectiveness. Economy rate measures the average number of runs conceded per over bowled. Again in Rashid Khan's ODI career:

MATCHES	OVERS
71	593

RUNS	WICKETS
2,467	133

$2,467 ÷ 593 = 4.16$

Rashid concedes 4.16 runs per over bowled in ODI cricket.

Thommo was halfway through a Test against India.[*] He had twanged a hamstring during the game, but announced, 'if Bradman's batting, I'm bowling.'

And it really was him, Sir Donald Bradman, at the far end of the net, ready to take strike. Neither Thomson nor the Beard boys were born when the Don had last batted. Thomson had already decided that he would bowl leg breaks as he didn't want to be responsible for any damage to a national icon about to enter his seventh decade, but as Bradman began to bat, Thomson found his run-up getting longer, his arm turning over more quickly. The Beard boys, being youngsters, bowled however they liked. And it all came the same to Bradman. Describing what happened, Thommo told his teammate Ashley Mallett:

> It was as if Bradman was wearing a suit of armour; he was invincible. That little old guy in glasses was suddenly transformed into Don Bradman, the human thrashing machine. He did not play a false shot in twenty minutes of the most amazing batting I've ever seen.[†] [When Thomson got back to the hotel, he recounted the story to the rest of the Australian team.] I said: 'Why isn't this bastard playing for us tomorrow?' He was that good.

---

[*] Test matches had rest days back then, almost always after three days of play and almost always on a Sunday, and they remained standard until the 1980s. The 1938–39 'Timeless' Test had two. Players used them for all kinds of purposes, mostly golf, sometimes fishing. Thommo once tore a shoulder muscle playing tennis. In 1985, West Indian spinner Clyde Butts got married on a rest day. English Tests first had Sunday play in 1981, and the rest day was eradicated almost entirely by 1997.

[†] Mallett told the story of Bradman's encounter with Thomson in his biography of Donald Beard, *The Digger's Doctor*. As befits a great yarn-spinner, Thommo himself has recounted several versions down the years. In one of them he said: 'I didn't believe anyone could be twice as good as Greg Chappell' until he bowled at the Don.

Bat, Ball and Field

KIT OF THE BATTER

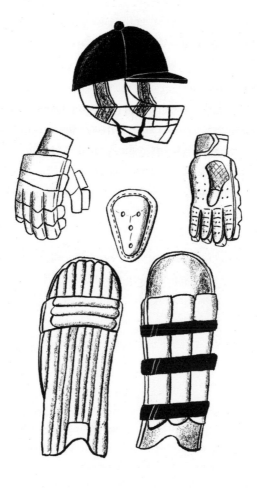

There is an old cricket joke: the first box was used in cricket in 1874 and the first cricket helmet was used in 1974 – it took men 100 years to realise that their head was also important.

Over lunch, Bradman told Thommo: 'You know Jeff, I enjoyed that knock, but I'll never do it again', and it seems that he never did. The greatest cricketer of them all, perhaps the greatest sportsman ever born, ended his days with his mystery and his mastery intact. The mastery has been pored over again and again. The mystery is less examined and yet unsolved, even though Bradman himself challenged cricket to do so (see page 124, 'Virat Kohli, Steve Smith and the Unknowable Future').

If that long-off afternoon in a sunlit garden was the end of Bradman as a batsman, it was an extraordinary one, as remarkable as the last Test innings he had played at the Oval in 1948, when he needed to score four runs to end his career with a batting average of 100. Instead, he had made the most famous duck of them all, bowled second ball by Eric Hollies,* and left behind cricket's most meaningful number, 99.94.

Bradman was anti-hype, beyond ego. His dominance was brutal and inexorable. There was something alien about it as it happened, and there still is now. Bradman's final Test appearance came in the 303rd such game ever played. Over the next seventy years there were two thousand more, and yet among the many records that Bradman

---

* Bradman was, naturally, Hollies' most famous scalp, but he was far from the only one. Hollies took 2,323 first-class wickets for Warwickshire and has a stand named after him at Edgbaston, where, as a loquacious sort, he would appreciate its reputation as hosting some of the most vociferous fans in England. Hollies was a famously terrible yet entertaining batsman himself, scoring 650 fewer career runs than he took wickets, and setting a record of 71 consecutive innings without reaching double figures. Australian cricketer and journalist Jack Fingleton once said that if Hollies could survive his first few deliveries, the crowd would be treated to 'something in batting unknown in any textbook'.

still holds are those for the most runs in a single day's play (309); the most times scoring a hundred in a single session of play (six); and the fewest innings to reach 2,000, 3,000, 4,000, 5,000 and 6,000 runs. During the innings that Bradman regarded as his best, his 254 against England at Lord's in 1930, he began with his fastest Test match half-century. Neville Cardus, *in situ* to observe the phenomenon up close, wrote: 'It was the most murderous onslaught I have ever known in a Test match.' These records highlight not just the weight of his scoring, but its speed – and the two are related. Bradman made 974 runs in the 1930 series – another record that stands today – and he would not have had the time to score that many had he not scored them as quickly. Bradman batted long before limited-overs cricket was conceived of, and long before the current revolutions in technique and equipment, but he has not been outscored.[†]

99.94.

Where did he come from?

It wasn't just his talent that was opaque and mysterious, in many ways it was Bradman himself. There is something about ability that isolates; in that respect it can act like the overwhelming amounts of fame or money that often accompany it. Consciously or not, Bradman closed parts of himself off in an act of self-preservation. Teammates and others thought of him as cold, aloof. He was teetotal, unclubbable and unknowable from the moment he recused

---

[†] I once met Henry Blofeld in the Test Match Special box at Edgbaston. He was talking about the Don, whom he'd known quite well, and I asked him whether the fielding in Bradman's day was as lacklustre as it looks on newsreel. He said it wasn't. Although fielders didn't really dive or slide or bother to chase a lost cause to the rope, batsmen still had to place the ball accurately to get it past them. Also, batsmen didn't run as hard as they do today.

COMPARING AVERAGES

CRICKET

Don Bradman
(1928–1948)

99.94

AC Vogues
(2015–2016)

61.87

SPD Smith
(2010–2021)

61.80

Bradman is 38 per cent ahead of any other player.

MEN'S 100 METRES

Usain Bolt

9.58 seconds

Tyson Gay / Johan Blake

9.69 seconds

Bolt would have to run 100 metres in 6.11 seconds to match Bradman's margin of dominance over the field.

WOMEN'S MARATHON

Brigid Kosgei

2 hours 14 minutes 04 seconds

Paula Radcliffe

2 hours 15 minutes 25 seconds

Kosgei would have to run the marathon in 1 hour 24 minutes to match Bradman's lead.

TENNIS – MAJOR CHAMPIONSHIPS

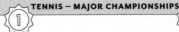

Margaret Court

24 Major Singles Titles

Serena Williams

23 Major Singles Titles

To surpass Court by Bradman's margin, Serena would need to win 33 majors (10 more than current).

himself with his obsessive childhood stump game. In his book *Farewell to Cricket*, you could almost hear him sniff as he wrote: 'I was often accused of being unsociable because at the end of the day I did not think it my duty to breast the bar and engage in a beer-drinking contest.'

The truth is probably that he lacked that social instinct so prized in cricket and other team sports. Writing for Wisden *Cricketers' Almanack* on Bradman's retirement from the game, RC Robertson-Glasgow acknowledged it: 'When cricket was on, Bradman had no private life. He paid for his greatness, and the payment left some mark. The informal occasion, the casual conversation, the chance and happy acquaintance, these were very rarely for him, and his life was that of something between an Emperor and an Ambassador.'

He published an autobiography at the age of twenty-one and was the subject of the umpteenth biography at eighty-seven. His story was well rehearsed in the Australian mind. He was the country boy who made it in the big city, a national symbol, a player greater than any ever produced by the mother country, birthplace of the game. John Howard, Australia's prime minister at the time of Bradman's death and a man who once described himself as 'a cricket tragic', mythologised the Don's story above all others: 'He reminded Australians they were capable of great things in their own right. He was the greatest, no-one will be anywhere near him.'

One of Howard's predecessors, Malcolm Fraser, described a visit to Pollsmoor Prison in Cape Town in 1986 to see Nelson Mandela: 'Mandela's first words for me were, "Fraser, can you please tell me, is Donald Bradman still alive?"' On seeing Bradman across a room during the tour of 1948, Winston Churchill said: 'Is that Don over there? I would like to be introduced.' Richie Benaud called him 'probably the most important Australian of all time'.

There are eight city thoroughfares in Australia named after him. His face appears on coins and stamps. The PO box number of the Australian Broadcasting Corporation is 9994. In 2000, a law was passed preventing businesses from registering a connection with Bradman if one didn't exist. And he probably received, and answered, more mail than any single individual ever – he is estimated to have sent more than one million handwritten replies.

As a figure from another age Bradman stood apart from contemporary fame, but whatever he was took its warping effect. In a piece for the Australian newspaper, David Nason reported that a nephew of Bradman's had said: 'Don Bradman only ever cared about Don Bradman.' Bradman's son John had for a time changed his surname to 'Bradsen' to alleviate its weight.

But there was, as one of Australia's foremost writers Gideon Haigh observed, a 'deferential incuriosity' about Bradman's life beyond cricket, perhaps because what Bradman came to represent was so important to Australia's vision of itself. 'Read most Bradmanarama and you'd be forgiven for thinking that his eighty Test innings were the sum of him', Haigh wrote. 'His family is invisible. Precious little exists of his three decades as an administrator. There is next to nothing about his extensive business career.'*

And perhaps the way to think of him is to imagine a pebble thrown into water. The outer ripples, wide and growing wider, are all of the cultural stuff, the iconography and its translations. Further in is the

---

* The list of Bradman's commercial and business dealings would become almost as long as his list of hundreds. He had signature bats and boots, book deals, a radio station contract, another with Associated Newspapers, another with a menswear retailer in Sydney called FJ Palmer. His career as an administrator was just as influential.

Bat, Ball and Field

cricket, perfect circles that contain great deeds, and at the centre, providing the energy for everything else, 99.94.

For decades and decades, no-one could touch it. The distance between Bradman and the rest was unbridgeable. The highest average attained by anyone playing more than twenty innings in their Test career was Graeme Pollock's 60.97, almost 40 per cent less than Bradman's. Then, in June 2015, Australia went to play West Indies in Dominica. Included in their team was a thirty-five-year-old from Perth named Adam Voges. Although Voges had enjoyed a solid career at State level, making 12,000 runs with an average in the mid-forties, and had scored a hundred for the Aussie one-day side, he was yet to make a Test debut, held at bay by a generation of stellar players. He'd achieved his late-career call-up on the back of a domestic season in which he'd averaged a Bradmanesque 104.46, but even so, no-one was quite expecting what followed.

Voges made 130 in Dominica, and became the oldest player to make a century on Test debut, a quirky record and one that had a certain melancholy about it. He retained his place for the 2015 Ashes but made only 201 runs in five matches, and by the time Australia played New Zealand at Brisbane a few months later, probably needed a score or two to hold on to his place. He made an unbeaten 80-odd there and then a second hundred in the next game on his home track at Perth, but both were contextualised by the really high-scoring matches they were made in – five centuries scored in Brisbane and two individual innings of more than 250 in Perth – and so Voges was, with an average that stood at 54.41 after ten games, doing well but far from exceptionally.

And then it began.

West Indies came to Australia, and Voges made scores of 269 not out and 106 not out. Australia travelled to New Zealand a month later, where, in the first innings at Wellington, Voges made 239, meaning he'd scored 614 runs since he was last dismissed, a world record. In the next game at Christchurch, he played the 20th and 21st innings of his Test career, scoring 60 and 10 not out. Beyond the twenty innings threshold that admitted a player to the record books, his batting average was now 95.50, as close as anyone had ever been to the Don.

Australia did not have any Test cricket scheduled for almost six months, when they would travel to Sri Lanka. For those months cricket had to consider a new reality. Sure, Voges had not approached the Don's weight or consistency of scoring. He was barely in the foothills of such freakishness. And no-one on earth thought that Adam Voges was the second-best player to have held a bat. He wasn't even the second-best player in the Australian team. And yet here it was, 95.50, a number that may somehow compromise Bradman's eternal dominance.

How would history regard it? Did 99.94 not hold the meaning that we thought? There was even a chance – unlikely, sure, but a chance – that Voges might make another double-century and retire ahead of the Don. What then?

As it was, a natural order restored itself. Voges stayed clear of injury and retirement and went to Sri Lanka, where he made scores of 47, 12, 8, 28, 22 and 1 as Australia lost the series three–nil, and then played Tests against South Africa, in Perth and Hobart, where he scored 27, 1, 0 and 2 in two more heavy defeats, and that was it. Steve Smith, Australia's new captain, said he was embarrassed by the losses and called for change. For the final match of the series, three of the top six batsmen, including Voges, were dropped, and at 36 there was no way back. The world had rebalanced itself, and Voges retired with the second-best Test average of all time: 61.87.[*] Like everyone else who'd ever pushed against the game's glass ceiling, he was almost 40 per cent below the Don.

———

The years have shaded the meaning of 99.94. In 1998, a study tried to contextualise Bradman's mark by taking account of improvements in fielding and changes in playing conditions and opposition and calculated that he would average 77 in the modern game.[†] And then, in August 2008, a scientist turned statistician called Charles Davis uncovered what he thought might be the Don's 'missing' four runs, the boundary that would produce that perfect, round average of 100.00. Davis was not sensation-seeking: his was an endeavour of forensic, almost thrilling, nerdiness. He spent some years re-scoring Bradman's entire career, and found along the way that there were many small anomalies in the books. He was diligent enough to confess that there were several plausible explanations for the Melbourne error, of which Bradman notching an extra boundary was just one. 'At least one resolution involves transferring the boundary to Bradman', he wrote. 'If so, a Holy Grail of statisticians has been found ... Is it really possible? Well, yes it is, but unfortunately it is unlikely.'

---

[*] After the Ashes series of 2019, Steve Smith's Test average stood at 64.56, but his career has a long way to run.

[†] In his 52-Test career, Bradman played 37 matches against England, and five each against India, South Africa and West Indies.

His regret was understandable from the view of a statistician panning his numbers for years on end awaiting that sliver of gold in the mud, but the truth was, the best thing about 99.94 — aside from its ability to inspire awe — was its imperfection. Contained within it was the story of that last innings, when the Don, with watery eye, let one from Hollies slip through. Along with everything else he was human, too. And Bradman deserved — he needed — to be remembered as that.

'Ninety-nine point nine four', when spoken, alliterates; anyone can remember it. While 'one hundred' might have its glassy, unapproachable sheen, the reality is that had Bradman survived that first over from Hollies, he was unlikely to have made just four. We would have been left instead with something like '100.32' or '101.09' or another figure that lacked both the lyrical fragility of 99.94 or the roundness of 100.

Buried now by time, unalterable, monolithic, we don't often stop to think about 99.94.

It just is.

The Wood that Makes the Bats

I once met a bat maker who told me about his greatest fear. His name was Chris King. We were standing outside in the yard where the newly felled willow was kept. Huge, fresh-cut trees were stacked on their sides, their bark the colour and texture of elephant hide. The trunks showed their ferocious capacity for growth: they had gone from the height of a toddler to sixty-five feet tall in less than twenty years. As a piece of natural engineering they were awesome. The giant trunks were actually a network of slender tubes designed to draw water from the roots to the leaves as rapidly as possible. They thrived in moderate climates and damp ground, and the corners of a few farmers' fields in England were perfect for them.

The trees that make cricket bats are one of four hundred varieties of willow, a genus called white willow – *Salix alba* – named for the colour of the underside of its leaves rather than the wood. Humans have used *Salix alba* for ten thousand years because it is tough yet pliable and doesn't splinter easily, rendering it perfect for weaving baskets and making tools. Tannin from the bark was used for tanning leather. Willow charcoal was a component in gunpowder. The Greeks and the Romans believed in its medicinal power to reduce fever, and they were right: *Salix alba*'s bark extract, salicylic acid, is a metabolite of aspirin. Within the genus there were many cultivars and hybrids that grew across Europe and Asia. In England, *Salix alba* var. *caerulea*, which had a single, fast-growing stem of a trunk, became the wood that made every high-grade cricket bat in the world.

The bat maker's greatest fear was a simple one: that *Salix alba* var. *caerulea* would one day fall victim to a plague or a blight like Dutch elm disease or ash dieback that had destroyed other species. It was a bit like the meteor strike on the dinosaurs. It would happen eventually, and the meteors were out there, orbiting – watermark disease, willow anthracnose and who knew what else. Cricket was uniquely vulnerable because only bats made from *caerulea* offered the precise balance between bat and ball on which the game survived.

Bat makers had tried to make bats from other types of *Salix* woods. Kashmir willow was the closest match, and produced a perfectly serviceable bat. But because it had lived with less moisture, it had a deadening hardness to it. In batter's parlance, the ball wouldn't 'ping' in the same way from Kashmir willow, and so a bat made from Kashmir sold for a tenth of the price of one made from high-grade English willow. Other woods had been tried too, mainly ash and poplar, but none performed in the same way. Cricket and English willow were inextricably bound together.

To one side of the yard lay the drying shed, a high-ceilinged barn containing rack upon rack of shelves that held the willow once it had been cut into clefts roughly the shape and size of a cricket bat. The clefts looked superficially similar, but judgement of them was the real art of the bat maker. The shaping and pressing of a cricket bat was, for someone as skilled as Chris, not difficult. He could make one in a couple of hours. But each of the clefts drying in the shed was an individual thing. Although they were cut to the same size, they could vary in weight by as much as twenty per cent due to the water content. Clefts cut from the centre of the trunk may have darker heartwood on them, which some players liked and others didn't. Some had little marks in the grain called 'butterflies', which meant they had to be downgraded. The grain itself was another issue. Each of the tree's annual growth rings formed a vertical line along the cleft, a little darker than the rest of the wood. Although the number of grains across the face had no effect on how the bat would perform, there was a fashion for the very highest grades of willow to have the closest and straightest grains from the trees that had grown the slowest.

Aesthetics were a consideration, but the major one was performance. And where aesthetics and performance met lay the rarest clefts of all. These would make the top-range bats that retailed for five hundred pounds and more. The first consideration was a cleft that had dried out but retained volume, which would enable Chris to keep the size of the bat imposingly big while reducing the weight; and then there was its density, which would affect how the ball rebounded from its surface.

From the thousands of clefts in the drying shed, Chris might find a couple of hundred each year that he would reserve for the bats used by professional cricketers. These clefts were engineered like racing cars, to perform at the very limits of the willow. And like racing cars, they weren't suitable for the regular punter, the amateur, because they might break at any moment. Chris took me inside to his workbench and showed me a bat so light and dry it felt like balsa rather than willow. It was an extraordinary thing, but it had split after a few innings by the player for whom he'd made it, a part of the spine shearing away and held in place by an elastic band that Chris had wrapped around it while he worked out if it could somehow be saved.

For bat manufacturers, having their stickers on the bats used by pro players, especially famous internationals, was important for their business. A player making a Test match century may be on screen for almost an entire day holding their product. The company that Chris worked for, Gray-Nicolls, had been producing bats since 1876. In their offices was a letter from WG Grace lamenting the loss of his favourite bat, made by them. But now that cricket had become so big internationally, and specifically in India, where the top players had the same commercial clout as Bollywood film stars and publicised everything from mobile phones to milk, giant sportswear companies had entered the market too. They would pay some of the best players vast sums to use their bats, or at least to have their stickers. It wasn't because Nike or Adidas thought they could make much money from selling cricket bats – they couldn't – but because it raised awareness of their training shoe and sneaker brands. In the game, there were always lots of rumours about who really made such-and-such player's bats, which were then stickered to the order of his sponsors. It was the bat makers' grassy knoll, another quirk of a fragile and insular industry that had limited ways of appealing to its market.

In 1972, a South African golf club engineer called Arthur Garner, and his business partner, Barrie Wheeler, who designed courses, approached Gray-Nicolls with an idea for a cricket bat based on something that had proven effective in golf. The backs of a set of irons had been hollowed out, which created a much larger sweet spot on the club face and made them more forgiving for the amateur player. They thought the same theory might work in a cricket bat, so John Newbery, who worked with his father Len as a bat maker at Gray-Nicolls, shaped a prototype.

Enter next Robert 'Swan' Richards, who was charged with expanding Gray-Nicolls' Australian operation. He made a Scoop, as the bat would become known,* and somehow got it into the hands of the Australian captain Ian Chappell, who used it in a Test match against

---

* The Scoop's official name was the GN-100. Gray-Nicolls followed it with the GN-500, which had four smaller scoops out of the back and was used by David Gower (who else?), and the Powerspot, all of which retain their place in the hearts of bat nostalgics.

HOW TO MAKE A CRICKET BAT

1
The trees are felled after 12 – 15 years of growth and the trunks cut into rounds.

2
The rounds are split into clefts, which are rough-sawn and seasoned in drying sheds for up to nine months.

3
The dried clefts are milled into a basic shape, and graded by the bat maker. Grading takes into account the potential durability and performance of the cleft, along with its appearance.

4
The clefts are machined into their more recognisable blade shape, with a variety of saws and planers used to create the length, width and depth, the bat maker judging which area of the cleft should form the various parts of the bat.

5
The handle, made of three sections of cane separated with rubber, is spliced into the blade and glued.

6
The blade is pressed several times during the shaping process to compact the fibres of the willow, increasing durability.

7
The bat is shaped by hand using the draw knife, spoke shave and block plane.

8
The handle is rasped into its final shape and then bound using twine.

9
The blade is finished by sanding using a variety of coarse and fine papers, up to eight times before the final finish.

10
The blade is burnished with wax, the handle covered with a rubber grip and the manufacturer's stickers applied.

11
The toe is usually protected with a rubber guard, glued into place.

England in the 1974–75 Ashes. Chappell's dashing younger brother Greg began using one too, and something old was made new again. The atom had been split, imaginations fired. Cricket bats no longer needed to look exactly like cricket bats always had. Stuart Surridge produced the Jumbo, a sort of anti-Scoop with a lump of extra wood added to the spine, and Viv Richards and Graham Gooch made the Jumbo as famous as the Scoop. Duncan Fearnley came up with the Magnum, a fearsome club used by Ian Botham. John Newbery, who left Gray-Nicolls to start out on his own, created the Excalibur, which had the shoulders shaved off to make it look more like its deeply evocative name. Dennis Lillee became involved with the ComBat, which was made not of willow at all, but of aluminium, and had a sticker of a rifle on the back.*

The truth was that the Chappells and Viv Richards and Graham Gooch would have been brilliant with whatever bats they used. But the new shapes and designs were objects of fetish, in the same way that guitars or motorcycles were, and they had brought into the light something that had been hidden in the folds of the game — the emotional relationship between the batsman and his bat, between player and willow.

---

* Lillee used the ComBat to infamous effect in a Test match against England at Perth in 1979. His first blow went down the ground for three runs with a dreadful metallic clank. Greg Chappell, Australia's captain, thought it should have been four and ordered the twelfth man to take out a regular bat for Lillee. At the same moment, Mike Brearley, England's captain, complained to the umpires that the ComBat had damaged the ball. The umpires told Lillee to change the bat. He refused, and the standoff lasted for ten minutes until Lillee gave up and hurled the ComBat somewhere over extra cover. Sales of the ComBat, in which Lillee had a small stake, briefly soared, but then the Laws of the game were amended to specify that the blade of the bat must be made of wood. I used a ComBat once in the nets. It just sounded wrong, and you can't mess with the sound of the game.

Although cricket was a team game, the batsman was essentially alone, ranged against the bowler and ten fielders. And everyone in a team had to bat. In this hostile universe, batsmen of all abilities had one thing in common: the bat itself. It was more than just a tool of the trade. In a drawer at the workshop, Chris King kept a series of what he called 'blanks', which were models of the type of handle that the pro batsmen he made bats for wanted. Each was a study in psyche: some round, some oval, some thick, others slender, some with extra grip points added on or shaved away. They all pointed to the intimacy between object and user.

Around the turn of the millennium, as cricket was about to undergo one of its futuristic shivers with the invention of a new format, Twenty20 cricket, the bat evolved once more. It perhaps began in India, where a trend began for bats that had a flatter face, thicker edges and a deep bow to the blade. Indian bats looked somehow broader, more weaponised. Bat makers changed the way that they pressed their bats, reducing the amount of compression to allow them to shape blades with long, sweeping lines and giant edges. They took weight from the shoulders of the bat and left it further down, rebalancing them. Within a few years the new-look bats had allied with a new mentality among batsmen to launch a revolution in technique and scoring. What had changed was not just the bat, but the psyche of the batsmen holding it.

Like a racing car, the willow had been pushed to its physical limits. There was nothing more a bat maker could do to make it drier or lighter or more efficient. So Chris King had begun to think about something else, a new frontier: how the bat might make its user *feel*. He'd designed a bat called the Nemesis, which looked like some kind of war hammer, with parts of the spine carved away to allow extra weight in the hitting areas. Sam Billings, a blindingly talented young wicketkeeper batsman at Kent, had agreed to use one.

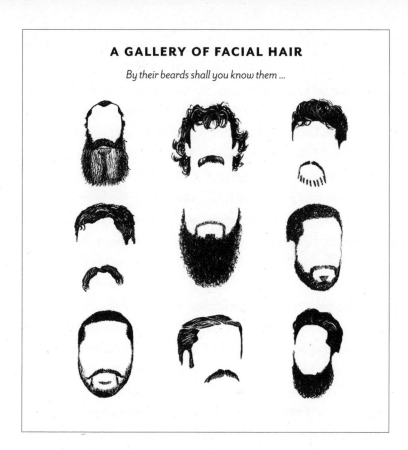

A GALLERY OF FACIAL HAIR

By their beards shall you know them ...

I went to see Sam bat against Hampshire at the Ageas Bowl. After lunch, the Hampshire bowlers were Matt Coles and James Tomlinson. Tommo bowled left arm over at sharp pace and was something of a cult hero on the south coast. He'd once taken a legendary catch when he walked out onto the field after the tea interval clutching a banana. He hadn't realised that play had restarted and when he looked up, the ball was flying straight at him on the boundary. He caught it in one hand while holding onto the banana in the other. Coles was a brawny all-rounder who had previously played for Kent and enjoyed what his profile on the cricinfo website called 'a roistering reputation'.

Tommo had grown a large hipster beard that he was refusing to shave off until the end of the season. He bowled rapidly, the beard jutting before him as he ran in. He looked like a ship's figurehead. Billings attacked him relentlessly. Coles was being barracked good-naturedly by both sets of supporters, and he started firing down some short stuff at Billings, who responded with a series of brutal pull shots. We were sitting side-on to the wicket, which is always where the bowling appears at its fastest, and Billings was hitting his pull almost from the front foot, weight going at the ball, whipping it off his nose with a flourish of the Nemesis in an exhibition of pure nerve and skill.

The Nemesis was a kind of thought experiment. As Chris put it, 'fast cars look fast', and the Nemesis was designed to look like something that would smash a cricket ball into small pieces. Yet it proved too extreme to catch the wider imagination in the way that the Scoop had done. Such was the nostalgic power of that bat, Gray-Nicolls were able to bring it back for successive generations. Brian Lara made his world-record Test match and first-class scores of 375 and 501 not out with a Scoop in 1994, two decades after the bat's first heyday, and in 2017, Chris came up with a beautiful new iteration that Kraigg Brathwaite used to open the batting for West Indies at Lord's.*

The future, Chris was sure, lay in this direction, where *Salix alba*, the wood that makes the bats, exerted its hold not just on the physical game, but on the one that lived on in memory and in the imagination.

---

* That bat featured in another record too, albeit when Brathwaite was bowled by Jimmy Anderson in West Indies' second innings to become Anderson's 500th Test wicket, the first Englishman to reach the mark.

Bat, Ball and Field

Phillip Hughes
and Youthful Promise

It was the start of the 2009 seaon. Phillip Hughes had been in England for a few hours, and looked like he'd never been so cold. This was a spring morning at Lord's, the skies as unyielding as iron, the wind sharp and terrible. It was the Middlesex CCC press day, not usually an irresistible draw for the world's media, but Angus Fraser, the chief executive, had pulled a couple of rabbits from the hat. One was Andrew Strauss, who as England captain played maybe one or two games per year for Middlesex, but who was also about to lead his country into an Ashes series that England appeared, for once, to have a fair chance of winning. Strauss certainly thought so, and he wore a steely look that he didn't always have.

Phil Hughes was Gus Fraser's other trump card. Between signing a contract to play the 2009 season for Middlesex and his arrival in London, he'd gone to South Africa and become Australia's latest batting sensation. In his first Test innings at the Wanderers in

Johannesburg he got out fourth ball for a duck, but in the second innings he made 75, and then in the second Test at Kingsmead he scored 115 and 160 against the most feared fast-bowling attack in world cricket. He was the youngest player in the history of the game to score a hundred in each innings of a Test. He'd got to his maiden century by hitting South Africa's spinner Paul Harris for consecutive sixes. He seemed fearless, and more remarkable still was the way that he played, often staying leg-side of the short delivery to carve it over the slips, and when he cut and drove, which he did a lot, he threw not just the bat but his entire body at the ball in a great kinetic rush. It was a thrilling high-wire act, utterly audacious and pulled off without once looking down. It was also completely contrary to any sort of wisdom about how to open the batting in Test match cricket.*

Hughes stepped forward to the interview table in the Lord's Tavern, right next to the Grace Gates at the home of cricket. He was swaddled inside a thick, new Middlesex CCC hoodie, which made him look even smaller than he actually was. He seemed about half the size of Gus Fraser, who had the air of a bear shuffling out of hibernation.

'This is him?' I thought. 'Scored 115 and 160 in a Test match?'

But there was a sharp brightness in his eyes that a lot of great cricketers seemed to have, and when he began to speak, everything he said and did that day conveyed the certainty of someone who'd not yet been stopped.

---

* Moving to the leg-side of the short delivery had always carried a stigma. Batsmen were coached to get in line with the ball in order to have the best chance of playing it safely, and not to do so carried with it the subtext of being afraid or somehow cowardly. The young Phil Hughes challenged that notion, and thrillingly so, at a time when batting technique was undergoing its greatest revolution since WG Grace. Some five years after Hughes' death, new thinking began to favour his technique.

So imagine for a moment that you are Phillip Joel Hughes. You come from Macksville, New South Wales, a town of 2,785 people on the Nambucca River. The most famous thing about Macksville – apart from the fame you will bring it – is that it lies equidistant between Sydney and Brisbane on the Pacific Highway, with Sydney five hours to the south, Brisbane five hours to the north. Your family run a banana farm. You have an older brother Jason and younger sister Megan. Jason is a fine cricketer, but you, you're something else. Special. By the time you're ten years old, you're hitting so many balls that the Macksville RSL Cricket Club lets Greg, your dad, take the bowling machine home. By the age of twelve, you're playing in A-Grade and have scored your first hundred. By the time you're seventeen, you're too good for a small town.

The local paper calls you 'The Macksville Express' as it sends you on your way ...

But Australian cricket is big. It contains multitudes.

You come from a dot on the map.

You may be the best player in Macksville, but so what?

Try driving five hours to Brisbane, see if you're the best player there. Or five hours to Sydney and see who's there. Try getting a game in First Grade cricket, where you'll come up against State and Test players who run in just as hard for their club team – harder, probably – because they're with their mates and they dare not do anything else.

Australia is not like England or South Africa, where most of the players went to public schools, or India, where it matters which caste you're from, or West Indies, with its inter-island rivalries, or anywhere else. Australia prides itself on giving everyone a fair go. And the country boy that makes it to the national team is one of Australian cricket's central myths. Don Bradman was a country boy. So was Kim Hughes. Glenn McGrath. So are you.

And you grow up watching the greatest era of Australian cricket, the teams of Mark Taylor, Steve Waugh and Ricky Ponting.

They win sixteen Test matches in a row.

Three consecutive World Cups.

People call them the best ever. Maybe they are.

Australian cricket is big.

Australian cricket is big and entire careers are swallowed. Men living at the wrong time. Stuart Law for example, who makes more runs for Queensland than anyone in history, gets one Test match, scores 54 not out in his only innings and never plays again. Ian Harvey, an all-rounder known as 'the Freak', plays 73 ODIs but never seals a place and doesn't get a single Test. Even a player like Matthew Hayden, who will become one of only three Australians to score more Test hundreds than Bradman, hangs by a thread for a long, long while, first selected in 1993 but dropped until a last-chance tour of India in 2001.

Australian cricket is big, and the culture can be brutal.

There are Good Blokes and there are Shit Blokes.

The Australian selectors pick a guy called Scott Muller in the same match that Adam Gilchrist makes his debut, right in the middle of that sixteen Test winning run. They play Pakistan in Brisbane. They win and Muller takes three wickets. He holds his place for the next match in Hobart, where Australia win again. Gilchrist scores an unbeaten maiden hundred. Muller takes another four wickets. But when he throws a ball in from the boundary over Gilchrist's head, an effects microphone picks up someone on or near the field saying, 'He can't bowl, and he can't throw.'

That evening a TV show airs the clip. Suspicion for the 'can't bowl, can't throw' comment falls on Shane Warne, who denies it vehemently. A Channel Nine cameraman called Joe Previtera comes forward to say it was him.

Scott Muller never plays another Test, and retires from all cricket four months later.

The point isn't whether or not a player had made the remark. It is simply that it is plausible that they had.

Big place. Brutal culture. Fair go.

This is how you win sixteen Tests in a row.

Three World Cups in a row.

From big to small: Australia is a big place with lots of cricketers, and you narrow them down and narrow them down, test them and test them, until you are left with the ones that can do it.

And maybe it's you. Maybe you can do it.

Maybe you're one of the few, one of the blessed.

You are seventeen years old when you arrive in Sydney to play for Western Suburbs. Wests might well be Australia's leading club side. Australia's star batsman and next captain Michael Clarke plays for Wests. So did all-time greats Alan Davidson and Bob Simpson. On your First Grade debut for Wests you make 141 not out.

You're selected for the Australian Under-19 World Cup squad alongside future internationals Steve Smith, James Pattinson, James Faulkner, Josh Hazlewood and Marcus Stoinis. You score a century for the New South Wales second team so they call you into the State squad. You make 51 on debut. And then, in the Sheffield Shield Final, ten days short of your nineteenth birthday, you score 116. New South Wales win the Shield. You are the youngest player in history to make a century in the final.

Biggest day of your life. So far.

The big place gets smaller. You make it smaller. You force New South Wales to offer you a contract. You force the Australian selectors to choose you; they choose you to replace a legend, Matthew Hayden.

Then you go to South Africa.

The kid from Macksville, pop. 2,785.

Phil Hughes was the one, the one whose combination of youthful abilities beat all the odds that the mad old game threw at people. He was a prodigy. There had been others. It was one of the game's tropes. WG Grace was a few days past his eighteenth birthday when he made 224 not out for All England against Surrey at the Oval, the innings that created modern batting. Don Bradman put up scores of 234 and 320 not out in club cricket at seventeen, made a century on debut for New South Wales at nineteen, got the then-highest first-class score of 452 not out at twenty-one, and broke Andy Sandham's world record Test score with 334 against England at the Oval a month before his twenty-second birthday. AEJ Collins was thirteen when he made 628 not out in a school game at Clifton College in Bristol,* a record that would stand as cricket's highest score for 113 years, until January 2015, when, in Kaylan, a town twenty-five miles from Mumbai, the fifteen-year-old son of an auto rickshaw driver called Pranav Dhanawade scored 1,009 not out playing in a school match for KC Gandhi against Arya Gurukul (see opposite).

---

* WG Grace scored thirteen centuries on Collins Piece, the outfield named after AEJ Collins, and sent his sons to school at Clifton.

AEJ COLLINS & PRANAV DHANAWADE
628 VERSUS 1,009

COLLINS' INNINGS is a score from a distant time. The boundaries on the college ground were so short on three sides that only two runs were awarded for striking the ball beyond them, and hits down the slope at the 'long' end had to be all-run. The wicket itself was crammed awkwardly onto this space and measured just nineteen yards. The innings' renown no doubt exceeded its brilliance, word spreading as the game unfolded, crowds growing and growing as Collins, to 'rapturous cheering', went past AE Stoddart's 485 to claim the record. After the third day the innings was reported in the *Times*, and when the game was extended into a further afternoon, 'the disruption to school life was considerable'. During his innings, he'd been dropped with his score on 50, 100, 140, 400, 556, 605 and 619. The chance offered on 400 was dropped by the youngest player on the field, eleven-year-old Victor Fuller-Eberle, who later held the catch that dismissed last man Tom Redfearn, thus ending Collins' innings.

Collins became famous almost overnight, with the game attracting more newspaper coverage than the Test match that began a day later. The *Guardian* offered some biography: 'The hero of the match is an orphan, and was born in India, where his father was engaged in the Civil Service.' Collins was asked for interviews and photographs, Stoddart sent a bat to commemorate his feat, and one journalist wrote: 'Who knew him a week ago except his schoolmates and his aunts? Today all men speak of him; he is a household word; he has a reputation as great as the most advertised soap; he will be immortalised in cricket guides; and his name will shine out conspicuously in the lists of records.' But Collins would never play first-class cricket, although he did appear for the Royal Engineers at Lord's. He died at Ypres on 11 November 1914, an hour after being wounded protecting the flank of his trench. He was twenty-nine years old, and had been married for less than a year.

Pranav Dhanawade's innings was separated from Collins' by more than a hundred years, but shared much in common. One boundary was little more than thirty yards, and the Arya Gurukul side was made up of much younger players after the school principal kept the usual team back to complete exams. Some had only played cricket with a tennis ball. They batted first and were dismissed for 31. KC Gandhi finished the first day on 956-1, with Pranav already having surpassed Collins. The Gandhi innings was declared closed the following afternoon at 1,465-3, once Pranav had passed four figures. Arya Gurukul were bowled out again for 52 to lose by an innings and 1,382 runs. During the Gandhi innings they dropped 21 catches. Nonetheless, the runs still had to be scored. Dhanawade received congratulations from India's captain MS Dhoni and Sachin Tendulkar. The sports minister of Maharashtra announced that the state would pay for the rest of Dhanawade's education. He's yet to play any form of representative cricket.

Sachin Tendulkar came to prominence in Mumbai as a schoolboy. At thirteen, the same age as Collins and playing against boys two years older, he made two double-hundreds and seven centuries in a summer. At fifteen, he made consecutive scores of 125, 207 not out, 329 not out and 346 not out. A year later, he became one of ten players in history to make a Test debut at 16 or under. His schoolboy record was beaten by a fourteen-year-old Prithvi Shaw, who made 546 in a Harris Trophy match for Rizvi Springfield against St Francis D'Assisi, four days after Tendulkar's retirement. He then matched Tendulkar's feat of scoring a hundred on debut in both the Ranji and Duleep Trophies, India's first-class competitions, before becoming the youngest Indian to make a Test hundred on debut, at 18 years and 329 days, against West Indies in Rajkot. In another twist of fate, Shaw had grown up as a teammate of Tendulkar's son Arjun at the MIG club in Mumbai.

Prodigies, just like you.

You don't know it yet, but curves can go down as well as up.

You play at Middlesex for twenty-seven days and score 882 runs, 574 of them in three County Championship matches, including three hundreds and two fifties. Against Surrey at the Oval, where you make 195, Andre Nel bowls you a beamer and you follow him back down the wicket and tell him: 'That's weak, fucking weak ...'

Lawrence Booth, editor of Wisden Almanack, writes in his report of the innings: 'At this rate England's best hope is that Hughes has peaked too early, but his dazzling left-handed strokeplay suggests a hand-eye coordination that does not do troughs.'

Everyone thinks the same. The endless upward curve.

In the first Ashes Test at Cardiff you make 36 in Australia's only innings, dismissed during a hostile spell on a flat pitch from Andrew Flintoff, who specialises in bowling at left-handers. In the second Test at Lord's, you make four in the first innings and 17 in the second, where Flintoff works you over with the short ball, and, maybe because they panic at being 1–0 down in the series, or maybe because you're twenty years old, or perhaps because they see flaws in the way you play, you are dropped for the third Test, news you announce on Twitter before it is officially confirmed.

This is how it begins, your next four years of international cricket, when you're dropped and recalled, dropped and recalled, in and out, from big to small.

There are still some highs.

You make 86 from 75 balls to rush Australia to victory over New Zealand in Wellington. You make a third Test hundred, against Sri Lanka in Colombo. You make a hundred on debut in ODI cricket, the first Australian to do it. Back in England for the 2013 Ashes, you and Ashton Agar have the world record tenth-wicket partnership when you put on 163 together in a mad game at Nottingham. You become the first Aussie to get a double-hundred in a 50-over game, 202 for the Australia A side against South Africa A, and then get 243, also for Australia A against South Africa A, your highest first-class score.

It is August 2014, and you are still just twenty-five years old.

Maybe another recall will come soon, now that you are back riding the curve.

The kid from Macksville, pop. 2,791.

It's easy, after what happened, to see Phil Hughes' career as one of unfulfilled early promise, but the truth is less clear. He died three days before his twenty-sixth birthday after being struck by a short delivery while playing for South Australia against New South Wales at the Sydney Cricket Ground. His injury was desperately rare and desperately unlucky, a result, the coroner found, of a 'minuscule misjudgement' of the kind all batsmen make many times. The sadness throughout cricket, and especially in Australia, was profound and profoundly moving. It seemed then, and still does now, trite to write about his career, because so much more was lost to Phil Hughes than just another decade of competing in top-level sport. But his life in cricket says something about the game. By conventional wisdom, he was an unorthodox player. Like Bradman, he'd worked out a way of playing that was entirely his. After his struggles began and his ride on the upward curve slowed down, he tried to adjust his game, a process that was ongoing at the time of his death. As a batsman, history suggested that his most productive years were still to come, in the sweet spot where experience coalesced with talent and produced a consistency of performance. For most it happened in their late twenties and early thirties, sometimes even later than that.

To look at Phil Hughes' career as complete gave a false perspective. His score stood at 63 in his final innings at Sydney, and following his death an amendment to the scorecard was agreed. Convention called for him to be listed as 'retired hurt'. Instead it reads 'PJ Hughes not out 63', a small distinction, but one that holds a life within it. Phil Hughes went undefeated that day, as he had been through his career. His indomitability is caught in those two brief words: 'not out'.

Beyond that were the powerful narratives we believe about youth and promise, within sport and outside it. There was something

Gatsby-esque about it, this dazzle of early success and beauty that can feel doomed as life plays out.

When I heard the news of Phil Hughes' death, I thought right away of that day at Lord's, when, half a world away from home and at just twenty years old, he stood out as something shimmering and rare, not here for long, but always to be remembered.

Phillip Hughes
2009–2014

Brian Lara and
the Urge for Beauty

Talent was a strange thing. Most people seemed to think of it as manifesting in a kind of effortlessness or aesthetic beauty, highest in players who didn't appear to have to try as hard as the others. David Gower is a classic example. He batted as though he was floating a couple of inches above the turf, every shot a dreamy waft of the bat that made facing Malcolm Marshall or Dennis Lillee look like an enjoyable afternoon diversion before cocktail hour. He finished his Test career with 8,231 runs at an average of 44.25. His England teammate and sparring partner Graham Gooch had similar figures, 8,900 runs at 42.58, but the way he made them was very different. Gooch was round-shouldered and ursine with a droopy moustache that seemed to capture his mood, and he scored his runs with brooding power. His training regime was legendary, and when he was England captain, he had lost patience with what he saw as Gower's casual approach and dropped him for a tour of India in 1993, which in turn prompted

Gower to retire. It caused an almighty row at MCC, who gave a vote of no confidence in the selectors, and everyone seemed to fall on one side or the other: either Gooch's pragmatic drive to improve the team by hard work or Gower's more romantic dilettantism that met this urge for beauty above all else.

Gooch carried on until he was forty-four and across all forms of cricket scored more runs than anyone who had ever played the game.* Gower floated effortlessly from the Test arena to the commentary box, where he made presenting live cricket on TV look very easy. It seemed like an open-and-shut case: Gooch had squeezed every run possible from his inbuilt supply of talent, while Gower had been far more casual with his allocation. Except Gower had often said that although it didn't look like he was trying, he was, and very hard: 'I was never destined to be on the ball 100 per cent of the time. I don't have the same ability that Graham Gooch has, to produce something very close to his best every time he plays. There were Test matches where I suddenly felt, at the end of it, "Well, I wish I'd really been at that one."'

The stats said that the talents of Gower and Gooch were broadly of the same level. The difference was more in how we perceived that talent: we gave more weight to making things look easy than we did to having the power to concentrate and focus.

The nature of cricket was that everyone who played would eventually hit the ceiling of their talent, whether they climbed there like a Sherpa on Everest or drifted angelically upwards like Gower. Only a very, very few, an infinitesimally small percentage, found that for

---

* Gooch's record total includes all international, first-class and List A (domestic limited-overs) cricket. Of the top five, Jack Hobbs and Frank Woolley did not play limited-overs cricket.

them there was no ceiling; that when they were at their peak, they were simply better than everyone else who was playing. Don Bradman was one, of course, just as WG had been, and Shane Warne, but it was a tiny, transcendent few. Another one of them was the Trinidadian left-hander Brian Lara, who was not set apart by his figures in quite the same way as Bradman or Grace, but who nonetheless produced passages of such sustained virtuosity it was impossible to think that anyone had ever batted better, or could do so.

The most remarkable of those passages began in Antigua on 16 April 1994, at the St John's Recreation Ground. The Rec was a wonderfully ramshackle place with piecemeal stands all around the field, packed with people squatting on rows of wooden benches. There was one double-decker that always looked on the verge of collapse, especially when it was crammed with fans dancing around to the music that blared from a sound system operated by a guy called Chickie. It was best known as the home ground of Viv Richards, who had made what was then the fastest Test century of all time, in 56 deliveries, out on the Rec against England in 1986.

Now it was Lara's turn. He was twenty-four years old and had played in fifteen Test matches to date. The great era of West Indies dominance was flickering to its end, but was not yet entirely extinguished. The game in Antigua was the last of the series. West Indies had won the first three matches quite easily before England, as was their wont, pulled off a quixotic dead rubber victory at Bridgetown, where Alec Stewart scored a hundred in each innings. Thus the visitors were perky enough in Antigua, and even more so when they had West Indies at 12 for two on the first morning, but then they only took one more wicket all day. When Lara had scored about sixty, Mike Atherton, England's captain, said to Phil Tufnell: 'He could break the record here.' It was a prescient comment because 'the record' he meant belonged to Garfield Sobers for the highest Test score of all time, 365 against Pakistan in 1958. It was a monolithic feat unchallenged in the intervening 36 years, and Lara still had more than 300 runs to go to beat it, but such was the certainty with which he played, the chanceless nature of every stroke and the speed at which he could score, anything seemed possible.

Lara batted all through the second day too, by which point the game had become entirely about whether or not he could surpass Sobers. As play began on day three, he required another 46 runs. The length of his innings had allowed the world to mobilise. There were film crews around the ground and Sobers had been secretly flown in from Barbados to congratulate Lara if he succeeded.

The England players were merely desperate for it to be over. 'His bat seemed about three feet wide', said Angus Fraser, who toiled through 42 overs in the heat and dust. The only uncertainty was whether Lara would make a mistake as nerves took hold and the enormity of the achievement dawned on him, but he kept them in check, and described a kind of premonitory feeling as Chris Lewis bowled him a short ball that he waited for and then swivel-pulled away for the record-breaking boundary.[*]

St John's went crazy. Chickie's disco reached an incredible volume and the crowd ran onto the pitch. Garry Sobers manoeuvred his way through them to embrace the new king. The government of Trinidad gave Lara a house on a prime plot of land above Port of Spain. He had been anointed, and nothing could stop him now. He would never be forgotten.

---

[*] England's wicketkeeper Jack Russell said that Lara's back leg actually brushed the stumps as he completed the shot that took him past Sobers' record: 'I remember the bail going up in the air because he had knocked it with his foot or his pad … I was watching the bail and realising I would need to appeal if it fell off. I also thought to myself that if I do appeal, I won't make it home – I'll be lynched. The bail didn't fall off in the end but it stayed slightly out of its slot.'

MOST RUNS IN ALL CRICKET

67,057

1. Graham Gooch
(1973–2000)

64,372

2. Graeme Hick
(1983–2008)

61,760

3. Jack Hobbs
(1905–1934)

58,959

4. Frank Woolley
(1906–1938)

58,521

5. Geoffrey Boycott
(1962–1986)

*Gooch's record total includes all international, first-class and
List A (domestic limited-overs) cricket. Of the top five, Jack Hobbs
and Frank Woolley did not play limited-overs cricket.*

The 375 in Antigua was Brian Lara's 25th Test innings and, amazingly, it wasn't even his best so far. By any objective measure the 277 he'd made against Australia in Sydney in his fifth Test match was a better knock, and one that had turned a series in West Indies' favour. That he was already a player of rare quality was obvious, but it was as if Antigua had opened a wellspring somewhere deep inside, and everything that he had promised would now flow out. The day after he broke the record, he flew to England where he signed a contract worth £40,000 to play the county season with Warwickshire, whose committee were already on their knees thanking the gods of cricket. At the first County Championship game of the season on 28 April, instead of the usual few hundred hardy locals scattered around Edgbaston, the sporting media had alighted for a glimpse of the new world record holder. They had to wait a day as Glamorgan batted first, but Lara simply picked up where he'd left off, stroking 147 from 160 deliveries, a knock that was somehow overshadowed by Roger Twose, a county journeyman who scored 277 (perhaps in unconscious tribute to Lara's innings in Sydney), an event made even more surprising given that it was more runs than Twose had scored in the whole of the previous season.

A week later, Warwickshire went to Leicester, where Lara made 106 and 120 not out, the latter squeezing a draw from an innings where no other batsman scored more than twenty, and then, a couple of weeks after that, he made 136 against Somerset, passing a hundred from just 72 deliveries. He now had five hundreds in five innings, and only Bradman, CB Fry and the great South African all-rounder Mike Procter had ever scored six in six. Lara didn't quite, getting to 26 against Middlesex at Lord's before being caught behind, but made up for it with 140 in Warwickshire's second innings.

He had now scored 1,050 runs in his last seven visits to the crease. It had taken him a little over six weeks. If what happened next hadn't happened at all, if it had been some kind of fever-dream or concocted, novelistic ending, then he had still produced one of the greatest sustained streaks in the history of batting.

Instead, what happened was this: Warwickshire played Durham at Edgbaston in a County Championship game that began on 2 June. Durham won the toss and went in on a pitch which, it's fair to say, was playing nicely. John Morris made a double-hundred that would go down as one of the more quickly forgotten of its type and Durham declared after 158.5 overs with their score on 556 for eight. Warwickshire went in and almost immediately lost Dominic Ostler, which brought Lara to the crease. When he'd got to 11, Anderson Cummins bowled him around his legs from a no-ball. On 18, he edged one behind and Chris Scott dropped it. 'He'll probably get a hundred now', Scott muttered. In fact, Lara felt he was batting so badly that at the end of the session he kept his kit on and went straight to the nets.

As Chris Scott had thought, Brian Lara did get a hundred. Then another, and then another. He wasn't batting badly now. Everything he hit flew by the fielders to the boundary. He went past the 375 he'd made in Antigua and then on beyond 400. The match was drawing to a close without any chance of a result. There was only one thing on anyone's mind as Lara flayed the Durham bowling across Birmingham, a feat that came gradually into focus as the overs remaining ticked away: the highest score in all of first-class cricket, Hanif Mohammad's 499, made at Karachi in 1959, the year after Sobers had set the Test record. Shortly after tea, Lara claimed the highest score ever made in England, surpassing Archie MacLaren's 424, and, as word spread across Birmingham that something extraordinary was happening, he advanced to 497. He was facing John Morris, who was bowling because all of Durham's regular bowlers had had enough of bowling at Brian Lara. He blocked the first four balls of Morris' stanza, and his partner, Keith Piper, had to

WEST INDIES CRICKET

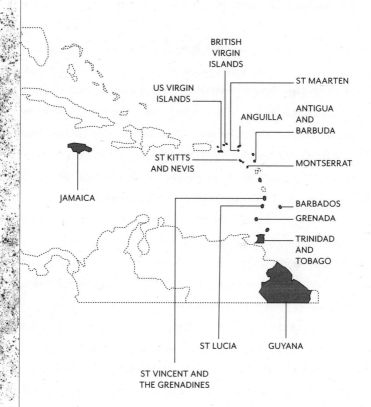

BRITISH
VIRGIN
ISLANDS

ST MAARTEN

US VIRGIN
ISLANDS

ANGUILLA

ANTIGUA
AND
BARBUDA

ST KITTS
AND NEVIS

MONTSERRAT

JAMAICA

BARBADOS

GRENADA

TRINIDAD
AND
TOBAGO

ST LUCIA

GUYANA

ST VINCENT AND
THE GRENADINES

*The West Indies cricket team is unique in that it comprises many nations
and territories rather than just one sovereign nation.*

run down the wicket to tell him that this was the final over of the match. Lara, still unfamiliar with the playing conditions, hadn't known. He thrashed the next delivery through the covers and walked off the ground 501 not out, now the holder of the highest scores in both Test and first-class cricket. It was an almost unimaginable feat that had taken him less than two months to achieve.

How had Brian Lara done it? And how would he go on, throughout his career, to build giant scores again and again? In 2003, Matthew Hayden went past Lara's 375 with a score of 380 against Zimbabwe at Perth. It was a prodigious achievement, but one that would always be asterisked by the comparatively low quality of Zimbabwe's bowling. It seemed as though Lara's reign was over but, extraordinarily, a year after Hayden's knock, he took the record back with an innings of 400 not out, again at St John's and again against England.

I had a friend who'd played in that game, the England fast bowler Simon Jones, who would go on to be a part of the famous attack that won the Ashes in 2005. Lara paid Simon a tremendous back-handed compliment after he'd got the 400 when he came up to him and said: 'I'm glad that Vaughan [the England captain] didn't give you the third new ball.'

Simon said that Lara had been impossible to bowl to. You could send down three identical deliveries, and he would hit each to a different part of the ground. Every time Vaughan moved a fielder, Lara put the ball exactly where that fielder had just been, as if he were proving a point. England were convinced that he'd been out caught behind from the fourth ball that he faced, but after that, his batting had been chanceless and remorseless, hour upon hour, day upon day.

This time, though, there was no pitch invasion and no Garry

Sobers. In Australia, perhaps because he'd beaten Hayden's record or maybe because he had regularly destroyed their bowlers, they were sniffy. They said that Lara had put personal achievement above a result on a wicket prepared specifically for him to bat for a long time.

The truth was that much had changed for Lara since he rode that endless blue curve through the summer of 1994. West Indies had declined dramatically. This time, when England showed up in Antigua it was the visitors who had already won the series. In the decade that elapsed, Lara had been captain several times and lost the captaincy several times, and his fate and the West Indies' were intertwined. They could almost only ever win when Lara succeeded, and that burden became bound up with lots of other things: his ego, his fame, his wealth, his battles with the Caribbean administrators, his separateness as a cricketer, the essential loneliness of his position.

Graham Thorpe, who played in both the 375 and the 400 matches, felt that Lara had become less certain as the scar tissue accrued. In 1994 he'd been almost infallible, but in 2004, in the three games before Antigua, the England bowlers had roughed him up, and for the first time that anyone could remember, he'd been rattled enough to drop himself down the batting order. It showed what the game could do, even to the very greatest of players.

Batting for the West Indies was chimeric in several ways. For a start, the team existed as an idea rather than a nation. The islands were autonomous countries with their own governments, and in every other sport competed on those terms. The 'West Indies' was a cricket team and a university, and that was it. At big tournaments when the national anthems were played before games, West Indies didn't have one, so they used a song written by

TOP BATTING STREAKS

BEST

Brian Lara
(375, 147, 106, 120, 136, 26, 140, 501)

FIRST

WG Grace
(344, 177, 318)

6 IN 6

CB Fry
(106, 209, 149, 105, 140, 105)

Don Bradman
(118, 143, 225, 107, 186, 135)

Mike Procter
(119, 129, 107, 174, 106, 254)

5 IN 5

Mohammad Yousuf
(192 and 8, 128, 192, 56 and 191, 102 and 124)

Jacques Kallis
(158 and 44, 177, 73 and 130, 130, 92 and 150)

Gautam Gambhir
(16 and 137, 23 and 167, 1 and 114, 167, 23 and 116)

Brian Lara had the greatest batting streak of all time. WG Grace had the first great streak.

CB Fry, Don Bradman and Mike Procter have all scored centuries in six consecutive innings in 1st class cricket. And Mohammad Yousuf, Jacques Kallis and Gautam Gambhir have hit centuries in five consecutive tests.

a famous calypso musician, David Rudder, called 'Rally Round The West Indies'. While the whole was greater than the sum of the parts, they were a marvel, a signal of hope and power to the diaspora, a model of co-operation and brotherhood that shone a light on the region. For two decades in the 1970s and 80s, they were the greatest cricket team in the world, perhaps the greatest cricket team that there had ever been. Players that would have walked into every other international side barely got a game (see page 216). Under Clive Lloyd and then Viv Richards, they had a powerful and macho internal culture too, a code that kept all of the stuff about the West Indies not really existing suppressed, but when Brian Lara became captain for the first time in 1998, that natural cycle was coming to an end, and he was a very different character than Lloyd or Richards.

The captaincy was taken from Jamaica's heroic, indefatigable opening bowler Courtney Walsh and given to Lara, a move that felt like the end of Boxer in *Animal Farm*. Jamaican fans were enraged, Trinidadians delighted. In short order, Lara led a players' strike over pay and conditions that alienated the West Indies board, lost his first series, away in South Africa, five–nil, and had his captaincy put 'on probation' for the first two games of his first home series against Australia, who, in Trinidad, won the opener by 312 runs, with West Indies bowled out for 51 in their second innings.

The second game was in Jamaica. On the eve of the match, Lara went to a well-known nightclub in Kingston called Asylum and missed the bus to training the next morning. Nehemiah Perry, an off-spinner who had known Lara since they played junior cricket together and who had been selected for the Jamaica Test, understood him as well as anyone.

'We were good mates. I knew that he liked to go out, but I couldn't go out, party and get up to play a game. I had to work too hard to get to where I was. He was so naturally good that he could go out and do all these things, then come out and make a double-hundred. I never knew how he did that.

Asylum was always packed. Good fun, music, you have a drink and a dance, then at three or four o'clock you roll out, go to bed, then get up by seven to go to cricket – well, I couldn't manage that. But anywhere the party was, Brian was there – he was that kind of fun person. Later on I learned that what he did was, as soon as a team meeting finished, he would go to his room and sleep. So he would go to bed at maybe seven o'clock, then get up at midnight or 1 am, and go down the road to some party for a drink and so on. That was his routine, and it worked wonders for him.'

When Lara went to toss up with the Australian captain Steve Waugh, he flipped the coin and murmured, 'this is the last time I have to do this shit ...'

Waugh, who was in his first Test as captain, cautioned himself against taking it seriously: 'He was a pretty cagey bloke, Brian. You were never sure what you were going to get, whether he was mucking around with your head a bit.'

Australia batted, Waugh got a hundred and then the Australian bowlers reduced West Indies to 37 for four by stumps on day one. Pedro Collins, who was the nightwatchman and found himself not out along with Lara, thought, 'oh no, not again ...'

The following day Lara scored 213, and West Indies won by ten wickets. In the next game at Bridgetown, he played what many consider the greatest Test innings of all time, a second innings 153 not out that steered West Indies to a knife-edge victory. He made another century in the final match in Antigua, which Australia won. He had somehow salvaged everything with almost unfathomable batting. Talking about the experience of bowling to him, Jason Gillespie said:

You're a fraction wide and he laces you through the off side. A fraction straight? He's smacking you through midwicket. A fraction full and he's jumping on it, driving you down the ground. A fraction short, he's pulling or cutting you. There's no margin for error. When a batsman's out of nick, you feel like your margin for error for where you can land the ball is the size of a beach towel. When they're on song, it's a hand towel. With Brian in that series, it was a tissue.

No-one made big scores as regularly or as rapidly as Lara.* No-one could match his range of shot or ability to hit boundaries. At his best he was better than anyone, perhaps even better than the Don himself. And the Don had never been to Asylum before any of his double-hundreds. As Angus Fraser, who had laboured for many hours trying to dismiss him, said: 'You look at the top fifteen or twenty innings ever played, and this fella has made half a dozen of them.'

In those first months of 1994, and on other days too, Brian Lara had no ceiling to his talent, nothing to butt up against, no-one to stop him. Unless you were old enough to have seen Bradman, there had been nothing else quite like it. We could watch it, we could describe it, we could capture it in statistics, but its nature, the nature of talent, remained elusive. How did it feel to bat that way? Ultimately, only Brian Lara could have that experience. It was enough to make you wish that time would loop and you could watch it all again, somehow knowing what it meant this time round.

Brian Charles Lara
16 April–6 June 1994
375, 147, 106, 120, 136, 26, 140, 501

---

* During his innings of 501 at Edgbaston, Lara struck 62 fours and 10 sixes, the highest number of boundaries in a single innings, and he made the most runs in a day's play – 390. At one point he was scoring so rapidly that, in his partnership of 314 with Trevor Penney, Penney's contribution was 44.

INTERLUDE
BAT NAMES

The makers of cricket bats sold a fantasy, and that fantasy had a language, a lingua franca of the areas in which men buy: sex, technology, power. Every spring, over four or five seasons, I watched the market boom forwards, each edition more fevered, more heightened, more alluring and more ridiculous than the last.

First was the common language used to describe the bat itself. Profiles were always 'massive', edges 'imposing', bows 'exaggerated' and 'deep', spines 'steep', middles 'huge', willow 'prime'.

And then there was the other language, the honey trap, reflecting the buyer's image of himself as a cricketer back at him. Here was how bat makers saw their public, in the way that they named their products. Each somehow identified the kind of player that might want it, and massaged his ego, a vision of his idealised self.

There were bats named after gods and kings, bats for myths and legends: the Newbery Mjolnir, the Gunn & Moore Mythos, the Vulcan Zephrus, the Red Ink Syrius, the H4L Devil 666, the Gunn & Moore Zelos, the Hunts County Aura, the Samurai Tessen, the Choice Saladin, the Ton Gladiator, the Kippax Colossus Genesis.

There were bats for soldiers and fighters: the Newbery B52 Bomber, the SF Sword, the Spartan Steel, the Kookaburra Recoil, the Instinct Sniper Upper Class, the Hawk X-Bow, the Gray-Nicolls Quantum Warrior, the Boom Boom Blaze, the Bulldog Spirit, the Choice Willow Teutonic, the Instinct AK47, the Newbery Uzi.

There were bats that sounded like an obscure Metallica B-side: the Hell4Leather 666 Monster, the Gray-Nicolls Oblivion Slayer, the Willostix Medusa, the SAF Hades, the Choice Willow Immortal, the Vulcan Fire, the Hunts County Mettle Monster, the Woodstock Festival.

There were bats named after nature's most powerful creatures, red in tooth and claw: the Buffalo Bison, the Shark Tiger, the Bulldog Growler, the Millichamp and Hall Raven Noir, the Kookaburra Rampage, the Warsop Stebbing Marlin.

There were bats for the esoteric, the believer in fate and destiny: the Salix Pod Finite, the Newbery Phantom, the Kookaburra Ghost, the Gunn & Moore Noir, the MRF Genius, the DSC Intense, the Hunts County Neo, the Solitaire Pink, the SAF Infinity.

And there were bats that appealed to the kind of rugged manhood that vanished with Charles Bronson and Clint Eastwood; bats that sounded like extinct clothing brands or pub machine condoms: the Chase Volante, the TP Willow Rumpus, the Samurai Keibo, the Kookaburra Rogue, the Woodstock Curve Platinum, the Vulcan Apollo, the Chase Lancer, the GM Epic DXM, the Willostix Anaconda, the Gladius Fire Heart, the Black Cat Phantom, the Puma Cobalt, the Adidas Libro, the Charlie French Recurve.

With a simple frame of language, almost identical objects could be subtly shunted towards their demographic, a demographic longing for their fantasy to be true. The names may be funny, but the psychology they describe was a fragile crossover of ego and id, a place where fantasy and desire intersect with commerce and reality.

1720 – The earliest cricket bats looked more like hockey sticks. There is a theory that the first games of cricket were played with shepherds' crooks.

1750 – The Laws evolved to allow 'length bowling', which was still performed underarm. The cricket bat became roughly parallel with a maximum width of 4.25 inches (still true today). These were extremely bottom heavy. Batting technique began to adopt a more vertical swing, rather than the earlier horizontal, 'sweeping' style.

1750–1820 – The cricket bat stayed at the maximum width, but the blade length and shape changed over this period.

1820s – Roundarm bowling was allowed, instigating more bounce so the cricket bat became lighter with a higher 'swell', more like the modern bat.

1830s – Until this period all cricket bats were carved from one piece of willow. Because of increased breakages as the ball travelled faster due to bowling advances, cricket bat makers started to splice handles into bats. Handles were either solid willow or ash.

1840 – The first recorded use of a spring being inserted into the handles of the cricket bat. These were initially whalebone, then later India rubber.

1853 – Thomas Nixon, a Notts cricketer, introduced the use of cane in handles.

1864 – Overarm bowling was introduced and as a result, bats become lighter and more carefully shaped. Handles were intricate constructions and were nearly all made of cane with rubber grips.

1870s – The modern bat shape emerges, and due to the MCC regulatory committee, remains similar today.

1974 – The first GN100 Scoop was released, the first bat to turn shaping on its head by removing the wood from the centre of the back of the bat. By removing this wood, the bat became lighter and its pickup improved.

AGES OF THE BAT

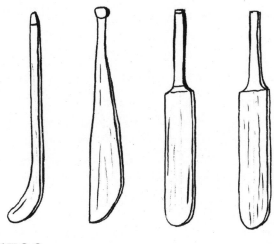

1720 ⟶

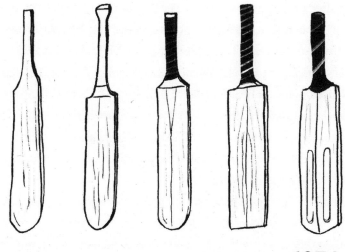

1974

The 3-2-1 of
the Universe Boss

Chris Gayle stood by the boundary at the Blundstone Arena in Hobart, Tasmania. It was a Thursday evening in January, nearly nine years after he had awoken to discover that he'd been bought by the Kolkata Knight Riders for US$800,000 in the first IPL player auction. In those nine years, he'd played for Kings XI Punjab, Royal Challengers Bangalore, Barisal Burners, Chittagong Vikings, Dhakar Gladiators, Karachi Kings, Jamaica Tallawahs, Lahore Qalanders, Matabeleland Tuskers, Rangpur Riders, Somerset, St Kitts and Nevis Patriots, Sydney Thunder and Melbourne Renegades, made many millions of dollars and become the Twenty20 format's defining star, its avatar, its Grace, its Bradman.

Tonight it was the Melbourne Renegades. He was clad in their bright red shirt, festooned with logos for KFC and True Value Solar, and the black bandana he wore under his helmet. He had a way of looking cool in such terrible clothing, which was lucky considering he spent so much of his life wearing it. It was all part of an image that he curated on various social media platforms where he had styled himself as the 'Universe Boss'. The Universe Boss lived the kind of life that the name suggested: one of money, travel, women and luxury. The Universe Boss spent most of his leisure time sitting by swimming pools in top hotels, drinking brandy and surrounded by pretty girls in bikinis. He broke this up with sessions in the gym, where he jacked up his considerable physique to universal proportions.

But the true substance of the Universe Boss came on the field of play. This January night in Hobart was typical. He had scored 41 runs from 15 deliveries, muscling Shaun Tait, one of the world's fastest bowlers, for consecutive giant sixes. The crowd were still buzzing and excited as Gayle prepared to speak to Network Ten's Mel McLaughlin, who was conducting the pitchside interviews for television.

And then Chris Gayle blew up the whole Universe Boss thing in a couple of sentences.

———

He had not always been Universe Boss material. After all, no-one is born the Universe Boss. It had been an act of reinvention. At first he was a tall, skinny left-hander from Kingston, Jamaica, who made his way into the West Indies side at the age of 21 just as their decline was becoming precipitous. They had Brian Lara, of course, and another left-handed batsman, Shivnarine Chanderpaul, who was from Guyana and was extraordinary in his own way, as ugly in style as Lara was princely. The West Indies players were underpaid and their organisation could be ramshackle and Chris Gayle got into almost as many scraps with the West Indies Cricket Board as Lara did; nonetheless he deserved to join Lara and Chanderpaul as a contemporary great of

West Indies batting. He did some remarkable things, including making two Test triple-centuries, joining Lara, Bradman and Virender Sehwag as the only men to do so. He scored a Test hundred from 70 deliveries, and hit the first ball of a Test match for six, the only time it had ever been done. He was also one of only three men to have scored a double-century in a one-day international.

But it was from Twenty20 cricket that the Universe Boss emerged. T20 had begun in England in 2003, the idea of a marketing executive called Stuart Robertson. At first the players thought it was a joke, a game of hit-and-giggle. They weren't sure of the tactics or what constituted a good score, or how you played a game in which it often didn't matter if a batsman got out. When Australia and New Zealand contested the first T20 international in 2005, the New Zealand players wore retro kit and comedy wigs. The Australian captain Ricky Ponting was particularly scathing about how much he hated it. But the public didn't share his view. From the format's very first season in England, crowds vastly exceeded expectations, enjoying a game that could be fitted into a summer evening after work. Television companies were delighted by a game which filled a night's viewing and offered an opportunity for adverts at the end of each over and during concocted 'time-outs'.

Twenty20 reached a tipping point when the first World Cup took place in South Africa in 2007 and India won it, beating their greatest rivals Pakistan in the final. In 1983, India had won the ODI World Cup by upsetting the holders West Indies at Lord's and it had provoked an apparently insatiable hunger for limited-overs cricket there. Now, the same thing happened again. As the new India emerged as an economic powerhouse and global player, Lalit Modi, the entrepreneurial son of a famous industrialist, came up with the idea of the Indian Premier League (IPL), a competition to reflect the new nation. He created a series of franchise teams that were bought by India's new, rich consortiums that included billionaires and Bollywood stars. Players were allocated to these teams by auction in which teams bid for their services, the player being paid the amount of the winning bid. At the first auction in 2008, seven players were sold for more than US$1m, and more than twenty, including Gayle, received bids of US$500,000 or above. Even players at the bottom end of the scale had offers of US$200,000 for six weeks' work. Modi had the vision to show the first IPL free on YouTube, which meant that the vast tracts of India with no cable TV could watch it. Six hits, the onfield currency of the new game, were referred to as 'DLF Maximums' after a canny sponsor, and Modi was a constant presence, giving TV interviews, dancing about in the stands and telling everyone who'd listen how brilliant he was. Even Ricky Ponting enjoyed it, signing to play for Mumbai Indians, where he joined up with Sachin Tendulkar to form an aged yet nostalgic partnership that quickly became known as 'Pondulkar' by the fans.

There were rumours of wild parties and rock star behaviour in the IPL's first few years, but it soon became too serious for that, a giant existential force that changed the shape of cricket. Similar competitions began across the world and the notion of the 'franchise player', a gun for hire who'd hop on a plane at a moment's notice, emerged. Cricket's often baroque financing was jolted into a new pattern. It had worked, broadly, on a trickle-down system where broadcasting and licensing revenues went to the individual national boards, who used the cash to fund their international and domestic programmes. But the distribution was not equitable, and after a series of internecine power grabs India, England and Australia emerged as 'The Big Three' that, one way or another, received or controlled the bulk of the billions. They could afford to pay their leading players centrally, and

A REVOLUTION IN TECHNIQUE:
REVERSE AND SWITCH-HITTING

The advent of T20 cricket in 2003 began the greatest revolution in batting technique since Grace started attacking the bowling in the 1860s. With the need to score from every ball, new and daring feats of imagination and skill came into the game.

REVERSE SWEEPING

While the principle had existed at least since the 1980s – England's Mike Gatting was pilloried for being dismissed playing the shot in the 1987 World Cup final against Australia – it has become a standard part of the modern player's game. While a conventional sweep, for the right-handed batsman, hits the ball into the leg side, the reverse sweep is a mirror image, hit into the off side, generally behind square. Some players reverse their grip in order to hit the ball harder.

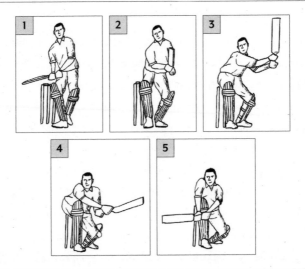

SCOOPING AND RAMPING

These shots are designed to exploit
the unguarded areas of the field behind the wicketkeeper.

The Scoop: Sri Lanka's Tillakaratne Dilshan popularised the 'Dilscoop', an insanely dangerous shot played by dropping to one knee and holding the bat horizontally in front of his face to flip it backwards over his own head and the wicketkeeper's (the scoop was arguably invented in 2002 by Zimbabwe's Douglas Marillier). It was soon adapted to lessen the risk of removing the batter's own teeth, the player moving to off or leg as the ball is delivered and then flicking the ball behind them.

The Ramp: A variation of the scoop played to a shorter ball bouncing higher, the player uses a horizontal bat to lift the ball upwards and backwards. When played to a fast bowler's bouncer, it's often referred to as an upper cut.

SWITCH-HITTING

First played by England's Kevin Pietersen against New Zealand in 2006, it takes its name from baseball sluggers who can hit both right- and left-handed. As the bowler delivers, the right-handed batsman spins around into a left-hander's stance and adjusts his grip accordingly. The benefit is in exposing new areas of the field to an attacking shot. MCC briefly considered banning the switch-hit as unfair, but as Pietersen pointed out, a bowler should have more chance of dismissing him left-handed than right ...

exert a degree of autonomy over the cricket they played. Further down the hierarchy, boards were powerless to stop their stars becoming freelancers, contracted by T20 leagues that followed the IPL model and emerged across the world. This was especially true of West Indies, where relations between players and the board were already strained, and half of the team were in demand as Twenty20 stars. The Universe Boss, for example, could make ten times as much money playing in an obscure Canadian T20 league than a two-Test series against India.

—

In the first game of that transformative 2007 T20 World Cup, Chris Gayle scored 117 from 57 deliveries, ten of which he hit for six. It was the first hundred in international T20 cricket and it was a heightened experience, foreshadowing what the Universe Boss would go on to achieve. Along with the ten sixes, he hit seven fours, meaning that 88 of his runs came in boundaries, more than three-quarters of his total. Gayle had fastened onto the value of being able to hit boundaries, and in particular, sixes. They were the primary currency for a batsman looking to maximise his potential in a shortened game, and the Universe Boss would hit more of them than anyone else who had ever played.

And India, with its small grounds and flat wickets, was ideally suited to his purpose. He missed the first season of the IPL due to a mixture of injury and unavailability, but once he joined Royal Challengers Bangalore for the fourth edition of the tournament, he became its dominant player, its defining force.

The figures that he produced in the IPL and around the globe were dizzying and vertiginously unapproachable. Like Bradman, he was more than 30 per cent better than anyone else. He had the records for the highest score, the fastest fifty, the most runs, the most sixes, the most centuries. Those last two records were the most telling. By the end of 2019, Gayle had scored twenty-two T20 hundreds. The next best was eight, by Michael Klinger. Gayle had hit 958 sixes. The next best was 625 by Keiron Pollard. Over his T20 career, Gayle had hit one in every nine deliveries he faced for six. He scored more than 13,000 runs in the format. The next best was Brendon McCullum's 9,922. His highest score, 175 not out made for Royal Challengers Bangalore against Pune Warriors at the 2013 IPL, featured 17 sixes and 14 fours, meaning that 154 of his runs came in boundaries, the greatest percentage ever recorded. About the only two records he didn't hold were for the highest average and the fastest strike rate. But those who could beat his average could not match his strike rate, and those who matched his strike rate didn't come close to his average. Gayle scored more runs more quickly than anyone else, and he did it by a distance that only WG Grace and Don Bradman had ever flown above the competition.

———

Ever since Gayle was sixteen years old, he'd been having episodes where he felt short of breath, and if they happened when he was playing he'd have to crouch down and ask the umpires to hold up the game for a moment. He was expert at hiding it, so no-one really knew. During the West Indies tour of Australia in 2005, while his teammates flew to Adelaide, Gayle remained in Melbourne for surgery to have a hole in his heart corrected. After the Universe Boss thing in Hobart blew up, he published an autobiography called *Six Machine* which began by describing what happened after the operation.

'We have a saying in Jamaica: "Use sleep an' mark death." Sleep foreshadows death. You get warnings in life and a wise man heeds them. In that moment, I realise I have changed. Looking down at the wires, the patches, my heart no longer jumping under my skin, I make the vow. From this day on, I'm going to enjoy life endlessly. Whenever – God's will – I get better, I'm going to do everything to the fullest. No waiting, no hedging, no compromises, no apologies. Night won't stop me, dawn won't stop me. Wherever I go, I'm going to have fun.'

Here was the birth of the Universe Boss, a hedonist at the crease and away from it. Coming at the right hour. Four years later, he looked different. He had laid slabs of muscle on his shoulders and chest and back. He grew his hair into long braids. He seemed less mobile but much more powerful. At the crease, he widened his stance, eradicating the need to play forward or back; instead, he simply rocked one way or the other to transfer his weight. His bat looked like a railway sleeper and he swung in a simple arc. In T20 cricket, the fielding regulations meant that in the first six overs of an innings the fielding side had to keep six men inside the thirty-metre circle around the wicket, rendering them almost useless in the face of Gayle's power. Even his mis-hits flew to the boundary. By the time more fielders were permitted outside of the circle, he was set and he simply hit it over them. He seemed to realise something else: that he could use his power to demoralise the opposition. There was something emasculating about his hitting. The ball didn't just go over the boundary rope, it usually went into the stands and sometimes onto the roof and out of the stadium. The bowler's self-image was as badly dented as his figures.

All the while Gayle made subtle adjustments that were sometimes lost in the general melee. He realised that he scored so quickly once he was set, he could permit himself time to get in. It wasn't unusual for his score after fourteen or fifteen deliveries to still be in single figures, because the investment was worthwhile.

MOST SIXES HIT (INTERNATIONALS)

553

1. Chris Gayle
(West Indies)
553 in 483 international
matches

476

2. Shahid Afridi
(Pakistan)
476 in 524 international
matches

464

3. Rohit Sharma
(India)
464 in 400 international
matches

398

4. Brendon McCullum
(New Zealand)
398 in 432 international
matches

359

5. MS Dhoni
(India)
359 in 538 international
matches

It was all part of the show, all part of being the Universe Boss. If cricket writers ever asked him about how he did what he did, he would shrug or smile and dodge the question. On the Boss's social media feeds, he communicated mainly in emoticons. He seemed to understand the value of image and of mystery.

Being the Universe Boss was like being in the magic circle. As T20 franchises began to employ armies of analysts and specialist coaches to deconstruct every ball of every game, there was a value to this mystery. The Universe Boss had them all on a string. When he batted, the opposition were trying to dismiss the image as much as the man. Underneath the smokescreen, everything Gayle did was carefully thought out, from the physical overhaul to the finer points of his technique, which was essentially a distillation of all he'd been trying to achieve. In one of his rare public comments on how he did what he did, he said: 'When a fast bowler runs in to me, my breathing is controlled. So you keep a still head, slow down your breathing. Sometimes I actually hold my breath, so I can be as still and well balanced as possible. If you get too excited, you overreact more, and with the adrenaline, you lose focus quickly.'

———

Then came the Blundstone Arena and the interview with Mel McLaughlin. Perhaps it was the adrenaline still pumping through him, or maybe the Universe Boss just got a bit too real:

Mel McLaughlin: 'Congratulations, were you just not in the mood to run today?'
Chris Gayle: 'It's a bit cold to be honest with you. It's a good wicket, the ball's standing up a bit when they bowl short. I mean it's all about rhythm. The first ball went for four and then everything you

know flew after that so it was fantastic, to be able to bat with Finchy out there ... his last game, so we want to entertain the crowd.'

MM: 'An incredibly aggressive approach from you. It looks like you're just smashing this innings.'

CG: 'Yeah definitely. I want to come and have an interview to you as well. That's the reason why I'm here. Just to see your eyes for the first time. It's nice, so hopefully when this game is over, we can have a drink after. Don't blush baby ... [laughs]'

MM: 'I'm not blushing. Er ... any injuries? The boys were saying maybe you picked up a bit of a twinge in your hamstring.'

CG: 'No, it was my back. It just flared up a bit. Just to look at some [inaudible] work and hopefully I finish the tournament, recover well and look in your eyes.'

MM: 'We'll leave it on that note. Well done, thanks.'

CG: 'Oh sorry.' [reaches out to touch McLaughlin's shoulder and laughs]

Mark Howard [from the commentary box]: 'One of the more extraordinary interviews you'll ever see on network television. Mel McLaughlin with an amorous Chris Gayle. Well done Mel, I thought you handled that very well, as she scurries off with bright red cheeks.'

Damian Fleming [from the commentary box]: 'Playing shots on and off the field, Chris Gayle.'

Chris Gayle didn't play in the Big Bash again. In the immediate aftermath of the Mel McLaughlin interview, he faced criticism for his comments, including by a former teammate at Sydney Thunder, Chris Rogers, who said they were part of a 'pattern of behaviour'. A few months later, in May 2016, Gayle gave an interview to the *Sunday Times*' Charlotte Edwardes, who quoted him as saying he had, 'a very,

very big bat, the biggest in the wooooorld', before adding: 'You think you could lift it? You'd need two hands.' He gave another to Donald McCrae of the *Guardian* that included the line, 'you're with men. You're good-looking. What do you expect?' When McCrae asked if Gayle would like his own new-born daughter to be treated that way in twenty-five years' time, he said: 'If you put yourself there, you have to expect that. You have to deal with it. Not all situations are going to be the best.'

The Universe Boss doubled down, even when the world was against him. 'I didn't mean to be disrespectful and I didn't mean it to be taken serious', he said. Part of it seemed generational. Gayle was approaching forty, a decade or more older than many of the players he appeared with. Partly it seemed cultural, some of the traditional machismo on which he had grown up. Some of it, to his eyes, was playful, a part of the hyper-real exaggeration that he brought to the character of the Universe Boss online. Another part was the anger at the iniquities and prejudice that he had to overcome, both in West Indian cricket and the wider world. In *Six Machine*, he talked about the racism in Jamaica, how cricketers with lighter skin and affluent families were favoured. He credited his first teacher, Miss Hamilton, for giving him the self-belief to overcome his background and succeed in cricket.

———

It was not the end of the Universe Boss in that he continued to circuit the globe, hopping from franchise to franchise, tournament to tournament, his returns diminishing only slightly as he approached his milestone birthday. But after the Mel McLaughlin interview, it was never the same again.

To me, being the Universe Boss was somewhat akin to a boxer before a fight. No athlete told themselves that they would be alright more often than a boxer. They had to build an impenetrable psycho-logical shield, and they often did it by speaking about themselves in the third person, as if they were observing themselves from the out-side, and by making outlandish claims about what they were going to do to their opponent. It was a condition exacerbated by pay-per-view companies that built up fights at stagey press conferences and weigh-ins to sell subscriptions. It became self-fulfilling until it all fell away at the end of the bout when the respect between the boxers and the relief at having come through the contest tended to show more of their real personality. I'd seen a few boxers who became trapped between the two, with the result that defeat could be a devastating blow to their psyche.

The Universe Boss was the super-confident pre-fight personality, the id manifesting as ego. But T20 cricket, unlike boxing, was aimed at families and children. However Chris Gayle saw himself, however he interpreted his morals and motives, whatever his view of the world, that world was entitled to stare back, to challenge what he had said and how he had behaved. Being the Universe Boss was not a free pass, whatever the pain of his creation.

And as the Universe Boss faded, the first age of T20 cricket, the age of T20 innocence, was ending with him. The Boss had offered a glimpse of what was possible, of what the future of cricket might look like. The game was changing, charging forwards. T20 had brought forth the biggest revolution in technique since Grace began playing forwards and trying to score rather than just defend his wicket. Bowling and fielding had responded, too, and it was now a heightened, spectacular game full of new skills that were unthinkable even a decade earlier.

MODES OF DISMISSAL

There are ten ways in which a player can be dismissed.

BOWLED Law 32	The striker is out bowled if his/her wicket is broken by a ball fairly delivered by the bowler. *Of the 63,584 wickets to fall in Test cricket, 13,629 were out bowled, or 21.43 per cent. Of the major modes of dismissal, being bowled is the one that has varied in frequency most through history. In the 19th century, it accounted for between 35 and 45 per cent of dismissals. As techniques and wickets changed, the percentage had fallen to around 20 by the 1970s, and with the rise in the number of LBW decisions due to the Decision Review System (DRS) technology, now stands at around 16 per cent of dismissals. In short, a good player will be bowled less than one in five times that they bat.*
CAUGHT Law 33	The striker is out caught if a ball delivered by the bowler makes contact with his/her bat and is caught fairly by a fielder within the boundary before it touches the ground. *Across history, most innings have ended this way, and it has hardly varied. More than half of all dismissals are caught, 40 per cent by the slips and other outfielders, and around 15 per cent by the wicketkeeper.*
LEG BEFORE WICKET Law 36	The striker is out Leg Before Wicket if a ball delivered by the bowler hits them between wicket and wicket without first touching the bat, and the ball, but for the interception, would have gone on to hit the stumps. *Now accounts for 17 per cent of dismissals in long-form cricket, up from 11 per cent in the 1970s. The force behind the change has been the arrival of the Decision Review System and its predictive element. Once umpires began to see, and be trained in, the number of deliveries that the system showed would go on to hit the stumps had they not been intercepted by the pad, the number of positive LBW decisions climbed exponentially.*
RUN OUT Law 38	Either batsman is run out if, at any time the ball is in play, he or she is out of their ground when the wicket is fairly put down by a fielder. *By the stats, a player has around a 3–4 per cent chance of their innings concluding in this most avoidable – and spirit-crushing – of fashions ... As Boycott once wailed at Botham, 'what have you done ... what have you done ...' (Botham's alleged, perhaps apocryphal, reply was said to be, 'I've run you out, you c**t.')*
STUMPED Law 39	The striker is out stumped if he/she is out of their ground when the stumps are fairly put down by the wicketkeeper without the intervention of another fielder, following a fair delivery by the bowler. *Around 2 per cent of dismissals, a figure that has remained steady across history. It's in part due to opportunity – the wicketkeeper spends much of his/her time standing back to quicker bowlers.*

Taken as a whole, these modes of dismissal account for less than two per cent of those recorded across more than a century.

HIT THE BALL TWICE
Law 34

The striker is out hit the ball twice if, while the ball is in play and before it has been touched by a fielder, he/she strikes the ball again after it has been in contact with his/her bat (unless they are attempting to guard their wicket).

One of cricket's oldest and most arcane modes of dismissal, and one of the rarest, this Law was introduced after the deaths of Jasper Vinall and Harry Brand (see page 26). In practice, the Law is unused – there has never been a Hit the Ball Twice dismissal in international cricket.

HIT WICKET
Law 35

The striker is out hit wicket if the stumps are broken by their bat or person while in the process of playing a shot or beginning to run.

The famous piece of commentarial corpsing between Brian Johnson and Jonathan Agnew on Test Match Special came when Ian Botham toppled a bail after playing a hook shot. 'He couldn't quite get his leg over', said Agnew, a line that resulted in both being unable to speak for several minutes.

OBSTRUCTING THE FIELD
Law 37

A Law that now incorporates Handled the Ball, offering a catch-all for any batter 'wilfully attempting to distract the fielding side by word or action'.

There has been just one instance of Obstructing the Field in Test cricket, in 1951 when Len Hutton prevented the Australian wicketkeeper from taking a catch by trying to steer the ball away with his bat (he thought that it was going to drop on his stumps). Handled the Ball happened seven times, after the batter has touched the ball with a hand not on the bat (unless trying to avoid injury). The growing application of Law 37 comes mostly in white-ball cricket, where a player is adjudged to have avoided being run out by deliberately changing course to obstruct the fielder's throw as it travels towards the stumps.

TIMED OUT
Law 40

An incoming batsman must be in position to take their first delivery (or allow their batting partner to do so if off strike) within three minutes of the previous wicket falling.

The Law has been applied just six times in the history of first-class cricket, and never in an international game. Australia's Ricky Ponting once told me that his recurring anxiety dream was getting lost in a vast pavilion on his way out to be bat, and being timed out.

RETIRED
Law 25.4

A batter can end his/her innings by retiring, with the consent of the opposing captain.

Most common in 'warm-up' type tour games, when a player will bat for a while and then retire to allow another to get some practice, it has happened once (or actually twice) in a Test match, when Sri Lanka's Marvan Attapatu and Mahela Jayawardene retired out against Bangladesh in 2001 after scoring 201 and 150 respectively, and were heavily criticised for it. It has become increasingly discussed as a potential tactic during white-ball games.

Fast bowlers had dizzying varieties of slower balls and yorkers; spinners learned to bowl with the new ball and the field up and prospered; fielding became supremely athletic, balls were caught behind the boundary and thrown back in for relay catches. Coaching became more specialist, and statistical analysts undressed performance in a way that had never been done before.

The effect went beyond a single format. In ODI cricket, which started in 1971, all of the top 20 highest team scores were made after 2006. All of the eight individual scores of more than 200 came after 2010. In Test match cricket, the drawn game went into rapid decline. In the seven years from 2010 to 2017, 140 of 168 Test matches ended in a decisive result, including a streak of 22 matches in a row during 2017. Such a run had occurred only once before, from 1884 to 1892, when results came for radically different reasons, and the calendar year of 2017 saw 89.2 per cent of Test matches end with a winner, an all-time high. When draws did occur, they were often intensely exciting because they happened in games where defeat was staved off at the last. Scoring rates increased, as did batting collapses, because the nature of batting had changed.

It had all begun not with the physical act, but with an act of imagination. To bat in the way that the Universe Boss did required him to first think about what was possible and then to figure out how best to do it. Others had travelled the same road, but none in quite the same way. He would leave the game with a unique record: the first – and so far only – man to have made a Test match triple-century (two, in fact), a one-day international double-hundred and a T20 international hundred: 3-2-1.

But who had done it: Chris Gayle, the skinny kid with the too-dark skin from a poor home in Jamaica, or the Universe Boss, a complex mediation of his personality? Six months after the Mel McLaughlin interview, *Six Machine* was published. After describing his transformational heart surgery in its prologue, the first chapter began:

I'm weird. I'm a weirdo.

You think you know me? You don't know me.

Yu cyaan read me. Yu cyaan study me. Doh even try study me.

Chris Gayle
2005–2018

INTERLUDE
THE MYTH OF THE NIGHTWATCHMAN

The use of the nightwatchman is one of cricket's implacable enigmas, a tactic that has been employed almost since the game began. Its effectiveness has always been disputed and never been proved. Nonetheless it persists and probably will as long as matches are played over successive days. It is a notion based on human fallibility, a defence of position, a counter-intuitive decision to place a player of lesser ability into a parlous situation that others are better equipped to handle. Beyond that, it is an identifier of the game's greatest single divide: that between batsmen and bowlers, men whose professional lives are consumed by thoughts of how to overcome one another. The very act of needing a nightwatchman, when wickets are falling at the end of a day, is indicative of failure: batsmen who have lounged in the field for hours have been unable to survive at the crease for a few minutes; bowlers who have trooped exhausted from the same arena are now

expected to clean up after them. It has a sacrificial element to it. It tells one member of a team that they are more expendable than another, that their abilities are more lightly regarded. It is about rank and position. In a game so finely attuned to psychology, the nightwatchman taunts a player with his mental frailty and displays it to the world and, when it is over for the day, the batsman who has declined to go in must change in the same room as the bowler he has required to do so. Some captains have banned the idea; others have exempted themselves from responsibility for it. In an age where the prevailing mindset is aggression, the nightwatchman is a laying-down of arms, a brief if temporary surrendering of the initiative. It's a move that piles pressure not onto the opposition, but onto the team employing it. And yet it lives.

Perhaps the position persists because it is so equivocal, so unprovably right or wrong. One study, which looked at 113 instances, found that the collective nightwatchmen had a mean career average of 15 in their usual position, and an average of 15 as nightwatchmen too. The effect of a nightwatchman on subsequent partnerships is examined, as is its effect on the final score. But what the data cannot provide is an answer to what would have happened without one in those precise circumstances. The study is called The myth of the nightwatchman, a title intended to be conclusive but that instead carries more weight when read another way. Nightwatchmanship eludes statistical clarity because its truth is very simple: it works when it works.

Chris Martin's Bike

When Chris Martin was growing up on New Zealand's South Island, the legal driving age was 15. It was one of the lowest in the world, because the bigger of New Zealand's two islands held less than a quarter of its population and large parts of the economy were based in agriculture and related industries. Being able to drive from teenagehood made life easier. But Chris didn't learn to drive until he was 28 years old, which meant that he went to most of his youthful cricketing engagements on his bike. It was hard to cycle and carry a bat, and so much of the time he didn't. As a result, Chris did not bat often, and he became one of the most celebrated number elevens in the game.

In cricket, batsmen did not have to bowl. But bowlers had to bat. And they had to bat against the same bowlers that had just finished dismissing their team's best batsmen. It was one of the game's paradoxes, and it didn't really happen in other team sports. Baseball, cricket's kissing cousin, allowed the pitcher to be replaced with a designated hitter when his team were at bat. Gridiron maintained entirely separate teams for offence and defence. In rugby, forwards and backs barely looked like members of the same species. Even a game as fluid as football maintained rigorous positional discipline – and any rare moment that an outfield player was required to go in goal contained all the levity and dread of an office party. And in any case, the skills required to play in different positions of the football pitch or the rugby field, or in basketball, hockey or netball, were at least comparable. But to bat and to bowl were two entirely separate disciplines, unalike in every respect. There was just one thread that connected them: the journey of ball towards bat.

Batsmen having a bowl were a cause for celebration. Indian crowds rose to Sachin Tendulkar's occasional medium-pacers. Alastair Cook took the one wicket of his 161-Test career, that of India's seam bowler Ishant Sharma, during a jokey over in which he did an impression of Bob Willis. Michael Vaughan, to general astonishment, once bowled Tendulkar as the great man reached 92 at Trent Bridge in 2002: Vaughan quickly christened it 'the Ball of the Century' (see page 185). Mike Atherton dismissed his England opening partner and captain Graham Gooch during a NatWest Trophy game between Lancashire and Essex, Goochie stomping off in high dudgeon. And despite being India's wicketkeeper, MS Dhoni managed one international wicket across his 500-plus appearances when he clean bowled Travis Dowlin of West Indies during the Champions Trophy of 2009. These moments are easily recallable because they are black swans, as unserious as professional cricket gets. The bowler batting, though, is prosaic, commonplace. There's no novelty in it, and it can be existentially terrible for them when overmatched.

Chris Martin can rightly be called a New Zealand great. His 233 Test wickets put him fifth on the list of their all-time wicket-takers.

To further contextualise that number, he took more than Andrew Flintoff, more than Andy Roberts, more than Jeff Thomson. His was a considerable career, and he had almost all of the champion batsmen of the era on his wickets' list: he got Graeme Smith out eight times, Jacques Kallis six, Mohammad Yousuf five, Ricky Ponting four, VVS Laxman four, Sachin Tendulkar and AB de Villiers three times each.

Chris Martin could bowl. But he couldn't bat. And he couldn't bat not in the way that most number elevens of the era couldn't bat – which was to average ten or so, and occasionally save a game or see a teammate through to a hundred or make a merry fifty when the bowlers were flogged and the pitch was flat and a declaration due. No, Chris Martin really couldn't bat, so much so that he became as famous for it as for his bowling, which seemed somewhat unfair.

But then Chris Martin's batting was funny, or at least the numbers were. In both Test and first-class cricket he scored fewer runs than he got wickets, which took some doing. In 104 Test match innings, he made 123 runs at 2.36, the lowest average of anyone to bat that many times. Thirty-six of his innings were ducks.* A further twenty-eight concluded with him scoreless but as the not out batsman, which meant that 59 per cent of the time he batted, he scored no runs at all. He made seven pairs, another record, and reached double figures just once, when he scored 12 not out against Bangladesh at Dunedin in 2008. In his 20 one-day international appearances, his highest score was three.

Chris Martin's figures stranded him at the bottom of the pile, but he was not quite alone. For most of cricket's history bowlers weren't

---

* The only player to have recorded more ducks, the great West Indian quick bowler Courtney Walsh, made 43 in 185 innings, a percentage of 23.24. India's revered leg-spin bowler Bhagwath Chandrasekhar is the one other Test cricketer with more than thirty caps to have taken more career wickets than he scored runs, 242 to 167.

really expected to be able to bat. Before helmets and decent protective equipment, fast men had their own code of not trying to kill one another. Umpires were happy to fire the tail out, safe in the knowledge that they were moving the game along. Eric Hollies, the man best-known for bowling Bradman for his fateful last duck at the Oval in 1948, took 2,323 wickets in his career, a figure that dwarfed his 1,673 runs, and he was far from unusual in his era. Phil Tufnell, himself a famous tailender, tells a great story about bowling at the end of a county game in which Middlesex, his side, were being held up post-lunch by a stubborn but pointless last-wicket partnership. Just 'it him on the pad, Phil, and I'll do the rest', the umpire side-mouthed. 'This lad's batting me into traffic ...'

It was only the rise of the modern game, with its marginal gains and central contracts and franchises, that ramped up the demands for bowlers to add value with the bat. Duncan Fletcher, England's unyielding coach of the early noughties, demanded that his players excel in at least two of the three disciplines of batting, bowling and fielding.* As captain of an era-defining Australian side, Steve Waugh introduced a 'buddy' system, where bowlers were paired up with batsmen assigned to work with them, an idea that spread quickly.†

---

* Fletcher's dictum, even unconsciously, favoured batsmen, who would never be expected to take up bowling, and could concentrate on fielding as a second discipline. Bowlers, especially quicker ones, needed periods of rest in the outfield. A batsman's deficiencies at bowling were never shown up, because they never did it. Bowlers, at international level, had all of their innings televised. There was no hiding place.

† David Lloyd adopted it as England's coach, and assigned Mike Atherton as Angus Fraser's buddy. Their first session ended in a stand-up row in the nets.

LOWEST AVERAGES IN TEST CRICKET

2.00
AVERAGE

1. Mpumelelo Mbangwa
(Zimbabwe, 1996–2000)

2.29
AVERAGE

2. Jack Saunders
(Australia, 1902–1908)

2.37
AVERAGE

3. Chris Martin
(New Zealand, 2000–2013)

2.54
AVERAGE

4. Jasprit Bumrah
(India, 2018–)

2.63
AVERAGE

5. Bert Ironmonger
(Australia, 1928–1933)

Australia's greatest tailender at the time was Glenn McGrath. McGrath made more Test runs than he took wickets – just – 641 to 563, yet in one-day cricket failed to score a single run in 27 of the 53 series that he played.* Waugh allocated himself the task of improving McGrath's batting. He discovered that McGrath's best shot was a flick through midwicket that he played, for some reason, with his back foot in the air, 'and if he missed, the ball would hit his leg and deflect onto the stumps', Waugh said.

'The batsmen get all this money for bat deals,' McGrath moaned, 'and Steve told me the best thing for me to do was to phone around the manufacturers and tell them to pay me ten thousand dollars or I'd start using their gear ...'

McGrath's story had a happy ending. He declared his ambition to score an international half-century, a feat so apparently unlikely that he negotiated a $10,000 bonus with his bat maker, the Sydney-based brand Sommers, should he pull it off.† In November 2004, he did, making 61 at the Gabba against New Zealand – where, rather deliciously, he was dismissed by Chris Martin. Sommers not only paid $10,000 to the McGrath Breast Cancer Foundation but produced a signature bat, emblazoned with a '61' logo, that McGrath wielded proudly during the 2005 Ashes.

---

* This was partly a sign of Aussie dominance. McGrath went through the entire 2007 World Cup without being required to bat, and in his 250 games went to the crease just 68 times. However, of those 68, he made just one double-digit score, 11 against New Zealand in Auckland. Australia lost.

† Steve Waugh's brother Mark had bet Shane Warne $1,000 that McGrath would never make a fifty of any variety, and had to pay out when he scored 55 playing for Worcester during a spell in county cricket in 2000.

There were special moments that the game offered, moments with the clock ticking and the light fading and matches on the line, that turned tailenders into strange kinds of heroes. James Anderson and Monty Panesar, bowlers with a combined batting average of fifteen, survived for eleven and a half overs to draw the first Test of the 2009 Ashes, a result that proved crucial to the series outcome. Graham Onions batted out the final minutes of two Tests on the same tour of South Africa, at Centurion and Cape Town, a year later. Jack Leach stayed with Ben Stokes as he somehow won the Ashes Test at Headingley in 2019, contributing a single run to their last-wicket partnership of 73. His was a feat on a par with Vishwa Fernando's, who'd hung in with Kusal Perera while Perera had made all but six of the last 78 runs needed against South Africa in Durban a few weeks earlier.

But these were moments as rare as a seam of gold in the riverbed. The quotidian was failure, ignominy and pain. It was demoralising and demeaning. In what other profession did its high achievers have the one part of the job that they could not do well televised, picked over, analysed and discussed?

Chris Martin played along gamely with a trailer for a fictional DVD release called Learn To Bat With Chris Martin – 'Like me, it's out now ...' – but failure hurt him in the same way it hurt any cricketer. He called his dismissals 'an exclamation mark on a poor performance ... I always feel like my wicket sums up our whole batting: "here comes the number eleven, he's not going to be around long ..." Boom, gone and we're all out in 50 overs and that sums up our whole day.'

He had periods where he worked hard on his batting in the nets, but then he would have to go out and face 'a couple of fast bowlers with a new ball bowling 140 (kph) and that's just a level I can't battle with.'

Iain O'Brien, who spent most of his 22-Test career batting at number ten to Martin's eleven, said: 'He took his batting seriously. It was just something that he couldn't do, and disliked. "Inept," he called himself. He netted every opportunity he got. By the time he got to have a hit, though, he was often left with the net bowlers, who were either knackered from a long session or not very good.'

The story of Chris Martin's bike seemed like a Malcolm Gladwell type thing, a piece of arcane knowledge that somehow explained the phenomenon of tail-end batting. All cricketers were shaped by where and how they learned to play. Bradman's rotary backlift existed because of his childhood game with a golf ball and a stump. Shane Warne bowled from a run-up of a few steps because he broke both legs as a kid and spent a couple of months wheeling himself on a trolley – his shoulders got so strong he didn't need the energy created by a run-up (see Warnie: The Magician's Fingers, page 178). Ricky Ponting learned to hook and pull full deliveries when he was playing with much older and taller boys. Lasith Malinga's slingshot action and Jasprit Bumrah's stiff arm were the result of bowling with tape balls or tennis balls as kids, working out their own way of doing things. They were acts of imagination, brought about by circumstance.

But these things alone didn't make players great, and having a bike rather than a car didn't explain why some cricketers can bat and some can't.

Bowling was a physiological thing, especially fast bowling. As the old saying about sprinters went: 'nobody born slow ever got fast', and the raw material was usually visible from an early age. Batting was less bound up with the physical, at least in terms of size and strength. It was about fine motor skills, instant judgement. Bowlers loved to moan that cricket was 'a batsman's game', but they had a couple of eternal advantages. One was that the batsman's first mistake often excluded them from the match, while the bowler simply bowled again after a bad delivery. The other was that the bowler knew what delivery he intended to bowl. One of the keys to batting was how early the batsman could work out what that delivery would be.

And here, whether Chris Martin had a bike or not, he was never going to get fast. The New Zealand squad went through many kinds of physiological and psychological tests, as all players did. One of the areas advancing most rapidly was in the analysis of vision. Chris Martin's eyesight was at the lower end of good for an international player. 'The guy said my eyes were fine and he had tested many New Zealand batsmen over the years with similar eyes, although they hadn't had consistent careers', he said.* In one test, the players watched a screen as rows of seven numbers were flashed up very briefly. They were asked to recall as many as they could. 'I can get five or six from the top line,' Martin said, 'but a guy like Brendon McCullum can do the whole first line and four or five from the second line; he can take in more information visually in that split second than I ever could.'†

McCullum, like other great batsmen, was in part a process of natural selection. By genetic fluke, he could interpret more visual

---

* Martin was talking to New Zealand's *Sunday Star Times* in 2009. As research on the vision of cricketers has advanced, it's clear that, while naturally good vision helps, it's not essential – and many players use contact lenses or glasses.

† McCullum played some of the most significant innings of cricket's modern age. On the opening night of the inaugural IPL he made 158, confirming the spectacular appeal of T20 cricket. And in 2014, he became the first New Zealander to record a Test match triple-century, with 302 against India at the Basin Reserve. In his final match, he made Test cricket's fastest hundred, in 54 deliveries against Australia. So yes, he does see the ball quite well.

information more quickly than Chris Martin. This was where the advantage lay. Other research found that the best batsmen picked up clues from the bowler's run-up and action before release, a kind of mental library that grew and grew with every ball that they faced.

And the great batsmen batted. They batted in matches and they batted in the nets as often as they needed. As long as they practised their fielding too, they were golden. In training, bowlers had to wait for their turn to bat, after they'd bowled at the batsmen and practised their fielding, at moments when they were frayed and tired and still thinking about their bowling and the coaches were losing interest. The worst batsmen batted less and practised least, and so it was a vicious cycle – bike or no bike.

So Chris Martin was, until someone worse came along, Test cricket's worst. Yet there was nobility in his failure and the way he dealt with it. There was something moving about the way that he would troop back out into the guns, day after day, sometimes with the weight of the match upon him, knowing that what he had was unlikely to be enough, knowing that he may be mocked, injured, humiliated, defeated once again. Chris Martin couldn't bat but he did, 104 times in Test matches, against the greatest bowlers of the age.[*]

Iain O'Brien had another story about his compadre at the bottom of the order. 'I remember Tommy [Martin's nickname] telling me over a coffee in a Dunedin cafe in January 2008 that this was his chance to get double figures. That series, against Bangladesh, was, in his mind, the best chance for a career best with the bat.'

---

[*] The list of bowlers Martin encountered included Dale Steyn, who dismissed him four times, Shane Warne (also four), Mitchell Johnson (three), plus Shaun Pollock, Glenn McGrath, Waqar Younis, Shoaib Akhtar, Brett Lee, Fidel Edwards ...

And soon O'Brien found himself at the crease with his friend as Chris Martin edged towards the promised land. He drove Shahadat Hossain to the mid-off boundary to move to five, inside-edged the next over his stumps for another boundary, and then, a couple of overs later, slid Sajidul Islam wide of point for the single that brought double figures. For once at least, Chris Martin could bat.

Chris Martin
2000–2013
233 wickets at 33.81, 123 runs at 2.36.
Highest score 12 not out, v Bangladesh, Dunedin, 2008.

Virat Kohli, Steve Smith
and the Unknowable Future

John Jacobs may have taught more people to play golf than anyone who ever lived. He taught major champions and municipal course hackers. He taught Jack Nicklaus, King of the Belgians Leopold I, José María Olazábal, Douglas Bader, Sean Connery and, he said: 'a good friend of mine who is a big slicer of the ball, but it starts left and finishes straight. I said to him, "if anyone says you're a slicer, tell them Jacobs says it's a power fade ..."'

In an interview with *Golf Digest* conducted when Jacobs was deep into his ninth decade, he revealed the guiding truth behind understanding the game: 'In my first book, *Golf By John Jacobs*, the first thing I wrote down on paper was, "golf is what the ball does". That was my breakthrough as a teacher. I look at what the ball does and I ask, "why?"'

All that mattered was the moment of impact. If the clubface was presented squarely to the ball and the strike was pure, then the swing was functioning properly, or at least effectively. 'The biggest step in becoming a good player is understanding how the flight of the ball teaches the correct geometry of impact', he said. 'Golf is such a difficult game because there are so many ways of playing it correctly.'

For a long time, more than a century, cricket had a prevailing orthodoxy. It was summed up in the MCC *Coaching Manual*. For all of its ubiquity within cricket, not many people had actually read it. It was a book that represented a mindset that ran through the bloodstream of the game. When anyone described a shot as 'textbook', this was the text they meant. And almost everything that was said or thought about it was wrong, or at least misinterpreted. That began with its title, which was actually *The MCC Cricket Coaching Book*, and when it was written – 1952, rather than carved into tablets and handed down the mountain a century earlier. Its author was Harry Altham and its noble purpose was to offer schoolteachers a quick and easy way of helping children who had never played before.* Its side-on, straightforward precepts fitted the post-war game and the post-war mind, with its need for order after chaos and its deference

---

* Altham's life was remarkable, like something out of 'Boy's Own'. He was educated at Repton, where the school cricket team he captained was considered the strongest ever schoolboy XI by EW Swanton. He was mentioned three times in dispatches and awarded the DSO for his service in the 60th Regiment (King's Royal Rifle Corps) during World War I, and then played first-class cricket for Surrey and Hampshire while a master at Winchester College. He began writing a history of cricket as a serial for *The Cricketer* magazine, which became so popular it was published as a book in 1926 and then revised in 1937, '47 and '48 in collaboration with Swanton. He was treasurer and president of MCC, President of Hampshire and, briefly, Chairman of Selectors for the England team. He died from a heart attack in 1965, just after addressing a cricket society in Sheffield.

to structure. The Baby Boomers learned it, and the children of the Baby Boomers, and even after Twenty20 cricket began the biggest revolution in technique since the introduction of overarm bowling, players that could reproduce its classical lines were the game's platonic ideal.

—

Gary Barwell stood on one edge of the square at Edgbaston. It was a bright, cold day in October and the 2018 season was over at last. For the groundsman, winters were very different to summers. In summer, the cricket was relentless, and so was the tension, not just because of the commercial and sporting pressure to prepare wickets that provided months full of exciting matches, but because of the pressure he put on himself. Like most groundsmen, Gary took everything personally. This earth had his heart and soul in it. In his office underneath one of the stands, he had a wallchart with a section for each of the pitches he'd prepared, filled with his notes on the Clegg Hammer reading and soil moisture content, the scores in the game, the grade awarded to the pitch by the match referee, and any personal reflections he had. In the seven years he'd been at Edgbaston, he knew everything about every pitch he'd prepared, even at the second-team grounds and the outdoor nets.

He could fit twenty-four pitches across the Edgbaston square, which stretched out beyond him to the far side of the ground like a pleasure beach. He took a breath and said: 'I was privileged to produce a pitch that Virat Kohli scored 149 on. When you see all the Tweets and people talking about the wicket, it's a joy to come to work.'

That game, the opening Test of the summer between England and India, had begun like every other Test, with Gary feeling physically sick as the first overs were bowled. His shoulders were knotted. What he was striving for in a summer of relentless heatwaves was a pitch that would offer a chance to bowlers and batsmen if they played well enough, a head-of-the-pin balance that would enable neither team to fully get on top but instead for them to fight for dominance, to gain slim advantage and hold it for as long as they could.

But as those first few deliveries went down, no-one, not even Gary Barwell, knew exactly what would happen.

Virat Kohli was 30 years old. He'd been voted 'Leading Cricketer in the World' by *Wisden Almanack* for two years in a row. He had been named as the captain of the International Cricket Council's (ICC) annual, notional, Test and one-day teams of the year. He was ranked as the number one batsman in 50-overs cricket and the number two in Test cricket. He had been awarded player of the tournament at consecutive Twenty20 World Cups. He was captain of India in all formats, and beyond that he was their most famous, richest and best-loved batsman, the successor to Sunil Gavaskar and Sachin Tendulkar in a land where cricket, and more specifically batting, was worshipped. He had just got married to Anushka Sharma, a Bollywood actress, in a union that compounded their celebrity, doubled it, cubed it. Kohli had thirty million followers on Twitter and another forty million on Instagram. His kind of fame came at a price, and Kohli coped by compartmentalising his day, his waking hours allocated rigidly and ruthlessly in order to preserve his training time and playing commitments.* He conceded only to superstition. As a young player he'd used the same pair of gloves for each innings, but that was impossible now so he moved on to various bracelets and bangles and bits of black thread tied around his wrists and in his pockets. He had a 'God's Eye' tattoo on his left shoulder, a samurai warrior on one bicep, his star sign Scorpio on the other, Lord Shiva on a forearm, his parents' names and his playing numbers. Above the God's Eye he'd added an Om symbol, important in the Dharmic religions. 'I have started to realise strongly that I am meant to be where I am', he said of it. Maybe he believed it or maybe it was just something he told journalists to keep them at bay, but it all added to his mystique.

Gavaskar and Tendulkar had each captained India on several occasions, apparently passively and reluctantly, but Kohli was

---

* It was a weight that had fallen upon great batsmen since WG Grace. The Doctor, a man of appetite, exploited these first notions of celebrity for money. Bradman was an introvert, aloof and remote even from other players, retreating to his hotel room to play records and reply to his fan mail. Neville Cardus wrote, 'no man is loveable who is invincible', and the Don was often invincible.

In Duncan Hamilton's biography of Cardus, *The Great Romantic*, he relates the story of Bradman asking Cardus for a reading list that would 'develop his mind'. Cardus obliged and Bradman spent a year reading them all, but when Cardus wrote about it in a column, Bradman flatly denied it had happened, leaving Cardus bemused and feeling foolish. Yet Bradman had also sought Cardus' company on the evening that he and his wife's new-born son was critically ill. Cardus sat in the car park outside the hospital until Bradman came out and told him that his son wouldn't survive. Cardus later wrote about the night so sensitively that Bradman kept the article in a scrapbook. Sunil Gavaskar and Sachin Tendulkar were equally worshipped, almost silent idols onto whom anyone could project anything. Tendulkar's one known escape was driving his sports cars on the Mumbai freeways late at night.

Bat, Ball and Field

different, seizing the job and steering them upwards by sheer force of will. His practice and training were ruthless. He demanded his teams be fit, so made himself the fittest cricketer on earth. He was not just the best batsman, but the best fielder, too. He patrolled the margins of marginal gains. On the field he was like a raw nerve in the wind, every small change of fortune showing on his face. He celebrated wickets and runs wildly. His hunger was palpable, insatiable, irresistible. He was the first player in history to score three hundreds in his first three innings as Test captain. He made double-centuries in four consecutive series as India twice became the number one Test side in the world. Being captain turned him into a king.

Virat Kohli had only failed – really failed – once in his life, in England in 2014, when India had lost a five-match series 3–1. In ten innings, he scored 1, 8, 25, 0, 39, 28, 0, 7, 6 and 20. Jimmy Anderson had dismissed him four times, and more than that, he had humiliated him, got inside his head, turned him inside out. The failure refracted the rest of Kohli's record in a new light. Great batsmen, really great batsmen like Gavaskar and Tendulkar, did it everywhere, against everyone. So must he, if he was to think of himself as great.

The game moved on quickly, series upon series, format on format, but Kohli still burned with it. When England toured India at the end of 2016, he made 655 runs in eight innings at an average of 109.16, but India was as alien to England's bowlers as England was to India's batsmen, and so it wasn't done, he wasn't avenged. Not really. Not yet.

Now, in 2018, Virat Kohli came to Edgbaston to bat for his reputation on Gary Barwell's pitch. James Anderson was waiting for him. Jimmy had just turned 36 years old, ancient for a fast bowler, but somehow he was defying time. He had become the first England player to take 500 Test wickets and he was sailing towards the magic number of 563, the most ever by a fast bowler.* The sportsman he most resembled was not another cricketer, but rather Roger Federer, an ageless sprite, loose-limbed and inexhaustibly elegant.

Anderson had created a character for himself, more of a caricature really, as a Grinch, condemned like all bowlers to long hours of poorly-rewarded labour, forever disappointed by dropped catches and a batting line-up that didn't back up his efforts. The reality was different. In England, with the swinging, seaming Duke's ball, he took his Test wickets at an average of 23. He was sublimely skilful, endlessly patient, a cunning old predator with sharp teeth and a leather hide. Anderson in England was the final frontier for Virat Kohli and for anyone who wanted to be the greatest batsman of the age.

There were no secrets in modern cricket. Every ball of every match was televised, analysed, logged. Everyone knew everything about everyone else. In a way, it made things more difficult, but in another, advantage was negated unless you were prepared to be audacious and radical. And that was difficult because modern cricket was endless. In the last year, Kohli had played international cricket against Sri Lanka, Australia, New Zealand and South Africa before going back to India to join his IPL franchise Royal Challengers Bangalore for two months and then travelling to Ireland for a couple of T20s,

---

* Anderson would take his 564th Test wicket from the final ball of the England–India series, when he clean bowled Mohammed Shami. With it, he went past the Australian great Glenn McGrath. In one of the statistical quirks that proliferate in cricket, Anderson had been McGrath's 563rd and final Test wicket, at Sydney in 2007.

Bat, Ball and Field

and then flying to England for T20 and ODI series before the Test matches began. He had juggled formats throughout, but moving from IPL cricket to Test matches in England was the most jarring change of all, and it was the one he had to make quickly. He'd signed up to play a few games for Surrey – even more cricket – to try and acclimatise, but the Indian board pulled him out after he injured his neck playing for Royal Challengers.

And everywhere he went, he was Kohli, captain, star batsman, main attraction, rock star. Every minute of every day chopped up, portioned out, consumed.

At Edgbaston, England batted first and had cruised to 216–3 when Kohli ran out his opposite number Joe Root with a direct hit from midwicket. Kohli had seized the moment, blowing kisses and mocking a 'mic-drop' celebration Root had performed at Headingley during an ODI a week or so before. The run-out began a mini-collapse that saw England all out for 287.

But he still had to bat. He came in amid the ruins of India's own innings, as 50–0 became 59–3, Anderson bowling at one end as if the gods decreed it, the crowd full of crackle and buzz, electricity in the air.

Anderson began: outswinger, outswinger, off-cutter, outswinger, inswinger. Kohli went leave, block, leave, leave, block. He squirted to gully to get off the mark. He hit mid-on with a sweet drive on the up. He left or blocked ten more, got a couple of singles and a boundary through third man. It was lunch.

He had one thought in his head, one thought he'd been keeping for James Anderson: 'Put your ego away.' It was no good hitting a couple of big flashy drives and then nicking off. His circumspection was exaggerated to almost comic effect. He blocked and then shadow-blocked, left and then shadow-left. His ego was subjugated under repetition and ritual. His plan became clear, and it was audacious in its way. Kohli had to stop being Kohli in order to win. He had made a couple of technical changes, batting outside of his crease to counter as much of Anderson's late swing as he could, and making sure that his hands did not get outside the line of his body. He played the line of the ball and trusted that anything wider would miss his bat.

After lunch, Anderson and Ben Stokes bowled together. Anderson had already bowled ten overs, and now, at the end of his eleventh, he had Kohli on strike and kept him there. Stokes offered nothing at the other end, and so Kohli faced twenty-six consecutive deliveries from Anderson as the great bowler gave everything to win this battle, to win this war that began four years ago and hung in the balance now. It was one of those sequences that could only happen in long games and in long series, when butterflies flapped their wings on one side and tidal waves rolled in at the other.

On the twenty-sixth delivery, Jimmy Anderson 'won'.

Kohli edged but Dawid Malan dropped it at second slip.

The sliding doors slid open. Virat Kohli walked through them and into his unknowable future.

No other Indian player got to thirty, so Kohli took their burden too; he scored their runs and his runs. He was on 97 when the ninth Indian wicket fell and Umesh Yadav walked in. Ben Stokes bowled short and wide and Kohli let his hands go at last, and carved the ball to the third man boundary. He screamed like a free man, free of the demons of four years ago, free of James Anderson, free of the shadows of Gavaskar and Tendulkar.

Great players do it everywhere, against everyone.

He kissed his wedding finger and blew the kiss along the bat to Anushka in the stands.

When he hit Adil Rashid's googly wide of Jimmy Anderson at long on, his score had risen to 135, more than he made in ten innings in

Bat, Ball and Field

England last time. When he was last out for 149, he had scored 54 per cent of his team's runs. The next-highest individual score was 26.

Australian batsman Steve Smith came to Edgbaston a year and a day after Virat Kohli.

Unlike Kohli, Smith hadn't spent his cricketing life as a nascent king of batting. As a kid in the Australian team he'd had the somewhat disparaging nickname of 'Piggy'. He had one of those faces, slightly upturned eyes and nose. I saw him get his first Test century, at the Oval in 2013. It was a strange game, the last of a series England were leading 3–0. It was a strange series too, in that England, in cricket's modern age, had won the Ashes in England just twice, and when they had, in 2005 and 2009, both occasions came down to the last Test, down to the wire, in terrible tension and then cathartic release.* So to go to the game with the absence of any real jeopardy felt odd.

England's selections had an end-of-term feel, too, a throwback to the bad old days of the 1990s when the team for the Oval would often contain some left-field choices that might make the winter tour party. With injuries to cover, they called up two uncapped players, the fast bowling all-rounder Chris Woakes and a slow left-arm spinner from Lancashire called Simon Kerrigan. Australia were on a generational downturn, euphemistically known in cricket as 'a rebuilding phase'

---

* As what we could see in retrospect was the finest achievement of this great England team, they had won the Ashes in Australia in 2010–11 by the margin of 3–1, with all three victories coming by an innings. It was the first time England had won in Australia since 1986–87, and on the two Ashes tours since, the team have failed to win a Test, losing five–nil and four–nil.

with a couple of great players, some old lags and a lot of will-they-or-won't-they kids, and had been playing mix and match all series. They had a new coach, Darren Lehmann, appointed in a hurry after Mickey Arthur had fallen foul of some senior players in a brouhaha referred to as 'homeworkgate'. Their batting order, which once had the feel of being as unalterable as Moses' tablets of stone, had been all over the place. The bullish opener David Warner was suspended after he scuffled with Joe Root in a bar called the Walkabout and missed the first two Tests.* The other opener was Chris Rogers, called up again at the age of 35 after playing his only Test five and a half years previously. He went to the wicket with Shane Watson, one of Australian cricket's great underachievers, until Warner was available again. Watson then dropped to three, a position occupied by Ed Cowan and then Usman Khawaja in the first two Tests. Phil Hughes (see page 63) played in the first two games and was then dropped. The only real mainstay was the captain, Michael Clarke, at number four. Steve Smith had not been selected for the original touring party but ended up playing every Test, batting at five and then six and then five again.

Even in Australia Smith was regarded as a novelty player. No-one seemed to be able to work out what he did well enough to be an Australian cricketer. He bowled hit-and-miss leg spin, a dangerous thing to try when you were young and blond and living in the post Shane Warne era. He was a brilliant fielder, but increasingly, so was everyone else. When he batted he could smoke it miles, hit searing square drives and smack good bowlers into the stands, but it was so ad hoc

---

* Warner's early nickname in the team was 'The Bull', later replaced by 'The Reverend' after he proclaimed himself a changed man. That lasted until his suspension for ball-tampering in 2018, at which point the jollity of nicknames ceased, at least for a while.

and idiosyncratic it seemed unsustainable. He was all eye and hands, as if he'd worked out how to play without watching anyone else. Smith was enigmatic in the most natural and naive of ways. He'd admitted that one of his roles was to tell some jokes in the dressing room. England, already dominant, saw Piggy himself as the joke, a symbol of Australian decline.

After ten Tests, he'd taken eight wickets at an average of 46.50. He'd made 493 runs with an average of 29.

Bits and pieces. Novelty player. In the team for his jokes. Piggy.

The first day of the Oval game was another odd one. Shane Watson, who seemed to avoid Test hundreds like vampires swerve sunlight, made his third in 84 innings and went on to his highest score, 176. He feasted brutally on England's debutant spinner Kerrigan, who had developed a distressing case of the yips, sending down a collection of full tosses and long hops. Those eight harrowing overs were the only ones he would ever bowl in Test cricket, a merciless execution of his lifelong dream.

At close of play, Steve Smith was 66 not out.

On day two, it happened. England picked up the nightwatchman Peter Siddle early, but the Oval pitch had expired during the night, and England captain Alastair Cook, after a long summer and with a back-to-back Ashes series looming in the winter, could not flog his frontline bowlers for much longer. They'd already sent down more than a hundred overs. He couldn't bowl Kerrigan either, so he turned to Jonathan Trott, a man whose medium pace was less part-time than unemployed, and some would say unemployable. The crowd were beerily delighted with the move. It felt like the last day of school, the teachers already half-packed for their holidays. Steve Smith had reached 94 and was on strike for the start of Trott's second over. He walked down the wicket to his batting partner, Brad Haddin.

'Do you think I can hit him over the top?'

'Yes. Keep a clear mind.'

He did, Trott's first delivery sent up and over mid-on, the ball a dark dot in the dark sky. I watched it come down beyond the rope at the Vauxhall End. The crowd cheered, for the six, for Trott, for Smith, for who knew what ... I didn't. England had gifted a Test hundred to Piggy Smith. I thought of the great innings I'd seen on the ground, the first on my first ever day of Test cricket as a little kid, Viv Richards making 291 in a match people still talked about. Steve Waugh's 157 with a torn calf. Kevin Pietersen's insane, unrepeatable 158 in 2005.

And Piggy Smith's counts as one, just like those? I don't think so.

How wrong I was.

—

Now it was August 2019, Edgbaston again. Gary Barwell had plenty of opportunities to feel sick. He'd made pitches for five World Cup matches, including the semi-final in which England had beaten Australia. Now he had the first Test of the Ashes series. The pitch he prepared was not like the one that Kohli had batted on. It was dry and slow and by the fifth day the ball was turning sharply from the dark footholds. Jimmy Anderson lasted four overs before he tweaked his calf and couldn't bowl. In his first Test match for eighteen months, after being sacked as Australian captain and banned for a year, after elbow surgery and some long, dark nights of the soul, enduring the boos of the crowd and the customary insomnia that accompanied almost every night before he was due to bat, Steve Smith made 144 and 142 and Australia won the game by 251 runs.* It raised his Test match batting average to 62.96, higher than anyone ever except for Bradman, the batsman to whom he was most often compared.

I thought again of that day at the Oval. Steve Smith, the new Bradman.

How did that happen?

---

* During the afternoon session of the third day of the third Test between South Africa and Australia at Cape Town in March 2018, with Australia in the field, television cameras showed Cameron Bancroft using a small piece of sandpaper to alter the condition of the ball – sandpaper he then tucked in his trousers. The incident escalated quickly, with David Warner and Smith relieved of duties as vice-captain and captain for the remainder of the game, which South Africa won by 322 runs. After the Australian prime minister denounced their conduct, Cricket Australia began an enquiry which saw Bancroft banned from cricket for nine months and Warner and Smith for a year. Warner was banned for life from any 'leadership role', and Smith for a further year. As was becoming the norm for social media storms, the punishment was first considered too little and then too much. Smith's tearful press conference hinted at a man swept away by events, and the incident prompted Australia to look at its wider cricketing culture (see page 63). Given the intensity of the cricketing calendar and the space it cleared for Smith to have an elbow operation and refocus on batting, the break itself – rather than the attendant damage to his reputation and career – seems to have only made him a better player.

When he was ten years old, Steve Smith decided he would play cricket for a living. He would be a cricketer. He was a kid with all the gifts, but his greatest gift of all was obsession. When he was seventeen, he left Menai High School, in the South Sydney suburb of Illawong, to go to England to play for Sevenoaks Vine in the Kent League. He'd had a meeting with the school principal at Menai to decide his future. The Cricket New South Wales Welfare Officer advised him to stay on in education, but his coach, Trent Woodhill, said: 'No disrespect to the school but Steve's going to make a million dollars per year for ten years of his life, he's that good a cricketer.' The school principal knew that all Smith thought of was cricket anyhow, and voted with Woodhill.

Steve Smith went to England, got called into the Surrey second XI, took 6–14 against Kent and caused a buzz because his mother had been born in London, qualifying him for a passport, citizenship and a place in the England team. But England had no chance. Steve had dreamed of the Baggy Green for as long as he could remember. It had his heart. He went back home and became captain of his Grade club, Sutherland, at the age of nineteen.

All the while he was blindsiding everyone with his bowling. He was the leading wicket-taker in the KFC Big Bash T20 tournament in 2008. He edged closer to the full Australian side with seven wickets for New South Wales against South Australia at the SCG. He made his international T20 debut against Pakistan as a leg spinner, and took eleven wickets, second-best of the tournament at the ICC T20 World Cup. He made his Test debut as a bowler batting at number eight. He was a stocky-looking blond kid who could give it a rip ... He must be a bowler.

And yet after thirteen first-class matches he had a batting average of fifty. He'd made four first-class centuries. He had a T20 strike rate of

130+. He took wickets in small cloudbursts but he scored runs in number. And it was about more than numbers. It was about personality, identity. When he was ten years old and he'd decided to become a cricketer, he played on Saturdays and Sundays, and trained on Tuesdays and Thursdays. On Mondays, Wednesdays and Fridays, he batted for an hour with his father, who could bowl all sorts of swing and spin. He played indoor cricket, where the ball skidded low on the hard floors, and on the crooked paving stones in his backyard with a cork ball and a bat with shaved-down edges. His father suspended a ball from a string in the garage, and Smith spent so much time in there that part of the ceiling wore away. Like Bradman, after ten thousand hours, Steve Smith was just getting started. Like Bradman, his method was home-cooked, imagined, created and perpetuated only by him. Batting was a place of retreat. Somewhere that the world made sense. He could spend hours choosing a new bat, because the choice was vital. It had to feel right because he would be holding it for so long. He liked to look down and see the toe sitting just so when he took his stance. When he was seeing that right, everything seemed to flow. He created little rituals between each ball, a touch of each pad, a hand on the box, a move across the crease, bat held out towards gully, just like Bradman.

It was all there, just hidden behind his bowling, tucked away beneath Australia's urge to find a new Shane Warne.

Trent Woodhill saw it. He looked at Steve Smith and understood what he was seeing. Trent had his own ideas about coaching cricket, mainly that you coached the player not the game. Orthodoxy was that one size fitted all; Woodhill was holistic and outward-looking. 'Australians,' Trent said, 'do not like things they're not used to seeing.' It was a line with echoes of Bradman's own when, towards the end of his life, an interviewer asked him, 'why don't the others bat like you?' and he replied, 'because they're coached not to'.

International cricket came along too early for Steve Smith, and in the years between his debut and his first hundred at the Oval, the Piggy Years, other coaches from all levels got into him. Woodhill said that Smith 'had to fight for his technique'. He had an on-field mishap with Ricky Ponting at the World Cup, when they collided going for the same catch. He had a shy at the stumps when India needed six to win the first Test in Mohali with one wicket remaining and he was on as the sub fielder, missing by a couple of inches and watching the ball rocket through cover for four overthrows. India won. He had his role as joke-teller at the 2010–11 Ashes. His bowling returns, never high, diminished. Shane Warne tried to help by slowing his run down and getting his left shoulder higher. Warne's coach, a maverick called Terry Jenner, felt Smith had been picked too soon. Kerry O'Keefe, another Australian leggie, said he'd always been more of a batsman than a bowler.

The Oval changed it all, the last day of the misfit Piggy Smith. In the 97 innings since, he'd made another 26 centuries at a rate of one every two Test matches. His overall average had more than doubled: it now stood at 62.84. Forty-two per cent of Australia's total runs in Test matches were made while Steve Smith was batting. He made half of those. The figures began to have a weird attraction of their own, as if reading them for long enough would reveal the secrets of their making.

It was insane, and you couldn't keep looking back and comparing him to someone who had played almost a century ago in the same way that you couldn't keep comparing Kohli to Gavaskar and Tendulkar. No, you had to look forward, at what Steve Smith and Virat Kohli said about cricket's future.

Bat, Ball and Field

John Jacobs watched thousands of people swing a golf club thousands of different ways and realised that the one thing they all had in common was the ball and what it did. How the club struck the ball was secondary to how *well* the club struck the ball. Golf diverged from cricket at that point, but the lesson John Jacobs learned had meaning. For a century or more the game of cricket had valued how the ball was struck rather than how well. A genius called Bradman had come along and been treated as an outlier, and the Don was grouchy that cricket revered his batting and ignored how he did it. He was the road not taken, so much better than everyone else that he could only be a fluke.

At his peak, Tiger Woods was the greatest golfer that ever played. He was so far ahead of anyone else that the player who was second in the world golf rankings at that time, Phil Mickelson, was closer in ranking points to the world number 1000 than he was to Woods. Yet Woods did not have the best swing in the game, far from it, but he dragged the rest of golf with him. A generation followed him into the gym as well as the driving range. They hit the ball as far as he did. They left behind the old mindset that winning one tournament per year was a successful season. They might not have been good enough to replicate his dominance, but they changed the sport and how it was played forever.

Woods' impact on golf was immediate and transformational. Cricket's batting revolution came not in the 1950s, with the first post-Bradman generation, but half a century later in the noughties.

Research into Bradman's 'rotary' method, begun by a club cricketer from Liverpool called Tony Shillinglaw and taken on by Bob Woolmer and Tim Noakes and then by Tim Noakes' PhD student Habib Noorbhai, found echoes in the techniques of other great players, most noticeably in Steve Smith, but also in George Headley, Brian

Lara and Shivnarine Chanderpaul.* And the rotary method was teachable. Its next application seemed sure to come in T20 cricket because a long and fluid flow of the bat was made for big hitting.

But a single new orthodoxy was impossible. Steve Smith may have been ahead of Virat Kohli in Test match run-scoring, but Kohli's record in the white ball game was just as dominant.† And he did it by heightening his method, not changing it. Kohli batted in the same way, just at different tempos.

T20 cricket was a swipe-right culture of fleeting hook-ups and brief infatuations, a temporary and transactional process. But it could make fortunes and it was like some kind of Jurassic era for technique, a time of rare fecundity and proliferation, where extraordinary things grew and lived. It had an unbalancing effect on longer-form cricket,

---

* At the time of his death in March 2007, Woolmer was in the process of completing *The Art And Science of Cricket*, a modern and sadly posthumous masterpiece that encapsulated much of his thinking about the game. His collaborator, the South African sports scientist Tim Noakes, completed the project. Before Woolmer left for the cricket world cup during which he died, Noakes had shown him a series of pictures that demonstrated elements of the rotary method in some of the game's great players. 'Well, Tim,' Woolmer said, 'we must look at this as soon as I get back.' Noakes and his student Habib Noorbhai have continued to do so. Habib's research is available online.

† At the time of writing, Kohli had made 43 centuries in 239 ODI innings and had a batting average of a touch below 60. Only Sachin Tendulkar had ever made more hundreds in the format, but his 49 were compiled over 452 innings. Kohli's average was fourteen more than Tendulkar's and seven above anyone else who has ever played. Kohli averages above 50 in Test, ODI, T20, First-Class and List A cricket, and stands at 40 in franchise cricket. He has 70 international hundreds compared to Steve Smith's 35. Smith in turn averages seven more than Kohli in Test cricket. He ended the 2019 Ashes series with the second-best average of all time, behind only Bradman, and after 73 Tests it was continuing to climb rather than level out.

but the history of the game suggested that it would soon be absorbed and accommodated, as change always was.

Franchise cricket commodified cricketers in a new and different way. They became more like golfers, freelance contractors moving from opportunity to opportunity. It seemed a logical extension to imagine that soon they would build their own support system of coaches and trainers and psychologists in the same way that golfers did, running themselves like mini-corporations to keep things in competitive shape. Cricket was atomising and it was impossible to play it or teach it in just one way. You had to start with the ball, and what it did.

Trent Woodhill watched Steve Smith grow up into the greatest batsman since Bradman, doing lots of the same things that Bradman did. As a coach, he didn't believe particularly in orthodoxy or in the game's existing organisations. He was a pure thinker, a radical, an outlier looking in. His fundamentals were simple and universal. 'You have to have balance, watch the ball, have the ability to play late and transfer your weight late through the ball, and read what the bowler is trying to do', he said. 'They are the things you can't get away from. But then if you look at the best batsmen in the world at the moment – Root, Williamson, Smith, Kohli or De Villiers – none of them look similar. It's when we pick a strength of one of them and try to put that into another one that we can come unstuck.'

Virat Kohli
2008–

Steve Smith
2010–

BALL

LENGTHS

A bowler's length is the distance the ball lands from the batsman's stumps

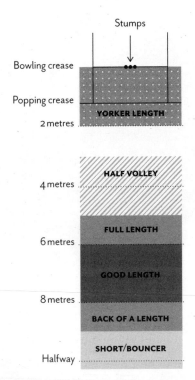

England's lead analyst (and novelist in his spare time) Nathan Leamon calculated from a representative sample in Test cricket that the average length of the seam bowler was seven metres +/- 0.5 metres. Of the bowlers to have delivered more than 1,000 deliveries in Test cricket between 2016–18, the four with the highest percentage of deliveries landing in the six- to eight-metre range had the best bowling average. His analysis broke the data down into morning, afternoon and evening sessions in different countries and conditions, so subtle questions were always being asked of bowlers, but, as a rule of thumb, the good length works because, with a ball travelling at around thirty-two metres per second, a batsman needs one to two metres after it has landed to judge the length and perceive bounce and movement, four to five metres to react and move, and then will intercept the ball two metres in front of the stumps. Deliveries pitching short of the eight-metre mark were twice as expensive.

LINES

The line a bowler chooses depends on a series of variables: their style, the conditions, their plans to opposing batters, the match situation and so on. There is, as Nathan Leamon has noted, a 'complex interplay between line, length and height (bounce)', but as a general guide:

FOR THE RIGHT-HANDED BATTER

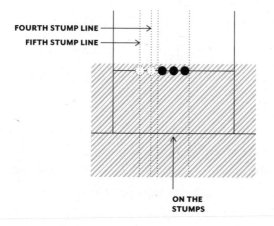

FOURTH STUMP LINE

FIFTH STUMP LINE

ON THE STUMPS

Most bowlers will concentrate on these lines, sometimes trying to drag the batter wider, and then bowl a ball on the line of the stumps to trap them LBW. Along with line, the angle of delivery is important – a bowler can vary that by using the width of the bowling crease, getting close to umpire, or stepping wide in delivery stride and angling the ball in. A further, and often effective, variation is for a bowler to come around the wicket (ie the leg side of the stumps), offering a new variety of lines across the striker.

At Stonyhurst

Robert Persons returned to England in 1580. He sailed into Southampton disguised as a choleric soldier and began his delicate insurgency. He was a Jesuit, born in Nether Stowey, a pupil and later a fellow at Oxford, but above all a Catholic in Elizabeth I's Protestant realm. He went to Rome in 1575 and was ordained there three years later. He had been 'touched by the sins of the world', a man of action drawn back to the land of his birth to serve as a 'shock troop' of the Church. With his friend Edmund Campion, a 'spiritual gladiator' who travelled under cover as a jewellers' merchant, he set up a clandestine printing press at Uxbridge that he had to relocate to deeper country at Stonor as the net closed in on them. Persons and Campion published the first Jesuit work in England, *A Brief Discors Contayning Certayn Reasons Why Catholiques Refuse To Go To Church*, and, provocatively, dedicated it to the queen. To Elizabeth's mind, if the old religion refused to pass away, 'it would have to be murdered'. Campion was captured, tortured and then, on 1 December 1581, hung, drawn and quartered at Tyburn alongside Ralph Sherwin and Alexander Briant. Persons, cast as the Machiavelli to Campion's martyred knight, escaped once again to France. He was to leave another, stranger, legacy to England there.

In 1582 he established a school for English boys at Eu, which transferred to St Omer in Lancashire in 1594 and became, with time, Stonyhurst College. The boys brought a curious Elizabethan game with them across the channel, a game fostered in the cloistered secrecy of Eu. The game was like a coelacanth, an evolutionary branch of cricket sealed off from the world in the way that pursuits like Eton's Wall Game and Field Game were, never played beyond the school boundary.

Stonyhurst Cricket was a derivative of Trap-Ball and Tip-Ball, played between Easter and Whitsun by teams of five on a gravel pitch 27 yards long with a stone wicket at one end and a running-in stone at the other, using bats made by the nearby villagers. Each batsman had 21 balls to face, which, once the first was sent down, could be delivered as rapidly and haphazardly as the bowler desired. Fielders were called 'faggers' and a 'second bowler' was assigned to keep the running-in stone clear of obstacles. The game survived at Stonyhurst until 1860, when it was absorbed into contemporary cricket, and would be just another obscurity for the history books but for the ball that they used to play it.

That ball had a core of cork covered in worsted and then soaked in glue and baked by the fire. Once it had dried and hardened, it was taken to the shoemakers for casing, two halves of leather sewn together with a thick, waxed seam that the bowler could use to make the ball veer one way or the other on the gravel.

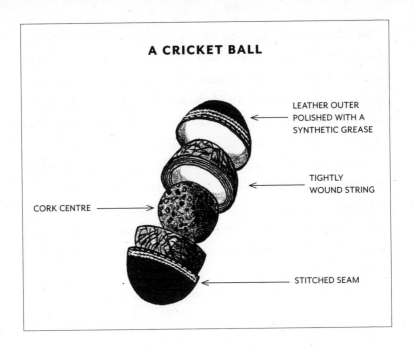

A CRICKET BALL

LEATHER OUTER
POLISHED WITH A
SYNTHETIC GREASE

TIGHTLY
WOUND STRING

CORK CENTRE

STITCHED SEAM

The history of the cricket bat, its curious journey from curved to straight, thin to thick, its response to the urgings of the game (see page 91), is almost too familiar. Less told, less considered, is the story of its other half, the ball, overlooked both as an object and as an agent of change. The ball exists at the centre of cricket's most delicate ecosystem; almost indiscernible differences in it can produce giant effects.

The seam on the Stonyhurst ball, wrote Hugh Barty-King, 'makes a raised belt ... like a ring of Saturn.' It was tough, and hard enough to be struck a hundred yards or so to a long boundary known as the Greener. In its stitching and in its conception, it was probably the first ball made just for cricket.

Yet with the Stonyhurst game stranded in its parallel universe, another evolutionary branch took life. Duke & Son, a bootmaker with a sideline in producing cricket equipment, read the runes and set up a specialist workshop at Penshurst, making a 'triple sewn' ball which, along with an externally stitched seam like the Stonyhurst ball, had an internally stitched quarter seam too. Duke's*, 'makers of the finest cricket balls', soon had a royal warrant, signed by George IV, an avid cricket follower.

The booming ball trade was a signal of cricket's popularity within the fancy – the dukes, lords, landowners and gentry obsessed with the game. With big money gambled on private matches, and with the wages of their professional players coming from their own pockets, the canny patron was unwilling to risk a result for the want of a decent ball. The level of craftsmanship was not just a matter of pride, but of commercial imperative.

It was a good business to be in – demand was high and the ball, although intricate and tough, was not particularly durable.† Every new game required a new cherry. Robert Dark had the monopoly on balls used at Lord's. John Small made bats and balls at his drapery business in Petersfield. Thomas Twort started up in Southborough, making balls for the Lion company and then striking out on his own. It was a tight little circle: Small's father sold some of his tools and some of his secrets to Dark, whose brother James was the proprietor

---

* Timothy Duke charged seven shillings for his best-quality ball. The Duke ball used for Test match cricket in England currently retails at circa £100.

† Manufacturers are experimenting with leather replacements to make a so-called vegan ball, so far with limited success.

of Lord's.* Dark passed on what he knew to Twort, and from Twort's fastidious nature came much of what is known about the production of these early cricket balls. He bought boxes of his rivals' products and cut them open in order to reverse engineer their processes. He kept detailed notes on his own methods, everything from the recipe for red dye to his cleverly constructed core, a layering of cork and worsted that has survived the centuries.

The weight and hardness of the ball built the game. Just as Edmund Gunter's chain brought its perfect dimension (see page 21) so the ball allowed for bowlers of all types to explore its limits, and gave cricket a scale by the speed at which it could be propelled and the distance it might be struck. Like the chain, its dimensions and construction have barely altered over the centuries. It was there from the start. Even the sound, the coming together of two natural substances, leather and willow, produced something unique and

---

* James Dark, the son of a saddler born in Marylebone in 1795, was player, umpire, property owner and developer, most notably of Lord's. He leased the ground from William Ward, who had in turn paid Thomas Lord for the rights. Dark's tenancy brought many improvements, including gas lighting in the pavilion, the addition of a billiard room and the real tennis court, and the draining of two ponds that lay on the estate. He planted hundreds of trees, and used the ground for all kinds of crowd-pleasing events, from Native American encampments to marathon walking contests. None of those helped the notorious pitch, the outfield kept short by sheep and the wicket so pitted with stones that it was a genuine health hazard (in 1881, sixteen years after Dark surrendered the leasehold, Fred Randon was struck on the head while batting and never really recovered, dying two years later from his injury). James' brothers Robert and Ben used the ground as a base for their equipment businesses, Ben producing bats and Robert pads and gloves along with cricket balls. The family name was synonymous with the ground for thirty years, and it was often referred to locally as Dark's rather than Lord's during that time.

magical, as recognisable then as it is now, the sharp crack of summer music.

The ball's capacity to hurt its players brought a profound psychological dimension, caught in the life of David Harris, the humble and unobtrusive potter from Elvetham in the north of Hampshire who became the first truly feared fast bowler in the game.[†] Harris bowled underarm, which doesn't sound terrifying until you consider the lack of protective equipment – no gloves or pads for the batsmen facing him – the decrepit, unprepared wickets that he bowled on, and the speed that softball pitchers, who also deliver underarm, can reach. Eddie Feigner, the greatest softball showman of all time, clocked 104 mph, and rather wonderfully characterised his niche in sports as 'like being world champion nose-blower'.

There's no record of David Harris' speed beyond the anecdotal: 'His mode of delivering the ball was singular', wrote John Nyren in *The Cricketers Of My Time*. 'He would bring it from under the arm with a twist and nearly as high as his armpit, and with this action push it, as it were, from him. How it was that the balls attained the extraordinary velocity they did by this delivery I never could comprehend.'

It must have been fearsome. Nyren again, this time on the toughness of Tom Walker, one of the leading defensive batsmen in the game: 'with his scrag of mutton frame, his wilted, apple-john face ... his skin was like the rind of an old oak, and as sapless. I have seen his

---

[†] Harris is well known because he was written about. I often think that much of the early history of the game, especially the narrative of Hambledon's dominance, is true but very much reinforced by the literature that exists about the place and its players. Was there an equally good club somewhere in England that simply never found its John Nyren?

knuckles handsomely knocked around from Harris' bowling but never saw any blood upon his hands. You might as well have tried to phlebotomise a mummy.*

The notion of the duel between heroic batsman and demon bowler had begun. Physical danger and psychological angst were at its heart. In 1836, Alfred Mynn, newly anointed as 'The Lion of Kent' after his single-wicket victory over Tom Hills, and fresh from bagging five wickets on his debut for the Gentlemen against the Players at Lord's, went to Leicester to play in a new fixture, South versus North. There he encountered Sam Redgate, like Mynn an exponent of the emerging roundarm style, a new and controversial challenge that would reshape the game and demand even more of the batsman. Redgate hit Mynn repeatedly on the inside of his right knee. Mynn, carved from Kentish oak, did not buckle. He made an undefeated 125, his highest ever score, but at the end of the game was strapped to the roof of a coach and dispatched to London, where he was taken first to the Angel Tavern in St Martin's Lane and then to St Barts, where the surgeon considered amputating his leg, so severe were the injuries.†

Such was the shock and sadness at seeing this amiable giant brought low, that even Lord Frederick Beauclerk, the usually intractable player

---

* Nyren was a wonderfully vivid writer, and John Arlott thought that *The Cricketers of My Time* was 'the finest study of cricketers ever written'. How much of it was down to John Nyren, the son of the publican at the Bat And Ball, and how much to his editor Charles Cowden Clarke, a handsomely connected Shakespearean scholar, remains open to debate. It really doesn't matter now: their book has life.

† Amputation would have been a gruesome fate for Mynn, without anaesthesia and with the high risk of infection. Even had he survived it, England would have been robbed of its earliest hero, a proto-Botham who forged a deep love for one of the game's archetypes, the buccaneering all-rounder.

and administrator who was captaining Mynn during the game, withdrew his opposition to the use of leg guards.[‡] After a pain-filled and sleepless night during which Mynn prayed for the courage to face his fate, the swelling on his leg began to subside, and the limb was safe.

A year later, Victoria ascended to the throne, and the prevailing Christian mindset adopted the game as a metaphor for Britishness and fair play, a symbolic interpretation that seemed bleakly, blackly comic given cricket's existential, unyielding nature, regular scandals and long dance with gambling. Beauclerk's view of the game as a kind of virility cult was absorbed into notions of muscular Christianity, and toughness and redoubtability became as prized as moral rectitude.

The grudging acceptance of protective equipment was a Victorian legacy that persisted for a century. In 1974, David Lloyd and Colin Cowdrey faced Dennis Lillee and Jeff Thomson with pads, gloves, box and rolled-up towels as thigh pads. Brian Close had his Waterloo with the West Indies in 1976 sans helmet – they didn't emerge for another few years, and were mocked when they did.

Each advance had the generation before snarling at it. Bodyline was designed to exploit the brutality and danger of the fast, short-pitched cricket ball. The West Indies' four-pronged attack of the 1980s was, too. Jeff Thomson said that he liked hitting batsmen, wanted to see blood on the wicket. All of these ideas were legitimate, and the ball was at their heart. The batsman's fight against it had a savage moral element that had run through the centuries. Cricket was meant to be difficult, a physical and mental test. Like the chain and the notch, this was seeded in the game from its earliest days.

[‡] Beauclerk had his own brush with mortality when struck on the hand, the wound later becoming infected. The injury almost cost him his life.

But the ball had other offers to make. In football, tennis, golf, rugby, snooker and almost every other sport, the object ball remained in the same condition throughout play, or it was changed. The condition of the cricket ball, though, altered during the course of play in a way that became central to the game. The lacquer came off, the leather scuffed, the seam got flatter, the ball grew softer. The players could work it into the state they wanted by shining one side and letting the other deteriorate. The variations it offered brought swing, reverse swing, seam and spin in a thousand different ways. It was a tool for the imagination, and, as always, imagination drove it forwards.

It was a miracle, this ball and the way it changed. So fine was the balance that a few threads of cotton could distort an entire season.

Take 1990. The English game was going through one of its spasms of self-loathing due to the failure of its batsmen. The groundsmen were ordered to prepare pitches that would last longer and be easier to bat on, and a change to the ball was made, producing a batch with a slightly flatter seam than usual.* In his book about the life of a county pro, *A Lot of Hard Yakka*, the Middlesex seamer Simon Hughes recalls the umpire Allan Jones pulling him aside to tell him: 'you're not going to like the balls this season ...'

---

* The move from three to four days was to allow more time for positive results, cut down on the number of draws and limit manufactured run chases (teams mutually in need of a result would often agree a fourth innings target, and then, in order to set it up, essentially fix the third innings with 'declaration' bowling – usually by non-bowlers – which would be smashed to all parts until the required number was set). Thus the need for pitches that would last for four days of play was logical, although conspiracy-theorist three-day fans felt that it would also guarantee fewer results than normal in the three-day games, given that better pitches mitigated against the taking of twenty wickets quickly, thus reinforcing the need for four-day cricket.

Hughes didn't, but the batsmen of England did. From the opening day on 26 April until the end of the first week of May, Jimmy Cook of Somerset and Neil Fairbrother of Lancashire made triple-hundreds, seven players got double-centuries and there were another 23 individual scores of 100 or more.[†] At the Oval, Surrey made 707–9 against Lancashire, a score surpassed a day later by Essex, who racked up 761–6 against Leicestershire, who then replied with 500 of their own. When Lancashire got their chance at the Oval they batted on into infinity, making 863, Fairbrother recording the highest-ever score on the ground with 366, and a young pup called Mike Atherton missing out: he had to settle for 191.

By the time this summer of hell – for bowlers, at least – had concluded, 108 games saw more than a thousand runs scored in them. There were a record 428 individual hundreds and another 32 double-hundreds. Ten batsmen got more than two thousand runs, including both of Glamorgan's openers, Hugh Morris and Alan Butcher. Graham Gooch, not a man to look a gift horse in the mouth, made 2,746 runs at 101.70. Compared to the previous season, 25,128 more runs were scored and 628 fewer wickets taken.

There were mitigating factors. The early season was unusually dry, and the wickets were flat. But the real difference was the ball. Instead of using a thread wound with fifteen strands to make the seam, the number was reduced to nine. This simple, almost unnoticeable, reduction in thickness resulted in carnage, an unbalancing of

---

† One of those double-hundreds came from Surrey skipper Ian Greig, brother of Tony, who made 291 in the game against Lancashire. Greig's previous best had been 147 not out against the students of Oxford University. At the Oval, an extra screw was placed in the scoreboard in anticipation of the first total of more than 1,000.

the game's infinitely delicate equilibrium. When the 1991 season began, the old-style cherry was back and so was the balance.

The ball would never be fetishised in the way that the bat was. Bat and batter had a connection that bowler and ball did not. A ball was used once and discarded, the bowler always looking ahead to the next. It would never have carefully designed stickers and players paid to advertise it. The ball would never be sexy, but it was the key to the deepest parts of cricket's nature, opening the door to what lay there.

BOWLING SPEEDS

Speed (mph)

95–100 mph+
Highest pace, attained by few, usually in single spells rather than every time they bowl

85–90 mph
Fast

80–85 mph
Fast medium

75–80 mph
Medium pace. Fastest bowlers in women's cricket

70–79 mph
Fast bowler's deliberate slower ball variations

65–75 mph
Amateur/club cricket fast bowling

50–60 mph
Average speed of spin bowling

40 mph
Club and amateur spin/slower bowlers

FASTEST DELIVERIES RECORDED

100.2 mph – Shoaib Akhtar, *Pakistan v England, Cape Town, 2003*
100.1 mph – Brett Lee, *Australia v New Zealand, Napier, 2005*
100.1 mph – Shaun Tait, *Australia v England, Lord's, 2010*
99.8 mph – Jeff Thomson, *Australia v West Indies, Perth, 1975*
99.7 mph – Mitchell Starc, *Australia v New Zealand, 2015*
99.1 mph – Andy Roberts, *West Indies v Australia, Perth, 1975*
97.4 mph – Mitchell Johnson, *Australia v England, Melbourne, 2013*

As impressive as they are, the fastest single delivery stats are heavily loaded towards teams that were/are covered by the correct television technology, which includes the speed gun. Bowlers of previous eras were undoubtedly as fast. As data becomes more complete, the speed of every ball is measured and logged. At Lord's in 2019 in the second Ashes Test, Jofra Archer sent down the fastest over on record by an England bowler, averaging 92.79 mph. His top speed was 96.1 mph, and at one point during his spell he sent down six deliveries in succession at over 90 mph. It's a quirk of the speed gun that deliveries which are fuller in length measure more quickly. During his spell, Archer struck both Steve Smith and Marnus Labuchagne fearsome blows on the head. Those deliveries were recorded at 91.3 mph and 91.6 mph respectively.

New Zealand's Lea Tuhuha has been recorded at 78.3 mph while playing in Australia's Big Bash T20 league. As with the men's game, data on highest speeds is incomplete. Australia's Cathryn Fitzpatrick and Elise Perry, India's Juhlan Goswami and England's Katherine Brunt have been clocked at in excess of 75 mph. Taking baseball as a model, where the fastest male pitch has been recorded at 105 mph and the fastest female at 82 mph, biomechanists have estimated that speeds of up to 81 mph will become possible.

*In the 2015 World Cup, Scotland spinner Majid Haq was clocked at 41.6 mph,
the slowest recorded delivery in men's pro cricket.*

The Over:
Holding to Boycott

An over lasted for six deliveries.

Those six deliveries could go like this:

Saturday 14 March 1981, Kensington Oval, Bridgetown, Barbados, West Indies versus England.

Michael Holding to Geoffrey Boycott.

The match: West Indies first innings 265 all out. Innings concluded morning session, day two. England to bat.

The Kensington Oval doesn't look like it can hold fifteen thousand people, but, nonetheless, there are fifteen thousand inside and more arriving, sliding through a gully under one of the stands and jumping over the pitch-side fence; climbing onto the tin roof of the Hall & Griffith stand. In the West Indies dressing room, Clive Lloyd asks Michael Holding which end he wants to bowl from. Holding has played twenty-six times for West Indies and is the fastest bowler in the world, but he's surprised to be asked, because to him Andy Roberts is the senior man, always will be.

'Whichever end Andy doesn't want ...'

They decide that Holding will come from the Northern end, into the wind, and bowl three or four overs flat out before resting and replacing Andy at the other end once his spell is finished.

Barbados is the eastern-most of the Caribbean islands that play cricket, so it was the first port of call for the earliest tourists. The Kensington Oval hosted West Indies' inaugural home Test in 1930. Legends of Barbados cricket have stands named after them: Worrell, Weekes and Walcott; Wes Hall and Charlie Griffiths; and the greatest of them all, Garfield Sobers. In the West Indies team to play England are four Bajans: Gordon Greenidge, Desmond Haynes, David Murray and Joel Garner. On the fringes of the team: Collis King, Wayne Daniel, Sylvester Clarke, Malcolm Marshall. Barbados is crazy for cricket, crazy for its heroes. The locals call the Kensington Oval 'Mecca'.

From the Southern end, Andy Roberts opens the bowling to Graham Gooch. The pitch is hard and green. Gooch takes a four and a two from the over.

Holding finds his mark. He is twenty-seven years old, six feet three inches tall. He's Jamaican, but the Barbados crowd goes wild at the sight of him. There is nothing in cricket, nothing in sport, like Holding. It's as if the air parts more easily for him, gravity yields just a little and offers him something that no-one else has – cleaner passage through the world. His run-up is the longest on earth; he comes in from nearer the boundary than the stumps. His nickname is 'Whispering Death'. The poet Roger Bonair-Agard, writing about this day, will call him 'Hypnotist Priest'. There's a story – untrue as it turns out – that he was a 400-metre runner until he found cricket, and it's believable, because he runs like an athlete, very quickly and without apparent effort. Seen from front on, the batsman's view, he begins as a speck near the sightscreen and rapidly fills the field of vision, a quirk of his running style making his head shift slightly from side to side. Some batsmen say it's best not to watch the full run-up because it lulls and seduces, and then he lets the ball go, and gravity seems reluctant to apply any brake, the air any friction, as it flies down, a red dot full of screaming energy.

At the Oval in London 1976, during a six-week heatwave on a scorched pitch with all of the pace deadened by the sun, he'd taken 14–146, the best figures in West Indies history, by bowling so fast and straight and full that the England batsmen couldn't keep him out. The year of '76 had been rancorous. Provo bombs and punk rock, rubbish in the streets, the National Front ascendant. Tony Greig, England's captain, said he'd make West Indies 'grovel', which didn't sound good coming from the mouth of a man born in South Africa. Holding, Roberts and Daniel let rip. At Old Trafford Holding brutalised Brian Close, who was 45 and playing what turned out to be his final Test. Close had no helmet, no chest pad, no arm guard, a rolled-up towel for a thigh pad. His almost lunatic bravery was famous throughout the game, but even Close buckled at the knees when a Holding rocket hit him in the chest.*

Close was Viv Richards' captain at Somerset. Viv Richards would walk through fire for him.

'Cappy, are you alright?'

Close told him in words of few syllables that he was.

●

---

* That incident, and others, prompted one of Eric Morecambe's best jokes:
'You can tell summer's coming when you hear the sound of leather on Brian Close.'

That pitch in Manchester had been crumbling.

The wicket at Bridgetown is green, greener than anyone can remember.[†] Holding thinks, 'It's sure to be as fast as lightning...'

Geoffrey Boycott takes guard. He doesn't like the pitch, hates it, knows it is too green for these bowlers. He wears a chest pad under his short-sleeved shirt, an arm guard inside a roll of Tubigrip on his left forearm, and a blue helmet with a clear plastic visor. He is the great enigma of English batting. He is approaching Garry Sobers' record for the most runs in Test cricket, 8,032.[‡] He wants that record. He deserves it. He has faced all of the great bowlers of the age, and he has done it while they are fresh, with a new ball in their hand.

But still, rumours follow him ... accusations. Accusations that he ducked the world's fastest bowlers during a self-imposed exile from international cricket.[§] He missed Lillee and Thomson in 1974–75 and

---

[†] Predicting the exact way that a cricket pitch will behave is a fool's game, but as a rule, a thin cover of grass decelerates the ball less than a bare surface, making it appear faster to the batsman (a cricket ball is always decelerating as it moves towards the batsman, although it may not feel like it is). Grass also acts as a binding agent, preventing the surface from crumbling or cracking, and it can also aid bounce and movement from the seam.

[‡] Boycott would surpass Sobers in India the following winter, finishing with 8,114 runs at an average of 47.72. Boycott's record would stand for eighteen months, when it was beaten by Sunil Gavaskar. The record has since passed from Gavaskar to Allan Border, Border to Brian Lara and Lara to Sachin Tendulkar, who tops the pile with 15,921.

[§] Boycott played no international cricket between 1974 and 1977, the reasons for which were complex. Many years after his retirement he said that he temporarily lost the desire to play Test cricket, and came to understand that he was suffering from stress.

Holding, Roberts and Daniel in '76, but he faced Lillee in 1970–71, Thomson in 1977, and Holding, Roberts, Garner, Croft and Marshall in 1980.

Boycott polarises, Boycott provokes. The rumours go on, yet here he is, forty years of age, almost forty-one, on a Barbados green-top, ready to take on the world's fastest bowler.

●

Ball one

Michael Holding will bowl six times in succession to Geoffrey Boycott.

An over has not always been this way. Six deliveries have been universal for just over a year. Law 17.1 (1980 code) now specifies, 'the ball shall be bowled from each end alternately of six balls'. Australia had a standard eight-ball over, which existed from 1936–37 until 1978–79. New Zealand used the eight-ball over from 1968–69 until 1978–79. Pakistan had it from 1974–75 until 1978–79, South Africa from 1938–39 until 1957–58.

During World War II, when, as Sir Alec Douglas-Home wrote in *The Cricketer*, 'the grim Test match against Germany had begun', England had eight-ball overs for the small amount of inter-services and charity cricket that was played.*

---

* Old Trafford was bombed in 1940, and then closed. The Oval was requisitioned as a prisoner-of-war camp, although no prisoners were held there. At Lord's the long room was filled with sandbags, and the ground was hit by bombing in 1941, and almost in 1944, when a game between the Army and the RAF was interrupted by a V1 that landed nearby (Jack Robertson is said to have hit the first ball after the resumption for six).

The game had first solidified around overs of four balls, a number that persisted into 1888 and the earliest Test matches. England and South Africa flirted briefly with five before moving to six with the arrival of a new century in 1900.[†]

But six is good, six is natural. Six gives the bowler a chance to find rhythm without getting tired, offers the chance to pin a batsman on strike and work them out, work them over.

Six offered Garry Sobers the chance to hit six sixes, a number that rang with magic.

Six gives Geoffrey Boycott an end point.

Michael Holding knows two things. The first is where not to bowl to Boycott. The game's greatest technician has a preternatural awareness of where his off stump is. Anything fractionally wide is left alone, wasted energy for the bowler. With Boycott, you have to bowl tight lines, make him play, make him do what he doesn't want to do.

Holding knows that Boycott is suspicious of the pitch. It's in his head. Tommy Pierce is the curator at Bridgetown. He tells Holding that Boycott arrived at the ground and said: 'What's this then? Where has all this green come from?'

Clive Lloyd sets a field of four slips and a gully, Joel Garner looming there with his endless arms, his huge hands. Desmond Haynes, in a white sunhat, crouches at short leg. Holding comes in, the run gathering pace, his Hypnotist Priest's head swaying as he jumps into his delivery stride. His wrist cocks back and then snaps as he lets go. The line is just right, inches outside the off stump where Boycott

---

† The launch of a new competition, The Hundred, in England in 2021 saw traditional overs abandoned and balls delivered in sets of ten from either end. Bowlers are permitted to deliver either five or ten balls each during those rotations.

must play or risk the ball landing on its seam on that green, green pitch and jagging in at the exposed stumps or at his pads. He jabs at it, hands too eager for the contact, the usual smooth certainty of judgement disrupted.

Bang. The ball hits the pitch and lifts. Boycott is not quite forward and not quite back, the ball smacking into the glove of his top hand. In fractions of seconds, he rides enough of the bounce to steer the ball downwards. It lands three feet in front of Gordon Greenidge at second slip.

Boycott turns away towards short leg, chest out, shoulders back. No weakness, no sign of hurt.

Michael Holding has gone from nought to ninety-plus in one ball, no warm-up, no loosener. Like a car crash, it comes from nowhere, happening before you know it's happening.

Five balls to come.

●

Ball two

Geoffrey Boycott has a standing joke about the best way to play fast bowling. 'From the other end ...'

Get off strike. Lean on your bat and watch the other guy.

At the other end, Graham Gooch leans on his.

Holding takes the long walk back. The crowd realise what they're seeing. The noise is a loud, low hum. Holding feels something rare. Everything about the first ball was right – run-up, delivery stride, action. That sometimes takes a few overs to happen. Sometimes it doesn't happen at all. The ground felt soft beneath his feet.

After the 1976 series in England, Michael Holding enrols at the

University of West Indies to study computer science.[*] Cricket in the seventies doesn't pay. He needs something else. He injures a shoulder and misses a tour of Pakistan, and then Clive Lloyd asks him if he wants to play World Series Cricket in a World XI captained by Tony Greig, and he earns enough to buy a car and a house, and when Kerry Packer has won his war with the establishment, he and the rest of the World Series guys re-join the West Indies Test side.

He comes in again, the air parting around him, the ground soft beneath his feet. Jeff Thomson once said, 'I just run up and go WANG ...' Holding is a different animal, but here is the same uncomplicated process, here is The Zone. Run up and let it go, make it go where you want it to go, like you're just putting it there ...

Bang. Ball two is on the same line as the first, the line that Boycott will later call 'the corridor of uncertainty'. Play or leave. Stick or twist. Your choice. You have 0.4 seconds to make it. Boycott plays, a reflexive jab of the hands, feet moving not forwards, not back, but up, up onto his toes. He misses it, or maybe it misses him. The ball is in David Murray's gloves before Boycott's feet are on the floor again.

Two gone. Four to come.

●

Ball three

Batsmen are often asked about the fastest delivery they have faced, but they tend to talk in terms of spells. Speed is empirical, but it is also

---

[*] This made Holding an extremely rare, maybe unique, example of someone being a member of both of the only two institutions in which the West Indies actually existed as a single entity, the cricket team and the university.

relative. What is survivable one day is not the next because so many things affect the batsman's perception of speed. Conditions. Bio-rhythms. Stress. Tiredness. Form. Sightlines. Match situation. A spell builds and builds, challenges them to believe that there is an end and they can get there.

An end point is important. Overs end. Spells end. Sessions end. Days end.

But the West Indies have a new strategy. Not one fast bowler, or two, but four, rotating through the day. No escape, no respite. No end. Roberts and Holding. Then Croft and Garner. Roberts again. Holding again. Croft again. Garner again. Through every session, every day, every match of the tour.

Michael Holding is in the far distance. He comes up again. This one is on the same line as the first two, but hits the seam and bounces, hits the seam and jags, sinks itself into Geoffrey Boycott's thigh pad.

The three-card trick. Two straight, one back in. Boycott survives.

Three gone. Three to come.

●

Ball four

If he has ever bowled faster, he doesn't remember it. Certainly not in his first over. Certainly not from the wrong end. Holding feels the strange lightness still within him. The crowd feel it too, in the stands, on the roof. Something is happening, something rare.

Ball four is rising from a length, seaming from that green, great pitch. Boycott gloves it downwards and it is fielded at gully.

Fast bowlers come in all types. Thommo scuttles up to the crease and then unfurls an extraordinary slingshot, his bowling arm drawn back low to the ground and swung in a huge arc. Andy Roberts rushes in, pigeon-toed, round-shouldered. Joel Garner is six feet eight inches tall and runs like a man climbing a ladder, his last jump into delivery so high that the ball appears to come from above the sightscreen. Dennis Lillee looks like a bounty hunter and has the most perfect sideways action. Colin Croft jags wide on the crease and spears the ball under the batsman's chin, seeking jaw and teeth.

Boycott has seen them all, resisted them all, and Holding is the quickest, right here, right now. He is making it seem effortless, and that is, as Boycott will say later, 'slightly scary, because he's the fastest you've faced and you feel that there is still more to come.'

And Mikey is gliding in, just gliding, no grunt or crunch, no strain, no problem, sweet as the Caribbean breeze in his face.

But Boycott survives.

Four gone. Two to come.

●

Ball five

Fifteen thousand in the Kensington Oval, and fifteen thousand more who will tell their children that they were.

This is special.

Holding comes in again and pulls his length back, the ball pitching in Boycott's half but only just, and then from nowhere ... WANG, like Thommo says, it hits that green Barbados pitch and rears, and in the remainder of the 0.4 seconds he has available, Boycott somehow computes that the ball will hit him in the upper chest or the throat and he gloves it away, a small miracle of reflexes trained over decades for deliveries like these. The ball bounces down to Joel Garner in the gully, and the crowd just ...

ROAR ...

The sound is like nothing Holding has heard in the ground before. It seems to come in waves, rolling end on end. It's a small ground anyway, and now, filled with air and sound, it feels even smaller, the stands on top of the players, every eye drawn inwards to the centre, where Holding and Boycott meet.

Five gone. Almost there. Almost over. An end in sight.

Five down. One to go.

●

Ball six

On the long walk back to his mark, Holding thinks, 'I've bowled five of the best balls I can bowl, and Boycott is still here.'

Usually it wouldn't bother him, but Clive Lloyd says this will be a short spell, three overs, maybe four, and it is hard to imagine the others will be as good as this one.

Then he thinks ... Boycott is probably guessing another short one. Fast bowlers with the crowd at their backs blow hot. It's a macho thing. And Boycott knows fast bowlers, knows how they think. Ordinarily, Holding would be thinking it too.

But this over is demanding something else, Holding feels it. As he runs in, he decides.

During a Test match career that began in 1964, Geoffrey Boycott has been clean-bowled twenty-seven times in 168 innings. Sixteen per cent of his dismissals come this way, compared to an average of more than 20 per cent. The exact number of deliveries he has faced is not recorded, but it is somewhere between twenty-five and thirty thousand. The chance of Boycott being dismissed by any one of them is in low single figures as a percentage. The chances of him being clean-bowled is 16 per cent of that already small percentage.

One ball to come. Boycott is thinking of nothing but survival. Survive, and the small battle is won. The battle of six.

Holding comes in again.

He bowls fast and full. Maybe because Boycott is, even subconsciously, anticipating another short delivery, his movement towards it is delayed, but everything is happening so quickly now it is impossible to tell. It's just a feeling that Holding has as the ball travels along the green Bridgetown pitch, hits the seam and then everything is obscured by Boycott's pad, his movement towards the ball finally under way, and for that tiny fraction of time Holding can't see what happens next.

Patrick Eager, who has photographed more Test cricket than anyone else alive, hits the shutter button on his camera. He captures Boycott half turned back towards the stumps, of which two remain in the ground, the other catapulted out of his frame and halfway to the boundary. The bail, it transpires, has travelled even further, almost to the sightscreen. Boycott holds his bat in his left hand, the right held out towards the broken wicket, his right foot not quite on this earth. Like a heroic, defeated general, he is staring somewhere into the middle distance. At short leg, Dessie Haynes is doing a strange kind of skip, his left hand waving. In the foreground, Gordon Greenidge has both fists raised above his head. Behind them all, on the tin roof, a long line of people are simultaneously trying to punch at the air and stop themselves from sliding off.

Holding is 'in a daze', still unsure exactly what has happened, conscious only of the noise that envelopes them all. He does not see Boycott turn and walk off.

From his seat in the press box, Frank Keating does. He writes: 'Boycott looked round, then as the din assailed his ears, his mouth gaped and he tottered as if he'd seen the devil himself.'

●

Aftermath

'Cricket is a game of war', Michael Holding wrote of that day. 'Some may call it a battle, but it is so much more, and the location of where it is played in the world often has a great bearing on the outcome.'

The over he bowled in Bridgetown in 1981 became a mythic thing, but only with time. England's tour had been a difficult one, cursed from the outset,* and that night England's assistant tour manager Ken Barrington suffered a fatal heart attack. The team were informed of his death before play the following morning. Graham Gooch made a stoic, emotional ton, but England lost by 298 runs.

In Antigua a fortnight later Geoffrey Boycott made a hundred, too.

It was not until October 1981, when Frank Keating published his book about the tour, *Another Bloody Day in Paradise*, that his vivid framing of Holding's over to Boycott in Bridgetown kick-started its second life. The television footage that remains is of poor quality but

---

* In St Vincent, the team's outdoor nets were surrounded by grazing livestock. There was a famous photograph of Boycott and wicketkeeper David Bairstow practising on a concrete strip with an old car tyre for a wicket. In Trinidad for the first Test, the team hotel ran short of food. England lost by an innings and travelled to Guyana for the second game, which was abandoned after the country's prime minister Forbes Burnham threatened to deport Robin Jackman, a late addition to the tour party, because he had once represented Rhodesia.

Bat, Ball and Field

that somehow adds to its power. It's easy to see that something extraordinary happened, and the symbolism of Boycott being the victim carried a resonance that other wickets did not.

Michael Holding thinks now that he did bowl faster in his career – he mentioned to the writer Andy Bull his dismissals of Ian Botham and David Bairstow on that same Bridgetown afternoon, and a spell at the WACA three years later – but he has come to acknowledge that his over to Boycott is one of the ways in which his greatness will be remembered. The over has its own section on his website, and a fan website dedicated entirely to it. He and Boycott have, he says, often discussed its decisive final delivery, Boycott still searching for the reason that the ball eluded his broad bat.

It seems to be as much about the human need for narrative as anything else. As a piece of storytelling and as sporting theatre, the over has a beginning, a middle and an end, a protagonist and an antagonist, a resolution both unlikely and inevitable.

The power of six.

Michael Holding
1975–1987

Geoffrey Boycott
1962–1986

SPIN BOWLING

There are two types of spin: finger spin and wrist spin.

	FINGER SPIN		WRIST SPIN
OFF SPIN	The ball breaks from the off side towards the leg.	**LEG SPIN (LEG BREAK)**	The ball turns from the leg side towards the off.
SLOW LEFT ARM	The left-armer's equivalent of off-spin. Delivered with the same method, and turns the opposite way, from leg to off for the right-handed player.	**LEFT ARM WRIST SPIN**	The ball turns from the off towards leg.

OFF SPINNER'S VARIATIONS		LEG SPINNER'S VARIATIONS	
TOP SPINNER	Delivered with a higher arm and more overspin than sidespin, the ball will go straighter and bounce higher.	**TOP SPINNER**	Goes straighter and bounces higher.
ARM BALL	Bowled with deliberately less spin, the ball will drift less, spin less and challenge the outside edge of the bat.	**GOOGLY**	Spins the opposite way to the standard leg break, from off towards leg.
STRAIGHT ON	Often bowled with a lower arm, the bowler uses a different seam position when gripping the ball. If the ball pitches on the seam, it will spin like a conventional off break, but if it lands on the leather, it will skid on to the batsman.	**FLIPPER**	Bowled with backspin, it goes straighter and skids on to the batsman.

Mystery spin is the generic term given to finger spinners that have produced new variations on the standard deliveries and methods. The best-known 'mystery' ball is the Doosra (though technically a variation of offspin), invented by Saqlain Mushtaq. It is bowled by the off spinner, and turns the opposite way to the standard off break, ie from leg to off. It is sometimes referred to as 'the off spinner's googly'. It is bowled by rotating the wrist until it is facing the batsman, and then imparting spin in the same way as with an off spinner.

Other bowlers, including Jack Iverson and Sunil Narine, have used their middle finger to impart both off and leg spin on the ball.

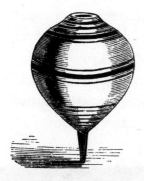

INTERLUDE

WHAT WAS IT LIKE TO SEE OVERARM BOWLING FOR THE FIRST TIME?

Sometimes, if you were in the right place at the right time, cricket would show you its future. At the Oval, for example, on 30 and 31 June 1866, when the eighteen-year-old WG Grace scored 224 not out for England against Surrey, an innings that essentially invented modern batting; or at Lord's on 25 June 1983, when India somehow beat West Indies in the World Cup final and ignited a love for limited-overs cricket that would reshape the game.

Grace ran from the field at the end of his innings, 'but experienced great difficulty in reaching his destination as his friends and admirers mustered in great force ...' At the end of the World Cup final, the crowd ran onto the ground from all corners, a human tide that massed around the pavilion as India received the trophy. Grace's followers and the Lord's crowd realised that they had seen something extraordinary and were celebrating it, but exactly what they had seen wasn't immediately obvious. As usual with cricket, it became apparent over time that things had changed, and could never change back.

But some changes were so radical and audacious and obvious that the shock hit right away. On 11 March 1843, the *Satirist and Sporting Chronicle of Sydney* published a single paragraph headed simply: 'Cricket.' Within it was the story of a revolution.

Five days earlier, 'Monday last', as the paragraph begins, the Australia and Victoria clubs had met each other, 'the game settled in favour of the natives (Australia) by a majority of 142 runs.'

Then came the kicker, a few lines that revealed nothing less than the future of the game:

> This is attributed entirely to the bowling of Still, on the Australian side, which was considered by many old Cricketers to be decidedly unfair; most of his Balls being thrown over his shoulder. This is NEVER ALLOWED in the Clubs at Home, nor is it right it should be, as the severe contusions most of the Victoria Club received while batting to it, shows that it is not only unfair but dangerous.

'The Australians must not boast of their achievement, as without Still they were basely beaten.'

There followed a rather sad coda, in which four Victorian batsmen went in against Still in 'a second match' to 'make up the deficiency', which, the *Satirist* recorded, 'showed much spirit but great want of judgment.' They lost again.

Still was years ahead of his time. The game took place five years before the birth of Grace, and Grace bowled roundarm (see page 230). The confrontation between Edgar Willsher of All England and umpire John Lillywhite at the Oval that tested the legality and the future of overarm bowling was still nineteen years away.

Those who watched Still bowl overarm in 1843 saw the future rushing towards them, shocking but maybe alluring too.

Warnie:
The Magician's Fingers

They were extraordinary, Shane Warne's fingers, like sausages that had just come out of the packet, slightly flat and squared off where they'd been pressed together. They seemed twice as thick as mine. His palms were broad, the heel and thumb-pad dense and meaty. Every now and again he looked down at them, as if he couldn't quite believe it either.

It was sometime in 2010, at a disused airfield in Surrey where the TV show *Top Gear* was filmed. On one of the runways was an old jumbo jet that was hired to movie companies and PR people as a location. The inside was still kitted out like a working aircraft, with uncomfortable chairs and zero room to move. An aeroplane seat was probably the last place Shane Warne wanted to spend any more of his time but nonetheless here he was, sat in one, on behalf of one of the many companies he spruiked products for.

I was working for the magazines published by another of the companies that Shane Warne was employed by, one of which was a sports title and the other some kind of celeb deal. The sports mag was fine. Warne was about to return to the IPL, where he had somehow, with typical Warnie smoke and mirrors, won the first title with Rajasthan Royals, something I was hoping we could bond over, but the celeb publication was a problem. They wanted me to ask him about the state of his marriage, something I had zero interest in doing – nevertheless, it had been made very clear to me that I had to. My plan going in was that, after bonding over Rajasthan Royals, I would couch an extraordinarily general question, something along the lines of 'how do you balance the interest in your life off the field', and then if he didn't mention anything about his marriage, just go back to the office and say sorry, but he'd refused to talk about it.

The only problem with that plan was that Warne rarely refused to talk about anything. He said, or at least he implied very heavily, that he and his wife were 'sorting things out', so I typed up a few quotes to that effect and gave them in, congratulating myself on a new role as celebrity hack. In the time between me filing the story and the magazine coming out, every tabloid newspaper in the land had the front-page news that Shane Warne was now in a relationship with Elizabeth Hurley.

Bowling Warnie

Everyone that met Shane Warne seemed to have a story about him. That was mine. He was like a Martin Amis anti-hero. His middle name was Keith, one of Amis' favourites, bestowed upon famously horrible characters: Keith Whitehead, for example, the acrid dwarf

of *Dead Babies* and Keith Talent, darts-playing liar in *London Fields*.[*]
But Warne was most like John Self, the protagonist of *Money*. He ran
on junk food and pop culture, heavy fuel. He smoked heroically. He
ate pizza and chips and lasagne sandwiches. He liked cheery music,
cars and poker. At his house in Melbourne he had commissioned a
mural, painted by Jamie Cooper, that depicted his 'dream' imaginary
backyard barbecue. Warne's own description of one half of this art-
work can't be bettered:

> There's Bruce Springsteen and me just chilling in the corner,
> having a drink. Springsteen's got a cricket ball in his hand, so
> he's sort of asking me questions about cricket. The legend Mick
> Jagger just sitting in the pool, chilling. And then you got Frank
> Sinatra and Muhammad Ali having a bit of a tune, singing
> along. JFK's just mixing with Sharon Stone and Marilyn
> Monroe. Two of my closest friends, Chris Martin and Michael
> Clarke having a chat ...

The other side of the panorama was, if anything, even stranger.
Sean Connery, James Dean and Warne's former Hampshire teammate Dimitri Mascarenhas were playing poker, while Angelina

---

[*] Another Keith, Keith Nearing, is a central character in *The Pregnant Widow*,
although he is most un-Warne like, and most un-Keith like. Amis' ear is viciously
attuned to a good name – Ainsley Carr, a low-rent footballer in *Yellow Dog*; Fenton
Akimbo, the acclaimed African novelist in *Money*. Keith Talent has a dog called
Clive, perhaps a nod to Amis' friend and contemporary Clive James. You suspect
Amis would have liked 'Shane' but rejected it alongside 'Warne', the chime of the
final 'e's not quite right. Warnie, in an Amis novel, would almost certainly be called
Keith, though.

Bat, Ball and Field

Jolie, naked and barely covered by a diaphanous sheet, lay at their feet. Warne's playing shirt number 23 was tattooed on her upper arm.[†]

The mural was a window into Warne's internal fantasy life. It was weirdly heightened, because the fantasy had to exceed reality and reality for Shane Warne was already pretty heightened. There were a thousand Warne stories that could be used to illustrate his reality, and many highlighting the strange dichotomy between Warne on the field, where he was courageous and unstoppable, the greatest of match winners with an acute understanding of the nuances of the game, and off the field, where he could blunder quite guilelessly into trouble anyone else would see coming.

---

† In a 2016 interview, Jamie Cooper said that Warne had designed the mural himself. The only part of the brief that Cooper had refused to follow was adding the words 'I love Shane' under Jolie's tattoo.

Martin Amis described the plot of *Money* as, 'a fat bloke trying to make a film'. John Self is that fat bloke, an ad man turned director from London who is assailed and seduced by America and all it has to offer. Following a catastrophic game of tennis against his producer Fielding Goodney, Self considers a series of increasingly radical makeovers, from a simple 'rug rethink' to total surgical intervention. Warnie too had been through a rug rethink. His had come courtesy of a company called the Advanced Hair Studio, which specialised in restoring the hair of balding cricketers. He appeared in one of their TV adverts despite not having any apparent problem with baldness. His rug was artfully bleached and cut to look as though he'd just stepped out of the surf, but with perfect hair. He was tanned and lined from all of those years in the sun. His eyes were two different colours, a condition called complete heterochromia, one blue, one brown. His presence had the heft of great fame. He wasn't like the usual inter-viewees on press junkets, spewing rote answers, bored by everything. Warnie gave it his best, his full attention. As the Australian journalist Jana Wendt wrote after her meeting with him: 'it was uncommonly easy to like him, and a little harder to explain why',* and by the time we shook hands at the airfield, mine disappearing deep into his, I felt much the same way.

●

---

* I found Wendt's line in Gideon Haigh's book *On Warne*, a series of dazzling essays about the great man. Haigh quotes an anecdote from Paul Foot about meeting Enoch Powell ('Oh my god, I liked him, I liked him!'), and writes that Warne was 'thoroughly engaging, not to say troublingly so ...' He goes on, 'I'm bound to say this was harder to set aside with Warne than almost anyone I have interviewed.'

Bowling leg spin is impossibly difficult. If you don't have a cricket ball to hand, take a tennis ball, or a good-sized apple and grip it in your fingers. The index and middle fingers need to come over the top of the ball, the ring finger held downwards against one side, with the inner parts of the knuckles snug against it. Use your thumb to steady to the grip on the other side of the ball. As you bring your arm over to bowl, the thumb should be pointing almost horizontally towards the batsman. At the moment of delivery, the wrist is rotated clockwise and upwards, the ring finger pulling up the side of the ball and imparting the bulk of the spin. Done properly and timed well, this will impart a combination of over spin and sidespin that causes the ball to dip late in its flight and, after pitching, move from leg stump towards the off for the right-handed batsman.

It is hard to do this accurately once, let alone for six deliveries in a row, but that is the minimum requirement. To get anywhere in the game, a leg spinner will need variations with which to spice up this stock delivery. There are three standard types. The best known is the googly or wrong 'un, which looks like a leg break but turns in the opposite direction, from off to leg.[†] The ball is gripped in the same way as the leg spinner, but at the moment of release, the wrist

---

† The googly was known originally as the Bosey, after its creator Bernard Bosanquet, who began bowling it around 1900 after devising it while playing a table-top game. The etymology of 'googly' itself is uncertain but thought to have originated when Bosanquet played in New Zealand. A century or so later, when the Pakistan off spinner Saqlain Mushtaq invented a way of bowling a ball that spun the opposite way to his regular delivery – by experimenting with a table-tennis ball on a table – he christened it the 'Doosra', which means 'wrong one' or 'other one' in Urdu (see page 209).

is rotated until the back of the hand is facing the batsman, meaning that the same action of the fingers imparts the opposite spin (it sounds counter-intuitive until you try it ... Grab that apple). A strong shoulder is needed to enable the wrist to rotate that far, and the googly alone is not always effective: a top batsman might pick it from the hand when they see the full wrist turn, or they may see the ball rotating the other way in the air. If they don't, they may well be able to pick the googly by the line it's bowled on – as it spins the opposite way to the leg break, it usually comes down on the line of off stump or outside. A third variant is the flipper, when, instead of being spun in the usual way, the ball is forced – or flipped – from the fingertips, undercutting it and producing backspin that makes it skid on much more quickly once it has bounced. Then there is the top spinner, bowled with the arm as high as possible in delivery, increasing overspin and decreasing the amount of side spin, producing a ball that bounces higher and keeps straighter than the regular leg spinner.

More than any other discipline in cricket, leg spin was referred to as an art. Beyond its physical difficulty, it had the fragile beauty often seen in art and artists. It had rarity. And it had geometry, an architecture that lay behind it that made it not only mysterious to face, but which had a kind of purity that yoked art to science. A leg spin delivery, spun hard, would drift in the air against the rotation of the ball, a phenomenon known as the Magnus Effect. Done right, it ascribed ellipses and arcs, it spun in perfect circles.

Australian captain Vic Richardson once said: 'we could have played any team without Bradman, but we could not have played the blind school without Clarrie Grimmett.' Grimmett was part of the lineage of Australian leg spin, along with his teammate Bill O'Reilly; Arthur Mailey before them, Richie Benaud and Bob

Holland afterwards, and others, Doug Ring, Terry Jenner, all part of the folklore of cricket in the big brown land.*

As Shane Warne arrived, it seemed to be all but over.

Leg spin had become that other cliché, the *dying art*, as anachronistic as an old master on the gallery wall. There were many reasons. Pitches were flatter, fast bowling was both dominant and terrifying, batsmen were less risk-averse, cricket was getting more powerful and concentrated. Test matches no longer meandered towards a draw; they no longer had rest days. Leg spin didn't seem to fit with a game that needed to accelerate up to the speed of the culture in which it existed.

Warne hadn't even wanted to play cricket. His first choice, his first *love*, was Aussie Rules football, a sport so deeply true-blue okker that it has never travelled beyond Australia's shores. To the uninitiated it looked like a pub full of men in singlets released onto a vast field and told to run riot chasing a distant ball. It was athletic and physical and superficially at least most un-Warne like, but he loved it and got as far as the St Kilda reserves before the heartbreak of being cut.

It was easy to see Warne in this alternative, knockabout life of the local footie hero, a matey kind of half-fame and a retirement of sportsman's dinners and pub quizzes, his great footie deeds fading gently with the years. Warnie would have suited that, easy and sunny and uncomplicated, and perhaps that's why he yearned for the career he couldn't have.

He came to cricket and to leg spin if not quite grudgingly, then not entirely committed either. The kid who met his destiny with a single

---

* Clarrie Grimmett was actually a New Zealander, born in Dunedin on Christmas Day 1891. He moved to Australia in 1914, and married a Melbourne girl. New Zealand at that time did not have Test status, and so Australia got what Bill O'Reilly called 'the best Christmas present we ever received from that country'.

delivery at Old Trafford in 1993, the one they call 'The Ball of the Century', was twenty-three years old, and an equivocal figure. He was being tested by the game. He'd had a season as the pro with an English club, Accrington, where he took a stack of wickets and made a heap of friends but was not re-engaged the following year. His first-class debut returned figures of 1–102, his first two Tests, against India, 1–228.

The initial glimmer came when he bowled Australia to a win over West Indies on his home ground at the MCG in the Boxing Day Test of 1992, but all stories demand a beginning, and Warnie's starts in his twelfth Test match, Manchester, 4 June 1993, a Friday. England are 80–1 in reply to Australia's 289 all out. Shane Warne's first ball in Ashes cricket is sent down wide of Mike Gatting's leg stump, where it obeys the Magnus Effect, which takes it wider still, before it dips, spins, then burns back across the pitch and past Mike Gatting to kiss the off bail. It happens so quickly, with such force, that no-one, including Gatting, realises what has occurred.

It suits the narrative to have this one ball as the moment something began, and it certainly changed the course of Warne's life. But that story demands it stand in isolation, a freak one-off never seen before, 'a fluke', as Warne will later call it. The truth was somewhat different, and more miraculous.

Andy Barker was the captain of Accrington CC during Warne's season there. 'We had a little chuckle when people called it the Ball of the Century, because we'd seen it week in and week out two years before against lesser batsmen, so we knew all about it when it got Mike Gatting out.'

A month before the Old Trafford Test, the Australians had begun their tour with a three-day game at Worcester, where the Worcestershire side included Graeme Hick, one of the batsmen England hoped would help them win the Ashes. Warne was taken apart by Hick, who made 187. His 23 overs went for 122 runs. Then, when Australia played Middlesex, Mike Gatting's county side, Warne was not selected at all.

Here were small clues that in the 1990s, in an era before the moneyball-ing of cricket, England did not see.* Warne was smashed by Hick because he'd been told by his skipper Allan Border not to bowl his any of his variations, just his standard leg spinner. At twenty-three years old, he had the self-control to do it. He was kept away from Gatting altogether, because Gatting was acknowledged as England's best player of spin and Border didn't want him to have an advance warning of what Warne could do.

The Ball of the Century was just one of 2,639 that Warne sent down during the 1993 Ashes, the most ever by one player in a Test series. Thirty-four of those deliveries brought him wickets, one every thirteen overs. That was an unremarkable strike rate: to find Warnie, his figures needed further parsing.

The 1993 Ashes was a six Test series, and Warne was one of two Australian bowlers to play every match. Of the 120 England wickets available (twenty per game), Australia took 114. Warne got 30 per cent of those. His 439 overs represented 39 per cent of Australia's overall 1,120. England scored 3,405 runs over the six games, Warne conceding 877, which was 25 per cent.

Of his 439 overs, 178, or 40 per cent, were maidens, and his economy rate of 1.99 compared to the team's 3.04.

---

* Named after Michael Lewis' groundbreaking book *Moneyball* on the use of statistics in baseball, published in 2003. Andy Flower, England's coach of the mid-2000s, was enamoured of *Moneyball*, and England began recording and analysing every delivery in every match anywhere that could be covered, something that soon became common practice. Gatting may not have stopped the Ball of the Century had it been bowled a decade later, but he would almost certainly have known it existed.

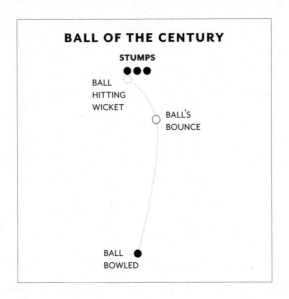

BALL OF THE CENTURY

STUMPS

BALL HITTING WICKET

BALL'S BOUNCE

BALL BOWLED

So Warne, a twenty-three-year-old purveyor of an art dying because it was too costly for the modern age, had bowled 39 per cent of his team's overs, taken 30 per cent of the wickets, conceded 25 per cent of the runs, at one run per over less than all of the other bowlers.

The Ball of the Century was, in Gideon Haigh's perfect analogy, 'the shark's dorsal fin rising out of the water', but the real story of 1993 was the other 2,638 deliveries that showed Warne was a spinner of uncanny control, relentless discipline. As a bowler, Warnie was never young. And as great a second-innings match-winner as he would become, his inimitable value lay in his ability to contain teams, to sit in with the patience of a croc at a waterhole.

The British chess Grand Master Tony Miles once described the experience of playing Garry Kasparov to Martin Amis: 'There are no quiet moves', he said. 'Everything is _sharp_ ...' Compare that with the England batsman Robin Smith's description of facing Shane Warne in 1993: 'He tormented me with demons that didn't even exist. He barely said a word but the way he looked at me really unsettled me – it was

Bat, Ball and Field

superior and knowing, as if he'd already decided how and when he was going to put me out of my misery.'

He was a young man feeling out his gifts, exploring the edges of what he found possible. His 34 wickets more than doubled the amount he'd taken in his first eleven games. Beyond that, he had expanded cricket's universe a little. His rarity itself had value. 'There was no feel for leg spin in the English game', said Mike Atherton, who played all six Tests. 'That was a real advantage for him.'

●

I had the vaguest inkling of what it might be like to face Shane Warne. In 2005, England won the Ashes for the first time in eighteen years in a series that was beyond fictional in its swooping changes of fortune and unlikely denouements. Warne had been one of its stars, a comet almost at the end of its run, both more majestic and more vulnerable than ever before.

In order to try and get a once-and-for-all hold on him, England's batsmen had been using a bowling machine called Merlyn, a creation that was in its way almost as miraculous as Warne himself. A man called Henry Pryor had built Merlyn using the parts from an old washing machine. By programming its on-board computer, Merlyn could mimic exactly any delivery by any bowler, including Warne. England's coaches had asked Henry and his son Matthew to bring it to various training camps and nets so that the players could practice against 'Warne' to their heart's content.

It was somehow appropriate that Warne could only be imitated by technology. It emphasised what a rare human he was. I went to Wales, where Merlyn was stored in a converted barn, and Henry and Matthew showed me how it worked. First Matthew fired a 100 mph

Yorker at a set of plastic stumps, which exploded from their base as if they'd been shot out. Then he reset the computer and turned an old washing machine into Shane Warne.

I strapped on my gear and faced six deliveries. I felt like a house painter staring up at *The Last Supper*. The utter magnificence of Warne was quickly apparent. The first delivery was the hard-spun leg break, the Ball of the Century, drifting outwards and upwards from Merlyn's lone eye. The Magnus Effect began about halfway down, making the ball sail as if on a current of air before it dipped sharply, screwed itself into the floor and zipped across me and over the off stump. It was amazing. The ball had been rotating so swiftly, I could actually hear it buzz past.

It was, through a bit of guesswork and a slice of luck, possible to hit one or two balls – or rather, for them to hit the bat – but the thought of actually constructing an innings against bowling like this, of being surrounded by fielders and the crowd, of surviving for more than an over or two, was unthinkable.

Merlyn offered a unique experience: the ability to face the bowling of Shane Warne without having to face Warnie himself. It was a fascinating division. I asked Matthew which of the England batsmen had been best against Merlyn: 'Ian Bell', he replied. 'He was like a wall ...'

In the 2005 series, Bell scored 29 runs from the bowling of Warne, and was dismissed three times.

It wasn't a fair fight. Bell was twenty-three, England's junior batsman who'd played three Test innings when the series began. Warne, by contrast was in his 123rd game. He was one of Wisden's five cricketers of the century.* It was like putting a promising featherweight in

---

* Chosen by *Wisden Cricketers' Almanack* in 2000. The others were Don Bradman, Jack Hobbs, Garfield Sobers and Viv Richards.

with Mike Tyson. And just as when boxers met a prime-era Tyson they were facing not just his punches but his brutal reputation, Bell faced not Merlyn's replication of Warne, but the real thing. He faced *Warnie*, a self-created force. Warnie's wickets could be muggings. There was the odd punishment beating. Often they were complex frauds, brilliantly conceived long cons. At their root was an understanding of the game and of players so acute that it may never have been equalled.

Warnie began with the observation of his foe. He would watch a batsman walk out onto the field and take in everything. Did he walk quickly or slowly? Was he licking his lips, fiddling with his kit? Did he seem at home or out of place? What did his voice sound like when he asked the umpire for a guard – strong, deep, confident ... or something else? Did he smile at the keeper, try and talk to the fielders?

He took in the stance and the way the player gripped the bat. If he'd bowled to them before, he would be looking for any changes to technique or routine, anything that hinted at uncertainty or angst. He would remember how they had been dismissed in the past, what had made them uncomfortable or unsettled. He'd think about their record against him and against Australia, about where they ranked in the game, where he'd last seen them drinking, anything and everything went in. And then it began.

Adam Gilchrist, who would succeed Ian Healy as Australia's wicketkeeper and Warnie's chief on-field accomplice, never forgot being on the wrong end of this in a Sheffield Shield game between Victoria and New South Wales in 1998. As he was taking guard, Warnie started on him: 'You're an arse licker ... That's how you got where you are ... An arse licker, mate...'

Gilchrist was upset and offended, not least because Warne and he had already played twenty-odd one-day internationals together. He took it to heart to the degree that he brought it up weeks later. Warne was astonished that Gilchrist had remembered: 'we were only trying to upset you ...'

Yet the remark highlighted Warne's ability to push his thumb into the sore spot of an opponent's psyche. Gilchrist was a nice guy who wanted to be liked, never one of the cool kids, not one of the smokers. Warne's insult burned in his head because it held a grain of truth, however exaggerated.[*]

●

Gideon Haigh felt that Warne's career had four distinct iterations. Cut forward twelve years, to the 2005 Ashes, the end of era three. Shane Warne – Warnie – is thirty-five years old, almost thirty-six. The hair is still bleach-blond, but now he looks like the guy who owns the surf shack, not the kid who works there. On the field, everything about him is familiar: the white sweatbands midway up his left forearm, the

---

[*] In *On Warne*, Gideon Haigh notes that the match between Victoria and New South Wales was Warne's first since shoulder surgery and the incident 'probably masked his own vulnerability'.

boot-cut flares he seemed to have specially made, the broad-brimmed sunhat, the zinc cream across the nose and on his lips.

Everything about him is familiar, and yet so much is different now.

The physical harrowing of Warne began early, brought about in part by his virtues. He bowled a lot because he was so accurate and so dangerous. He bowled from a run-up that wasn't really a run-up at all, just a couple of steps, and so all of that torque and fizz that he put on the ball, all of the freakish energy, was generated by his body, specifically his shoulder and his hand. By the end of theee 1995–96 series against Pakistan and Sri Lanka, he was having anti-inflammatories injected into his spinning finger. In the middle of '96 he had finger surgery. In 1998 he had a shoulder operation. In the second half of the decade he missed a quarter of Australia's matches.

The googly went first because it put a strain on his shoulder and he had to grip the ball harder than with his other variations, which caused his spinning finger to blister. In place of the flipper, he perfected a slider, a ball released from the front of the hand but with less strain on the fingers, a real Aussie ball taught to Warne by Terry Jenner, who'd had it passed to him by Richie Benaud, a bit of history that Warne burnished into a glowing bullet. During the second half of his career, he bowled, basically, two deliveries: the leg break and the slider. The problem for the batsmen was that they were delivered by Warnie, the highest IQ bowler that ever lived.

2005, and Warnie was in an autumnal sweet spot. His past two and a half years of Test cricket had brought him 167 wickets, but at his age, thirty-five, almost thirty-six, the end could come at any time, and often did. He knew that this would his last act in England. He and Australia cast a long shadow. It was a measure of their dominance that of the English team that faced them, Andrew Flintoff was nine years old the last time England had won the Ashes. Kevin Pietersen was six. Ian Bell had been three.

At Lord's in the first Test these young and fearless men hit Australia hard, draw blood from the skipper's cheek, but get hit back even harder. Warne eight wickets, four in each innings. Australia 1–0 up.

At Edgbaston, England hit Australia harder still, 400 runs on the first day, won by two runs, the second-smallest margin in Test history. Warne ten wickets in the match and 42 in the second innings run chase. 1–1.

At Old Trafford, ten thousand people are locked out of the final day as Ricky Ponting bats for six and half hours to save the Test. Warne four wickets and 90 with the bat in Australia's first innings. Still 1–1.

At Trent Bridge, Australia are made to follow on for the first time anyone can remember. England need 129 to win, and after falling to 57–4, pull it off. Warne eight wickets in the match and 45 in Australia's second innings. England 2–1.

And so to the Oval, where Australia need to win to level the series and retain the Ashes. Throughout the series, as before it, odd little things have been happening. Prior to Lord's there is talk of the Australian team going home after the 7/7 bombings in London. A couple of days before the Edgbaston game, a mini-tornado blows through Birmingham. The storm dumps an inch of rain in sixty seconds directly onto the playing surface. On the morning of the opening day, Glenn McGrath rolls his ankle on a stray ball and can't play. Ricky Ponting wins the toss and bowls anyway. There are rumours of a big bust-up between Ponting and Warne over that decision. Two days before Old Trafford, Brett Lee is admitted to hospital with an infection in his knee. McGrath plays but he's not really fit. Lee plays although he's been in the hospital. Before Trent Bridge, Glenn McGrath fails a fitness test on his ankle and doesn't play. Ricky

Ponting is run out by England's substitute fielder, Gary Pratt, and walks off shouting up at England's coach Duncan Fletcher. Before the Oval, Ponting and Simon Katich are fined, Ponting for shouting at Fletcher, Katich for something he said to the crowd.

Does Warne feel it, with his senses so attuned to the fractions of advantage that changed games? If he does, he has little to compare it to because Australia lose so rarely. If he does, he doesn't acknowledge it, even to himself.

At the Oval, England bat first and reach 62–0. The sky is blue, the pitch is flat, the score is clattering along. Ponting needs something, anything, and so he throws the ball to Warne, and it begins.

Part of the art of spin bowling is to make the batsman think something is happening when it isn't. – Shane Warne

Nothing is happening. But Warnie is here. The trickster's hair is teased up. On the wrist of his bowling arm, he has a couple of white thread bands, surf-bum chic. He bowls around the wicket from the pavilion end. He bends down and rubs his fingers in the dust of the bowling crease, as he has done thousands of times before. Two steps and then in, his first ball a well-flighted leg break that doesn't turn much and that Andrew Strauss lets go past the stumps.

'Owww ...', goes Warne.

'Aahhh ...', goes Hayden.

'Yes Shane ...', goes Gilchrist.

A look down the wicket. A smile at the umpire, Billy Bowden. In again. Tossed up, looking for the drive. Strauss goes for it, edges through gully for four.

'Arrhhh ...', goes Warne.

'Ohhh ...', goes Hayden.

Warne smiles at Strauss. Smiles at the umpire. The next one turns past Strauss' edge.

'AAAoooohhh ...', goes Warne, and Gilchrist and Hayden.

Warne says something to Strauss, something else to Bowden. Strauss steals a single, Trescothick hits a boundary. Shaun Tait bowls from the other end.

Warne bowls again, to Trescothick this time, dead straight, he plays and misses. Next ball is too short, Trescothick pushes for a couple. The next is tossed up. He misses again. Warne smiles. Warne says something.

Tait bowls again.

Warne bowls again. Strauss sweeps and gets off strike. Warne brings Ponting in even closer at silly mid-off. Ponting doesn't bother with a helmet, just his ancient baggy green, crumbling on his head. Perfect day, flat pitch, 82–0, the Ashes slipping away. Warne rubs his hand in the dust, bowls again, Trescothick defends. Warne bowls again, Trescothick prods, Hayden takes a sharp low catch at slip.

The art of making the batsman think something is happening when it is not.

McGrath returns at the other end. Australia's two champions back in harness. Warne bowls to Vaughan. Vaughan pulls a short one through midwicket for four. Warne throws one higher. Vaughan drives it through extra cover for four.

McGrath bowls again. Warne bowls again. He has Vaughan back on strike. He bowls over the wicket with a man under the helmet at short leg. He remembers the pull shot. He remembers the drive. A lot of shots for a short innings ... What does that mean? Edgy? Trying to push the game faster than it will go? Or loose?

Bat, Ball and Field

Vaughan has made one big hundred this series and not much else. Twice he's been dismissed by occasional bowlers, Katich in Manchester and Ponting in Nottingham.

Yeah, maybe loose ...

Warne rubs his hand in the dirt. Stops at the end of his run, bowls. Vaughan tries to drive the first one but hits mid-on. Warne bowls again, on the stumps again, Vaughan gets inside this one and tries to beat extra cover. No run. Warne bowls again, shorter, flatter, Vaughan blocks. Warne bowls again, slower, fuller, Vaughan drives again, Warne stops it. Warne bowls again, shorter, flatter, outside leg stump. Vaughan goes back and plays another shot, this time a nondescript flick off his pads that hits high on the bat and goes straight to Michael Clarke at midwicket. Perfect day, flat pitch, nothing happening, England 102–2.

Ian Bell comes in. Warne has been working Bell over all series. He has given him a nickname, 'The Sherminator', after an alleged resemblance to a character in the *American Pie* films that Warnie (naturally) loves.

Warne bowls again. Five at Strauss until he can get one at Bell. Final ball of his seventh over. Four minutes before lunch. He makes Bell wait. Silly point, slip, leg slip, short leg. They could reach out and touch him.

Warne stops at the end of his mark. Looks up at Bell, comes in, bowls. The ball fires from the front of his hand on the line of middle and leg stumps. Bell thinks it's the leg break and leaves his pad there, playing for the turn that never comes, the ball sinking deep into his pad, right in front. Billy Bowden's finger is up as the appeal leaves Warne's mouth.

From 82–0 to 104–3 in a moment.

●

A few months after we met at the aerodrome, it had happened. Warnie had got the full John Self. He'd shed 10 kilos. He had new teeth, so white they were almost blue. His hair looked as pricey as the teeth, lustrous and styled. His eyebrows had been 'reshaped'. He had a peanut-butter tan. He wore tailored suits and form-fitting t-shirts. The media had their fun, but Warnie was having the last laugh. He and Elizabeth Hurley had fallen for one another and were patching together a life in the Cotswolds and Melbourne. Here was a new level of fame.

And the truth was, Warne had always had a streak of vanity. One of the biggest scandals of his career was brought about when he took 'a fluid pill' given to him by his mother because he had a double chin. The fluid pill was a prescription diuretic called Moduretic and on the list of banned substances. Warne failed a drug test taken a week before the start of the 2003 World Cup and was notified the night before Australia's first game. It cost him a year of his career.*

Although the Australian Cricket Board hearing found that the evidence Warne and his mother gave was, 'vague, unsatisfactory and inconsistent', and Warne admitted that it wasn't the first time he'd used Moduretic, it seemed like the kind of brain fade he sometimes had, the ones that led him into trouble.

---

* Diuretics are not performance enhancing – certainly not in a sport like cricket, although abuse could lead to kidney problems. Their major use was as a masking agent for steroid abuse, eliminating traces of the drug more quickly. Warne had dislocated a shoulder six months before his positive test, but there was no evidence that he had used steroids, or recovered more quickly than the usual parameters for such an injury.

I admitted to the hearing that I had taken a tablet in early December [Warne said afterwards]. I was doing a lot of wine promotions. I'd had a couple too many bottles of wine and had a few late nights. I took a fluid tablet then. It was to get rid of a double chin. The December test showed small traces of the same thing. That was before my [shoulder] operation. That proves I didn't take the fluid tablet to mask anything.

The source [of the diuretic] is not relevant', said Dick Pound, the head of the World Anti-Doping Agency. 'You cannot have an IQ over room temperature and be unaware of this as an international athlete.

Did Warnie have an IQ over room temperature? On the field, sure. He was genius level, off the charts. Off it, he referred to himself as 'a dummy' or 'stupid' often enough for Jana Wendt to pick up on it when she interviewed him again some years after their first meeting. 'There is something gnawing away at his sense of self when it comes to the subject of intelligence', she said. It ran deeper than a convenient excuse for poor behaviour.

Some of the great comic turns in *Money* come when John Self misunderstands the literature he's exposed to. He proclaims Iago, 'a fun-loving kind of guy I took to immediately', and is attracted to the nightmare dystopia depicted in *1984*: 'Airstrip One seemed like my kind of town. I saw myself as an idealistic young corporal in the Thought Police ...' There's a dichotomy between the world that Self instinctively comprehends – the pub, the streets – and the one he's thrown into. 'It's exhausting, not knowing anything', he says.

Self becomes trapped by the culture that he aspires to. The same thing, stripped of Amis' satirical exaggerations, happened to Warne when he stepped beyond the boundary. He told Australia's most famous TV interviewer Ray Martin: 'Whether, rightly or wrongly, mate, whether you hate me or like me, you love the way I play or whatever, the facts of the matter are I don't read much, I don't take a lot of interest in the outside world. I just play cricket.'

Ultimately, it was Warne's Self-like guilelessness that bailed him out of the diuretics ban and other scrapes. 'It is one of those quirky, Warnian paradoxes,' wrote Gideon Haigh, 'that it was his testimony's vague unsatisfactoriness that made it credible.'

●

It didn't quite work out for Shane Warne at the Oval in 2005. That first morning was about as good as it got. He took six wickets in England's first innings, six in their second, dragged Australia along, but on the final day Kevin Pietersen made 158 after Warne had him dropped at slip. When Pietersen was finally dismissed and the Ashes were gone, it was Warne that ran over to him and shook his hand. He and McGrath walked from the field together, haloed by the sun.

I had watched all of his career, and to me he had never been greater than in those moments. Defeat allowed him to show it. Sure, he could be like John Self, a caricature framed by overwhelming and unwanted fame, but he was honest and friendly and polite and unpretentious, and loyal too. 'Warnie' was something he conjured from the game, a wizard, a true star, but not real. Philip Hensher once wrote that Martin Amis had, 'a Dickensian belief that character and name were the same thing.'

Shane Keith Warne was someone else altogether.

Shane Warne
Wisden Cricketer of the Century
1993–2005

Postscript

Shane Warne died on 4 March 2022 at the age of fifty-two. It's hard to think of a passing that has affected cricket more. There were some extraordinary moments in the weeks that followed, none more so than a state funeral at the Melbourne Cricket Ground attended by more than 50,000 people and watched by an audience estimated at one billion. That reflected not the shock of Warne's death but the size of his life, and there could be no greater tribute to him as a person than the words spoken at the service by his three children, Jackson, Brooke and Summer. Any parent would wish for those words, if too, that they should never have to be spoken.

This essay was written long before then, and as Warne the cricketer will always be vibrantly alive to anyone that got to watch him play, I didn't think I should rewrite it. I'm glad I got to shake the magician's hand. *Vale* Shane.

Spedegue and
the Quest for Novelty

You see, it was my ambition to invent an entirely new ball. I am sure it can be done. Look at Bosanquet and the googlie [sic]. Just by using his brain he thought of and worked out the idea of concealed screw on the ball. I said to myself that Nature had handicapped me with a weak heart, but not with a weak brain, and that I might think out some new thing which was within the compass of my strength. Droppers, I call them. Spedegue's Droppers – that's the name they may have some day.

– Tom Spedegue, from 'The Story of Spedegue's Dropper'
by Arthur Conan Doyle

Most cricket fans have a handy hat-trick of facts to hand about Arthur Conan Doyle and his life in the game. The best known is that he once dismissed WG Grace, a wicket so personally meaningful he composed a poem about it. The second that he was set on fire while batting for MCC against Kent at Lord's in 1903, when a delivery from

Bill Bradley hit a box of matches Conan Doyle had left in his trouser pocket.* The third is Spedegue's Dropper.

I first read it in an anthology of cricket stories compiled by John Arlott when I was a kid. I don't remember any of the other pieces in

---

* Conan Doyle was a modest cricketer by first-class standards, making 231 runs in his ten matches, with a best of 43. Grace's wicket was his only top-level scalp, the great moment coming after the Doctor had made 110 in the London County second innings against MCC at Crystal Palace Park on 25 August 1900, the final day of a three-day match. Grace was almost fifty-two years old at the time, and nearing the end of his thirty-sixth professional season. Doyle's celebratory poem was called 'A Reminiscence of Cricket', published in 1922, seven years after Grace's death. In the lamplight of memory, it casts him as 'a statue from Thebes or Knossos' with 'the beard of a Goth or a Vandal', and describes the wicket as fortuitous, the Champion top-edging a hoick that was pouched by the keeper, Bill Storer. 'Out – beyond question or wrangle', the poem went on – which, given WG's famous reluctance to leave the crease, wasn't always the case. And Grace was playing with Conan Doyle in an MCC side when the fire incident happened. Conan Doyle wrote:

> [Bradley's] first delivery I hardly saw, and it landed with a terrific thud upon my thigh. A little occasional pain is one of the chances of cricket, and one takes it as cheerfully as one can, but on this occasion it suddenly became sharp to an unbearable degree. I clapped my hand to the spot, and found to my amazement that I was on fire. The ball had landed straight on a small tin Vesta box in my trouser pocket, had splintered the box, and set the matches ablaze.

He threw the matchbox on the wicket, and soon afterwards was left not out when the final MCC wicket fell. In the pavilion, Grace told him (perhaps apocryphally): 'they couldn't get you out, Arthur – they had to set you on fire ...'

A final aside: Conan Doyle attended Stonyhurst College (see page 148) where the student body included a boy called Patrick Sherlock, and the Moriarty brothers. Doyle met EW 'Willie' Hornung through cricket, Hornung later marrying Doyle's sister Connie. And Hornung created another literary cricketer, the gentleman burglar Raffles.

A tall, thin young man was lobbing balls from one end.

An illustration from the original publication of 'Spedegue's Dropper' by Arthur Conan Doyle in *The Strand Magazine*, October 1928.

the book, and, for a long time, didn't know or recall who had written Spedegue, but the story itself was unforgettable. Deep in the New Forest, Tom Spedegue, a school teacher who is suffering from 'a weak heart but not a weak brain', devises the dropper, a delivery bowled fifty feet into the air that comes down over the batsman's head and onto the top of the stumps. Walter Scougall, an 'old cricketer' out for a walk, discovers Spedegue and his brother practising the dropper by firing the ball up and over a clothes line suspended high in the trees. Scougall writes to the England selection panel, and, after some entertaining derring-do, Spedegue makes his final appearance on a cricket field at Lord's for the last Ashes Test where ... well, you can guess, I'm sure. Spedegue is chaired from the field by his teammates and immediately retires from cricket on the advice of his doctor. Conan Doyle, thoroughly enjoying himself by this point, finishes the story with the unlikeliest lines of all: 'The Australian papers were at first inclined to be resentful, but then the absurdity that a man from the second eleven of an unknown club should win a Test match began to soak into them, and finally Sydney and Melbourne had joined London in its appreciation of the greatest joke in the history of cricket.'

'The Story of Spedegue's Dropper' was published in *The Strand* magazine in October 1928, less than two years before Doyle's death at the age of 71. It was one of his last pieces of fiction, and when it appears now, it's usually bundled together with his mystery or occult stories. But it is based on one of the great tropes of the game, an idea that has run through its history, real and imagined: the unplayable mystery ball. It is a quest for novelty, a way of the bowler maintaining their biggest advantage – the batsman not knowing what they are going to bowl. In the imagination, these deliveries can be as wild as any their creator can dream up. Three-quarters of a century after Spedegue, in Shehan Karunatilaka's novel *Chinaman* (see page 215), Pradeep

Mathew, the mysterious, absent figure at the heart of the book, can bowl ambidextrously and skim a ball down the pitch 'like a stone'.

In both cases the stories fulfil a yearning for 'a ball that can bring a nation to its feet', in Karunatilaka's phrase. And in both cases the game has proved strange enough to do it. Four years before Spedegue, Conan Doyle published *Memoirs and Adventures*, in which he recalls facing a dropper bowled by AP 'Bunny' Lucas, best known as an opening bat who played five times for England. The ball rose thirty feet by Conan Doyle's estimation, and he tried to swot it away like a fly, only to hit his wicket on the downswing and break his bat. The ball descended into the general chaos beneath, but an idea was born.[*]

RJO Meyer, the eccentric founder and head of Millfield School and former captain of Somerset, who would certainly have been familiar with Spedegue, was said to have landed a dropper on top of the stumps in a game against Kent, which brought the equally eccentric wicketkeeper Godfrey Evans to the crease. Evans countered Meyer's droppers by playing one-handed tennis shots.

Shehan Karunatilaka's notion of ambidexterity arrived in 2015, when Kamindu Mendis, a right- and left-arm spinner, debuted for

---

[*] Bunny Lucas bowled roundarm, so whether events unfolded exactly as Conan Doyle recalled is impossible to say. It has the ring of a well-crafted yarn. A further source may have been *Cricket*, a book in the Badminton Library series by AG Steel and the Hon RH Lyttleton, which described a deadly ball that 'reached its highest point when almost directly over the head of the batsman and should pitch on the very top of the stumps'. The authors claimed to have seen such bowling in a match that 'afforded the greatest merriment to players and spectators alike' and proved effective until the batsmen decided attack was the best line of defence and walloped the dropper to all parts.

Colombo in Sri Lanka's domestic limited-overs competition. He has since broken into the national side, primarily as a batting all-rounder, but the value of a bowler who can beat both right- and left-handed batters on the outside edge, is obvious.[†]

For almost all of cricket's history, bowling's prized quality has been accuracy, repeatability. Bowling was and is attritional. The greatest bowlers took a wicket with around one ball in sixty. The fewer runs scored from the other fifty-nine, the better. They sometimes bowled great deliveries, great overs, great spells, but to remain useful outside of those times, they had to be accurate. And accuracy, repeatability, having a great stock ball that the batsmen thought only of defending, was the piecemeal of the game.

It was this reality that allowed the fantasy to exist, that made writers imagine extraordinary deliveries that upturned the balance of the game. Cricket, in its nature, is a game of lulls, of tidal contrasts. The slow, prosaic, sometimes boring passages were as necessary as the symphonic swells of action. One could not exist without the other. In many ways, it was a game made of its inconsequential parts and very few bowlers escaped these demands. All of the consistently great ones had it as part of their game – the same dynamic made internal.

Notions of new, unthought-of and unplayable deliveries broke the circle, provided dreams of escape in the same way that batsmen fantasised about hitting six sixes or a hundred before lunch. And sometimes it really happened.

---

† I once played in a game at Wormsley in which the Test Match Special scorer and comedian Andy Zaltzman bowled with all four actions – right-arm over, right-arm round, left-arm over, left-arm round – in the same over.

It was 1994 or '95. Wasim Akram couldn't quite remember the year, but he remembered the game. It was a semi-final in the Pakistan Cup, one of the few occasions he had enough time away from the national side to play for PIA.* The team had a spinner he'd not met or seen before, a seventeen-year-old from Lahore called Saqlain Mushtaq. After eleven or twelve overs, Wasim called Saqlain on to bowl. He began well, Wasim thought, with good length and good pace through the air, keeping it tight. Then, from nowhere, with no change of action, he bowled a ball that bounced high and turned the other way, from leg to off, a ball so unusual that Wasim, who had faced just about every off spinner in world cricket and a fair few that weren't, thought it was a fluke. It wasn't, though. Saqlain bowled the delivery several more times, always with the same control he had over the off break.

He had come up with it years before, when he was a child playing with his brothers on the roof of the family house. They would chalk a wicket onto the wall and play a game with a table-tennis ball. While he was waiting for his brothers to come home from tuition, Saqlain practised on his own and discovered how to do it – make the ball spin from leg to off, but not like a leg break, rather with the same action he used for his regular off breaks. His brothers couldn't tell which was which. The ball, he said, 'became very famous on the roof'. As he got older and began to play street cricket with a tennis

---

* The cricket team of Pakistan International Airlines, based in Karachi. The team formed in 1960–61, and have won the domestic first-class title more than any other side.

ball, he saw boys that could bowl leg spin the Lahore way, by flicking the ball with their middle finger from the front of the hand. He began bowling his trick ball for them, and soon he was famous not just on the roof but in the streets of Lahore. It took him two or three years to work out how to bowl it in organised cricket, because the ball was heavier and the wicket longer, but he persevered. Now here he was, bowling it in front of the captain of Pakistan, who thought it was a fluke, but knew that it wasn't.

The strange, short life of the doosra had begun.

'Don't believe there is anything new in cricket', the former Australian captain Vic Richardson told his grandsons, the Chappell brothers Ian, Greg and Trevor. But sometimes new things happened. The quote from Richardson is from the first page of Gideon Haigh's book *Mystery Spinner*, which brought back the life and the story of Jack Iverson, a long-forgotten cricketer from St Kilda: 'He was thirty-one when he took the game up in 1946, thirty-five when he played Test cricket, thirty-five when he withdrew from it, thirty-eight when he played his final first-class match.'

Iverson's life seemed a little like Spedegue's, a thing of fiction, something a writer might dream up. Just as Spedegue found his method in the New Forest, so Iverson developed his mystery in Papua New Guinea while serving in the army. He held the ball between his thumb and his middle finger, the finger turned down at the second knuckle and held against the side of the ball. From there he could make the ball spin both ways and produce a top spinner, all dictated by the direction his thumb was pointing. It was a secret that would wreak havoc until it was worked out: as Haigh wrote, 'For the seven years from his unannounced appearance in the sub-district ranks to the end of his first-class career, he was perhaps the world's most destructive bowler, harvesting in all classes of cricket more than 500 wickets at a cost of just over twelve runs each.'

Iverson's story was far sadder than Tom Spedegue's. Once opponents had figured out what he was doing, he faded from the game, became an estate agent, and died at the age of fifty-eight from a self-inflicted gunshot wound. He was suffering from depression caused by atherosclerosis.

Iverson was an original, an outlier. No-one else could have or has bowled like he bowled. 'For sheer originality,' Haigh wrote, 'no-one else came close.' Saqlain's magic ball was different to Iverson's. It didn't have a name until the stump mics began to pick up Moin Khan, the Pakistan wicketkeeper, urging Saqlain on with 'doosra, doosra', and Tony Greig up in the studio worked out that Moin was referring to the type of delivery he wanted Saqlain to bowl. In Urdu it meant 'second one' or 'other one', and soon it wasn't just Saqlain bowling it but a method passed around through the game's back channels. It was transformative. For the first time in the history of cricket, finger spinners – as opposed to wrist spinners – had a delivery that turned the opposite way to their stock ball. Saqlain became the fastest player to reach 100 ODI wickets, and took 208 Test wickets in 49 games, including a legendary routing of India at Chennai. Muttiah Muralitharan, on his way to becoming international cricket's highest wicket taker, began bowling the doosra, so did Harbhajan Singh, who would finish his Test career as the second-highest wicket taker among off spinners. Saqlain's Pakistan teammate Shoaib Malik bowled the doosra, as did the South African spinner Johan Botha. From nowhere, it was everywhere.

And then came 2004.

Murali was reported for chucking his doosra against Australia in

March.* Harbhajan was reported in December against Bangladesh. Shoaib was reported in December against Australia. The remedial testing that they underwent revealed something new: almost all bowlers – and not just spinners – flexed their elbows more than anyone thought during the act of delivery. In the light of this, the ICC amended the Laws to allow all bowlers to straighten their arm by up to 15 degrees.† It wasn't enough. Johan Botha was reported in January 2006 against Australia, Saeed Ajmal in April 2009. The problem with the doosra seemed endemic and terminal. At a meeting in 2009 at the Australian Centre of Excellence, a committee including Shane Warne, Stuart MacGill, Terry Jenner and Ashley Mallett concluded that the doosra could not be bowled legally, and decided that the

---

* Chucking, aka throwing, breaks the essential law of bowling – the requirement to keep the arm straight and the elbow locked throughout delivery. For a hundred years it was a mark of shame to be called by the umpire for chucking, and careers were ruined by it. And then came Murali, and also the science and technology that began to take apart what actually happened during the act of delivery. Murali was born with a congenitally bent arm and an ability to hyperextend his wrist, which meant that he could generate prodigious spin, but also appeared, to the naked eye, to be chucking. When he was called in Australia by the umpire Daryl Hair, it led to changes that would go a long way to removing the stigma that dogged Murali and others down the years. The responsibility of the on-field umpire to call a bowler for chucking was removed and replaced by a system of reporting once the game was concluded. This was followed by biomechanical testing that revealed the degree of flex in the arm, and if necessary remedial work that continued until the player was again cleared to bowl. The biomechanical analysis revealed that bowling with a fully straightened arm, or with one that did not bend at all, was impossible. All bowlers had some degree of flex. The permitted limit is now 15 degrees, which sounds a lot but is difficult to see with the naked eye.

† The previous limits were nine degrees for spinners and twelve for fast bowlers.

SEAM AND SWING

*Seam and swing movement for faster bowlers are not exclusive.
Both can be happening at the same time.*

SEAM

A seam bowler is so-called because
they will often aim to land the ball on
its seam, which creates movement
away from or into the batsman.

LEG CUTTER	OFF CUTTER	NATURAL VARIATION	CROSS SEAM
Moves from leg to off, challenging the outside edge of the bat. The ball is gripped with the middle finger along the seam, the thumb underneath. The index finger drags down the outside of the ball to 'cut' it (effectively to impart revolutions).	Moves from off to leg, bringing bowled and LBW dismissals into play. The index finger is held along the seam, the thumb underneath, and this time the middle finger is dragged to impart the cut.	Often the ball is gripped with index and middle fingers either side of the seam, with the aim of landing the ball on it and allowing the wicket to do the work – the ball may move slightly either way, or not at all – any could be problematic for the batsman.	The seam is held horizontally rather than vertically. If the ball lands on the seam it will often bounce more sharply than if pitched conventionally (the grip is often used for the shorter delivery and bouncer), and if it misses the seam and hits the leather, can skid lower and more quickly onto the batsman.

WOBBLE SEAM	SLOWER BALL VARIATIONS		KNUCKLE BALL
A newer variation, it is bowled with the fingers either side of the seam and then dragging them backwards at the moment of release, causing the ball to move slightly from side to side as it travels down the pitch. Whether or not it seams to off or leg depends on how it lands – neither bowler nor batsman can tell until it does.	Now a vital part of any quicker bowler's armoury, especially in the white ball game. The aim is to produce a ball that is travelling 10–15 mph more slowly than the standard delivery without reducing the speed that the bowling arm comes over. There are several ways a bowler can do this, and most develop their own variation based around gripping the ball more lightly, holding it slightly deeper in the palm or with the end of the fingers, or by sliding the thumb out from under the ball and up the side, to reduce the force imparted at release. The wrist can also be rotated slightly more, gaining some back- or side-spin. The key is to disguise it as much as possible, so the change in grip should be hard for the batsman to see.		Another slower ball, this one adapted from the baseball pitcher's variation. The bowler begins their approach with a conventional grip but then before delivery slides the middle and index fingers backwards so that the fronts of the lower knuckles are resting on the leather. The ball comes out far more slowly, and will often move unpredictably in the way a wobble seam delivery does.

SWING AND REVERSE SWING

Why, how and especially when a cricket ball swings is one of the game's enduring mysteries – not even NASA have been able to fully unravel it. There are two broad types, both dependent on the condition of the ball. When one side of the ball is shiny and the other side rough, swing will occur.

SHINY   ROUGH

CONVENTIONAL SWING	OUTSWINGER	INSWINGER
Can happen immediately with a new ball, and when an older ball is looked after in a certain way by the fielding side. It works, broadly, when the shinier side of the ball travels through the air with less friction and thus more quickly, pulling the ball in its direction of travel.	Moves from leg to off. To bowl it, the shinier side of the ball is held on the right (leg). The ball is gripped with the seam at a slight angle in the direction that the bowler wants it to swing.	Moves from off to leg. The shiny side is held on the left (off side).

BALL CONDITION FOR CONVENTIONAL SWING	REVERSE SWING
The fielding side will shine one side of the ball while allowing the other to deteriorate. Most sides appoint one fielder to 'look after' the ball, and shine it.	Requires an older ball. The fielding side allows one side to deteriorate and scuff, and that side of the ball is kept as dry as possible (some teams do not allow players that sweat heavily to touch it unnecessarily). As the ball gets older, the rougher side becomes heavier, and, when combined with the right grip and pace, pulls the shiny side along, moving the ball in the opposite or 'reverse' direction to conventional swing. Reverse swing tends to happen late in the ball's flight, making it more dangerous to the batsman.

While conventional swing is well suited to the lush outfields and microclimates of grounds in England, reverse swing originated in the hot, dry and abrasive conditions of the sub-continent, specifically Pakistan, where bowlers had to develop a way of moving a ball in poor shape. England, of course, regarded it with great suspicion until they learned how to use it.

LAW 41.3

A fielder may polish the ball on his/her clothing provided that no artificial substance is used and that such polishing wastes no time.
[A fielder may] remove mud from the ball under the supervision of an umpire.
[A fielder may] dry a wet ball on a piece of cloth that has been approved by the umpires.

Australian Academy would no longer teach it. Bruce Elliott, a professor from the University of Western Australia who consulted with the ICC in the biomechanical testing of Murali's action, felt that spinners from the sub-continent found it easier to bowl the doosra than Caucasian players.

The problem was that the doosra required an element of contortion to achieve. The wrist had to be rotated almost 180 degrees to impart the opposing spin, and this, combined with the need to flip the ball out of the fingers, meant that the triceps muscle needed flexion in the elbow to generate the speed required to make the delivery effective. Saqlain had been doing it since he was a child, and so his body and bowling action had adapted. He had the strength in his arm and shoulder to do it legally. But the others had learned the delivery as adults, and it was harder for them to control, especially as they became fatigued through the day's play. Ajmal was reported again in September 2014, and although other players experimented with the occasional doosra, it began to fade from the game, its potential to devastate overwhelmed by the problems it brought.

●

Bowling continues its dance with novelty. The urge for the mysterious is strong, both as narrative and as relief from the grind. The spread of analysis, the quality of TV coverage and the mingling of players in franchise teams make its conception and preservation ever more difficult. There may be nothing new in cricket, but there is also nothing secret – at least not for long. Saqlain's effectiveness was mitigated by exposure, as was Sunil Narine, the West Indies spinner who subtly moved the ball both ways with a flick of the fingers. I remember having a long-ish argument with a reasonably well-known coach about why no-one had tried to teach the roundarm style of Sri Lanka's lethally effective quick bowler Lasith Malinga, who retained the ability to take wickets in destructive bursts deep into his career. While batting techniques in the T20 age underwent their greatest revolution since Grace resolved to start hitting the ball as hard and often as he could, bowling fell back on clever variation, primarily of the deceptive slower ball.

In 'The Story of Spedegue's Dropper', the character of Walter Scougall, the 'old cricketer' who discovers Tom, is essentially an avatar for Conan Doyle himself, a straightforwardly reliable narrator. The arrack-addled WG of *Chinaman* is the opposite, a journalist who cannot be relied on. His search for Pradeep Mathew is both mystery and spin; it's actually a search for himself and everything he has lost. It transpires that Pradeep's most famous game took place in an empty stadium, with no cameras or reporters because of an attack by Tamil Tigers; or maybe it was all an invention, a story to tell, an act of imagination that will one day come to life.

Cricket and Sadness:
Sylvers and Maco

'Have you been to Wrigley Field?'

'No. Should I? What is it?'

'It's the ball park. It's sixty years older than any other ball park in America. The slopes, the hardboard. It's sad there, as it should be. Even the best teams lose fifty games a year. That sadness gives the game its poetry. Like no other. Just look at the writers it attracts. Lardner. Malamud ...'

That exchange is a little more from Martin Amis and his novel *The Information*, an on-air conversation between radio DJ Dub Traynor and the book's protagonist, the failing and vengeful writer Richard Tull. It's part of a viciously comic section in which Richard is trying to promote his unreadable novel 'Untitled' on Dub's show while Dub juggles breaking news about a baseball sponsorship deal, reads out 'messages' from advertisers and wishes he wasn't interviewing Richard Tull. It stands as the only moment either says anything of any depth. In a book about literary envy, it is perhaps also a nod to the place that baseball occupies in the American novel. Along with the sadness, baseball has seriousness.

The sadness stands out, though. Sadness in cricket is important, too, and resonant. It is always there, in the weft of things. It is the game's low hum, one that your ear tunes in and out. This is not sporting sadness of the 'we just lost the cup' kind, although that is, as Amis suggests, in part responsible as it accrues over the years. It is something more fundamental, maybe something that has always been there, a feeling you get looking at empty cricket grounds in autumn, at the memory of matches played or left unplayed, at the people who have passed through, at the great melancholy of time itself. Cricket is sad.

In 2019, *Wisden Cricket Monthly* asked me to help compile a new list of the best cricket books ever published. The game's literature is vast and no-one can read everything, but several of the books that emerged as contenders dripped with some particular sadness or other. There was *Golden Boy*, Christian Ryan's biography of the former Australian captain Kim Hughes, a man with an uncomplicated love of the game who became stranded by the icy loneliness of his position; Shehan Karunatilaka's wonderfully offbeat novel *Chinaman* had the kind of languorous despair and yearning that only very good writers can sense and then write; *Rain Men*, Marcus Berkmann's memoir of his amateur cricket team, taps a wry sadness of loving a game that never quite loves you back; the poignancy of cricket in Pakistan lay in Osman Samiuddin's history, *The Unquiet Ones*; and *Beyond a Boundary*, a book described by one of the judges, William Fiennes, as 'a geological feature of the landscape', has, amid its idiosyncratic sweep through history, CLR James' melancholic and beautiful pen portraits of truly great players like Leary Constantine alongside the almost forgotten Winston St Hill.*

John Arlott and Neville Cardus had at the heart of their work empathy for the player. Arlott wrote essays and pamphlets about all kinds of jobbing county cricketers. He held down friendships with men as different as Mike Brearley and Ian Botham. His advice to new cricket writers was, 'get to know the players.' Cardus made stars of his unheralded favourites, the first of whom, Cecil 'Cec' Parkin, Cardus developed an almost symbiotic relationship with, Parkin playing up to the character Cardus created in print. Cardus idealised his heroes to the point that he would put words in their mouths, attributing asides and aphorisms that they never quite said in a strange kind of esprit de l'escalier. It wasn't confined to print. His biographer Duncan Hamilton wrote of him: '[He] made the dead live again. This occurred especially when describing the man he called "my idol, my hero", the imperious RH "Reggie" Spooner. He spoke in bursts of love about Spooner, compelling you to love him too.'

Cardus paid it forwards, successive generations of writers, beginning with RC Robertson-Glasgow and Dudley Carew, and

---

* The judges' final choice was, narrowly, for *Golden Boy* over *Chinaman*. Both are wonderful, although I'm not sure any exercise in ranking things like books can be entirely successful, given their different aims and outcomes. Cricket in fiction, while not quite accorded the respect that baseball gets, has been a vehicle for a kind of sadness that the best have found; from Conan Doyle's 'The Story of Spedegue's Dropper' (see page 202) through the comedy of PG Wodehouse, it has always been there. *Chinaman* has it, as does Joseph O'Neill's *Netherland*, the pseudonymous Jennie Walker's *24 for 3*, and, most recently, Nathan Leamon's *The Test*.

on through Arlott and Alan Ross to Frank Keating and Alan Gibson, David Foot and David Hopps found their own ways of communicating the feeling. Recently I found this passage from Vic Marks, the player turned writer and broadcaster, in his memoir, *Original Spin*.[†] It's a scene in the Somerset dressing room in the late 1970s, as Merv Kitchen prepares to face Colin Croft on a pitch with a deadly ridge in it at Southport: "'I'll never see it. And I'll never be able to get out of the way. I'm done for," he said (maybe to Derek Taylor, who was definitely there), as he removed his false teeth and put them delicately in his blazer pocket for safekeeping.'

It does a lot in a very few words, but as his bracketed sentence suggests, Marks is writing decades later. For many years, he remembered the game for his own dismissal in the middle of a Croft hat-trick. But when he looked up at the scorecard, there was no hat-trick, and Croft took only three wickets in the match.

It's a brilliant and revealing piece of writing, because it is about the fallibility of memory, and the human urge to complete stories, to round them off. At the heart of it all is Marks' tone, which is funny and sad, a combination that somehow pulls higher truth from the game.

Marks played most of his career with Peter Roebuck, another player turned writer, who, when I was growing up, published two books I loved, *It Never Rains* and *Tangled Up In White*. Roebuck had a complex relationship with the game, with his teammates, and most of

---

[†] Players, or more accurately their publishers, are suckers for dreadful, punning titles on cricket autobiographies, a trend that reached its nadir with off-spinner Graeme Swann's *The Breaks are Off*, which came out around the same time as wicket-keeper Matt Prior's *The Gloves are Off*.

EVOLUTION OF BOWLING

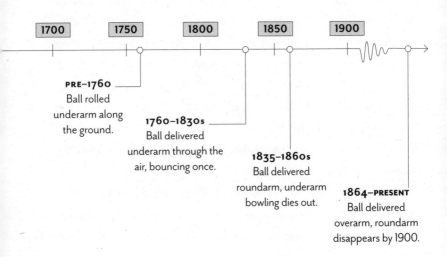

| 1700 | 1750 | 1800 | 1850 | 1900 |

PRE-1760
Ball rolled underarm along the ground.

1760-1830s
Ball delivered underarm through the air, bouncing once.

1835-1860s
Ball delivered roundarm, underarm bowling dies out.

1864-PRESENT
Ball delivered overarm, roundarm disappears by 1900.

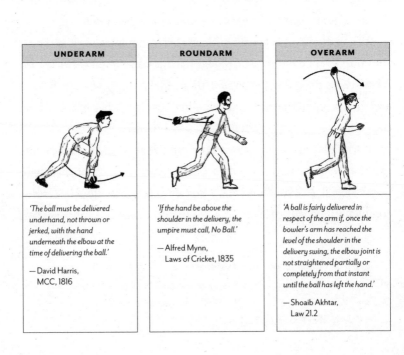

| **UNDERARM** | **ROUNDARM** | **OVERARM** |

'The ball must be delivered underhand, not thrown or jerked, with the hand underneath the elbow at the time of delivering the ball.'

— David Harris,
   MCC, 1816

'If the hand be above the shoulder in the delivery, the umpire must call, No Ball.'

— Alfred Mynn,
   Laws of Cricket, 1835

'A ball is fairly delivered in respect of the arm if, once the bowler's arm has reached the level of the shoulder in the delivery swing, the elbow joint is not straightened partially or completely from that instant until the ball has left the hand.'

— Shoaib Akhtar,
   Law 21.2

all with himself. *It Never Rains*, which is a diary of the 1983 season, is in parts vividly sad as Roebuck becomes conflicted about cricket and his ambitions in it, his struggles contrasting with the men sitting in the other corner of the dressing room, Viv Richards and Ian Botham, whose masculinity and innate sense of the culture make inhabiting it a breeze.

●

When I think about Roebuck and the other cricketers that I have somehow invested in, they share this unease in one way or another. My early hero Barry Richards grew bored of his stratospheric talent towards the end of a career that was denied all but the briefest taste of international cricket due to the apartheid ban. Mark Ramprakash carried the sadness of an unfulfilled England career while he laid waste to county attacks and became the last man to score one hundred first-class hundreds. Kevin Pietersen could never quite find the love he needed in a restless, rootless quest for acceptance. When players like these come along, it's easy to develop a relationship with their work that leads you to think that you know more about them than you do. All you really know is that their talent speaks to you in some way. So you can become like Cardus, turning them into idealised versions of something in your head, or like Vic Marks, remembering things that never really happened.

●

Sylvester Clarke was another of those players whose story held great force. He seemed star-crossed, somehow benighted. He was a fast bowler born at a time when, by cosmic fluke, West Indies had more great fast bowlers than any other nation at any other time. So Clarke, who took 942 first-class wickets at an average of 19.52, played exactly eleven Test matches, a number exceeded, in other eras, by players like Darren Powell, Pedro Collins, Corey Collymore and Jermaine Lawson.

Had he arrived ten years later or twenty, he might have played a hundred times, but instead of bowling alongside Roberts and Holding, Marshall and Croft, Daniel and Garner in the great theatres of Test cricket, Sylvester took his wickets on quiet afternoons in empty grounds, at Northampton and Leicester, in the Transvaal and Orange Free State. He played for the most part in the shadow of others.

The players knew how good he was, though: Graham Gooch had his helmet split down the middle; David Gower the thumb of his glove torn off; Viv Richards was 'uncomfortable' for the only time in his life facing Clarke; while Steve Waugh felt the will of his teammates 'disintegrate' at the thought of him. Waugh had gone on to write that, 'facing him was an assault, physically and mentally'.

Not only was he quick, he was dangerous, the ball coming in at the right-handed batsman from Clarke's natural angle of delivery. Seeing him bowl in the flesh was a shock. He had a short, shuffling run, and when he entered his delivery stride he held the ball lowdown, tucked next to his thigh, but from there everything happened with amazing coordination and power. There was something sullen about it, too. He was more like a boxer than a cricketer, and the boxer he seemed most like was Sonny Liston, an almost wordless outsider, happy to let others talk while he took care of business.

Bat, Ball and Field

If Clarke did talk on the field, because he didn't say much else, it became part of his myth. From the outside, he embodied the existential threat of the fast bowler as destroyer, implacable as a gunslinger. As it had with Sonny Liston, the world saw what it wanted to see in him.

His plight seemed lonely, isolating, bad for the soul. In 1983, his Test career apparently concluded, he signed up for a rebel tour of South Africa, one of seven that took place during the apartheid era. If he had anything to prove he proved it then, with 37 wickets in the unofficial Tests, another 20 in the one-day games, and the tour began a long relationship with South African domestic cricket, which he'd play through each English winter.

The rebels from the England unofficial tours, which included at various times Graham Gooch, Geoffrey Boycott and Mike Gatting, were briefly controversial but soon reintegrated. The West Indies tourists had no such luck, no such forgiveness. They were all banned for life. The captain, Lawrence Rowe, moved to Miami to leave the stigma behind. Richard 'Danny Germs' Austin died after a life of homeless drug addiction. David Murray, the wicketkeeper behind the stumps for Michael Holding's over to Geoffrey Boycott (see page 160), sells trinkets to tourists on the beach.

Clarke returned to Barbados after he retired, and died there of a heart attack at the age of forty-five, three weeks after the passing of Malcolm Marshall from cancer. It seemed that his story, like Sonny Liston's, had its early and inevitable end.

Those who had seen him play, and those who had played against him, never forgot Sylvester Clarke, but as the years passed, his name was spoken less and less often. In 2015, I wrote a piece about him. I wrote him as I saw him from the outside. I bought into the myth. A few days after it was published, I got a message from Alan Butcher.

Alan had played with Sylvester for his whole Surrey career; indeed, he'd been instrumental, in a way, to him joining the club in the first place. And Sylvester, Alan said, 'was nothing like what you wrote'.

●

It was the end of the 1978 season. Surrey were playing Lancashire at the Oval. Alan Butcher was Surrey's opening batsman. The manager Micky Stewart had asked him to come to the ground early – he needed someone to bat against a triallist, a possible signing for the following year. Butcher was still half-asleep after his journey through the morning rush hour. It was 9 a.m. Stewart sent him out to an unprepared, end-of-year practice strip on the far edge of the square, dry and roughed up by a season's footfall. The triallist marked out his run, 'no more than fifteen yards,' Butcher said, 'which was reassuring.' He did notice something strange, though. Clive Lloyd, Lancashire's captain as well as West Indies', was already out on the opposition balcony along with half of his team. Butcher ignored them and took his lefty guard. The triallist ambled in, 'almost waddling', he said. 'This was only going to be a loosener ...'

Alan Butcher loved facing fast bowling. It was scary in the way that a horror flick or a rollercoaster was scary – it got the adrenaline pumping, the fight-or-flight reflex ready. Butcher's was finely tuned to 'fight'. He'd been hit on the head by Imran Khan, John Snow and Andy Roberts and played on. It was an occupational hazard of the era, an era when every county seemed to have a lethal quick bowler waiting for him. Nonetheless, he'd built a career on his ability to play it, day in day out, on all pitches, in all weathers.

The triallist finished his amble to the crease, did a strange kind of double-whirl with his arm and WHOOSH ... It was no loosener. In the early morning light Butcher just about picked out a red missile that pitched on the back of a good length, then catapulted upwards and across him and disappeared over his left shoulder. It was still on the rise when it hit Jack Richards' gloves.

From the Lancashire balcony came some awed shouts, 'followed by some excited hooting and hollering and useless advice ... "Wake up Butch ...", "Hook him ...", "Get forward ..."'

Sylvester Clarke had arrived. Butcher faced one more ball, an even more terrifying repeat of the first, turned to Micky Stewart and said, 'that'll do for me, manager', and headed for the dressing room.

Many years later, Alan Butcher wrote this about the day:

A brief encounter with barely a word exchanged but it felt like something had been forged, a comrades-in-arms thing. It led to me being present to witness the childlike, wide-eyed wonder at his first sight of snow; his despair and anger at the banana throwers and monkey calls he endured in the north of England. Later, when I had moved counties, a brute of a ball from Clarkey which smashed me on the gloves elicited a genuine, "sorry 'bout dat, Butch. Didn't mean dat, Butch." Later still, a family holiday coincided with his wedding to his long-term girlfriend Peggy. I still chuckle when I think of the reception; sharing a drink in the shade with Sylvester when Peggy, in her wedding dress, hoves into view like a Spanish galleon in full sail, "Butch, dat dress mek no sense at all!"

In April 1979, Sylvester Clarke arrived at Heathrow on the same flight as Malcolm Marshall. Sylvers went one way along the M3 to play for Surrey, Maco the other to play for Hampshire. Each county was permitted two overseas players and the only team that refused to have them were Yorkshire, who would hold out for another thirteen years.* It was a time, almost gone now, when overseas players became emblematic of the clubs they played for, often staying a whole career, their arrival each April as regular and welcome as the swallows on the jet stream. The names were easy to tick off: Imran Khan and Garth Le Roux at Sussex, Andy Roberts, Barry Richards, Gordon Greenidge and Malcolm Marshall at Hampshire, Viv Richards and Joel Garner at Somerset, Faroukh Engineer, Clive Lloyd and Wasim Akram at Lancashire, Sarfraz Nawaz at Northants, Wayne Daniel at Middlesex and so many more. Mike Procter's genius with bat and

---

* In 1968, the summer after the Summer of Love, the Advisory County Cricket Committee agreed to Nottinghamshire's suggestion that each county be allowed to appoint one overseas professional. Nottinghamshire went all out to recruit the game's greatest star, Garry Sobers, with a contract worth £7,000 plus apartment and car. Sobers repaid them with one of his most famous feats, hitting Malcolm Nash for six sixes in an over. Cricket that had become, in the words of *Wisden Almanack*, 'dour and attritional' was now, like youth culture, awash with new glamour. Among the first recruits were Barry Richards, Mike Procter, Clive Lloyd and Alvin Kallicharran, soon joined by so many other great players as the regulation changed from one to two per county. Yorkshire held with their tradition of fielding no player born outside of the county until 1992, when they signed up the young Sachin Tendulkar. Now, given the global nature of the game and the rise of franchise cricket, county spells for overseas stars tend to be stints of weeks or months rather than years. The nomadic South African spinner Imran Tahir has, so far, appeared for Derbyshire, Durham, Hampshire, Middlesex, Nottinghamshire, Warwickshire, Yorkshire and Surrey, almost half of the eighteen first-class counties. In addition, the Kolpak ruling by the European Court of Justice has meant that overseas players willing to relinquish their right to play international cricket can be employed by county teams without occupying one of the two overseas spots. Among its other effects, the ruling made Maros Kolpak the most famous Slovenian handball player of all time.

Bat, Ball and Field

ball saw unfashionable Gloucester transform into 'Proctershire', an often-irresistible force. Teams arriving at Trent Bridge found an opening attack as great as Richard Hadlee and Clive Rice awaiting them, and a pitch so green it looked like the outfield ...

The overseas pro's job was simple: to do the business day in and day out through the long grind of the circuit. In return, they were feted and loved in the low-key way that English county cricket offered. Sylvester Clarke found a home at Surrey and he gave an already powerful team its edge. Colleagues became friends on the endless ring roads and pub grub pit-stops, and they grew to know his quirks and idiosyncrasies, his love of a practical joke, his strength and relentlessness, his rebellious heart. 'For him,' Alan Butcher wrote, 'it was get on the pitch, bowl like the wind, dismiss the opposition and then enjoy. And there were others of us who shared his philosophy.' He was engaging company, kind and gentle with the families of his teammates and young fans. He would never bowl short at Malcolm Marshall, although Maco happily bombarded Sylvers when he got the chance. He once won the Walter Lawrence Trophy, awarded for the season's fastest century, biffing a 62-minute ton against Glamorgan batting at number nine, but he didn't much like fast bowling, and Butcher felt that his often brutal treatment of tail-end batsmen was a case of hating in others what he saw in himself.

Some of his fastest spells came from his pain. After the monkey chants at Hull, he reserved plenty of fire for his encounters with Yorkshire, one scrap in 1980 sticking in Butcher's mind for its untrammelled violence, with Boycott worked over and Bill Athey's helmet split apart. When Clive Lloyd, the captain who had shunned him in his West Indies side, came into bat for Lancashire wearing a sunhat, the pair engaged in a duel for the ages. At times like those, Sylvester lived up to Garry Sobers' assessment of him as potentially the best of the golden generation, and also to Alec Stewart's long-held view that he was the fastest bowler he had ever seen.

Yet Alan Butcher's judgement of Clarke as a player concurred with Clive Lloyd's. In his penultimate game for West Indies, against Pakistan in Multan, Clarke responded to having rocks thrown at him by hurling a brick back over the fence, badly injuring a spectator. He went on the rebel tour in part because he could see that there was no way back into the official side, but also because, in Butcher's words, 'he had a problem accepting authority'. He didn't believe in gym work and training. During an interview after his playing days were done, he gestured to a bottle of rum on the table in front of him and said, 'that ruined my career'. His total of 942 wickets – 591 of them for Surrey – was astonishing, but way short of Malcolm Marshall's 1,651.

He returned to Barbados, played club cricket, worked as a carpenter and, in 1993, famously turned out as a net bowler for the English tourists. Wearing his customary plimsolls, he bowled what Graham Thorpe felt was the fastest spell he faced on the tour.

Alan Butcher arrived in Barbados the day after Sylvester Clarke died, to lead a Surrey Under-19 tour. Instead of catching up with his old friend, he found himself delivering an address at his funeral. Sylvester left his wife Peggy and sons Shakeem and Sasha. Here was true sadness, compounded by the death a month earlier of Malcolm Marshall from stomach cancer. The pair had arrived in England on the same flight and left together, too.

Sylvester Clarke seemed to embody what fast bowling was in the same way that Sonny Liston embodied what boxing was. Both disciplines had romance, but at their heart they required a coldness that had to somehow be accessed. To turn ball or fist into a weapon that could harm and kill, that could humiliate and destroy great players, required Sylvester to go to that place, the same journey that Sonny Liston often took. It was what we, as outsiders, saw, and although it could be thrilling and exhilarating to watch and to write about, it had its own melancholy. It built them up as myth, but it reduced them as a man.

As Alan Butcher said, 'He was nothing like that.'

Sylvester Clarke, born 11 December 1954,
died 4 December 1999
Malcolm Marshall, born 18 April 1958,
died 4 November 1999

With thanks to Alan Butcher.

WG Grace: Bowler

The batsman, seeing an enormous man rush up to the wickets with both elbows out, great black beard blowing on each side of him and a huge yellow cap on the top of a dark, swarthy face, expects something more than the gentle, lobbed-up ball that does come; he cannot believe that this baby-looking bowling is really the great man's.

Those words came from a Lancashire amateur called Allan Steel, and they are a vivid description of facing the bowling of the Leviathan himself, William Gilbert Grace. You know WG Grace. Everybody knows Grace. The beard and the cap. The paintings and the statues. Staring out from the Coleman's Mustard advert that became a piece of gift-shop kitsch. The face of God in Monty Python's *The Life of Brian*. A century after his death, he remains more recognisable than most of the current England team, the emblematic symbol of cricket. The most famous man in Victorian Britain and its

WG: FIRST AMONG EQUALS

Bradman may be cricket's outlier, uncatchable statistically, but Grace was its great engine of creation. His first-class career began at 16 and ended at 60, 44 seasons, a record that will never be matched. If I could watch one innings from all of those ever played, it would be his 224 not out for All England against Surrey at the Oval when he was 18. He essentially invented modern batting.

Grace didn't just do things that no-one had done before, he did things that no-one had imagined. His career coincided almost perfectly with the arrival of overarm bowling, and he dominated this new form. On the bombshell wickets of the Victorian era, centuries were rare. In the 1871 season, just 17 were registered in first-class cricket, and Grace made 10 of them. By the time he had made 50 first-class hundreds, he had as many as the next thirteen batsmen on the list put together.

He was the first man to score a hundred before lunch, the first to make a triple century, the first to score a thousand runs and take a hundred wickets in the same season. He scored England's first Test century. In 1895, at the age of 46, he became the first to climb batting's true Everest and make 100 first-class centuries. It was a total many thought no-one else could meet. As it was, it took another 18 years for Tom Hayward to join him on the list. In 2008, Mark Ramprakash became the 25th and very probably the last to achieve this high mark of batsmanship. The structure of the game no longer allows a player enough opportunities in first-class cricket (Ramprakash will certainly be the last man to both score 100 hundreds and win Strictly Come Dancing, too).

empire created an image long before anyone knew what one was, and it perseveres.

Grace's fame is not the empty contemporary kind. He conceived the modern game: he imagined and then played it, and then, by the force of what he did and who he was, dragged it along with him into its new golden age. No-one else will be as important to cricket. No-one else can be. He scored the first triple-century,[*] England's first Test match century, and was the first man to score 100 first-class hundreds. He is still the fifth-highest first-class run scorer of all time. As Bernard Darwin, the grandson of Charles, wrote after he'd made that 224 not out as an eighteen-year-old for England against Surrey at the Oval: 'He was no longer climbing the ladder, he had got to the top, although he was destined to add a few more rungs to it, dizzy rungs utterly beyond anyone else's reach.'

He became the 'Champion' at eighteen, and he stayed that way, at least until Bradman – but then how would the Don have fared on the wickets Grace had to bat on?

●

Yet cricket and its establishment had no real idea of who he was, what he became, how he did what he did. The opinions of him, dripping with metropolitan prejudice, still have the power to shock. Darwin, he of the 'dizzy rungs', also wrote that Grace was 'simple-minded'. MCC's official history, published – astonishingly – in 1987, contended that WG had, 'a simple, even puerile, mind'. Even John Arlott, the

---

* Grace scored 344 not out against Kent at Canterbury in 1876. Two days after that he made 177 against Nottinghamshire, and then, two days after that, scored cricket's second triple-century, 318 not out against Yorkshire. In three innings he'd made 839 runs and been dismissed once.

most empathetic and poetic of men, called him 'rustic', and that was the view of him, the Gloucester bumpkin with a high squeaky voice and its Bristolian burr, a naive giant, a cricketing savant.

It's true that Grace was no intellectual. It took him eleven years to qualify as a doctor, and you probably wouldn't have wanted him treating you once he had. He wasn't particularly sophisticated, he was dreadful with money and he was a notorious glutton, but he was also a visionary, a strange kind of genius.

As his biographer Richard Tomlinson wrote in *Amazing Grace: The Man Who was WG*, 'Grace had a deeply analytical, creative mind, as is instantly plain from his own writing on cricket, as distinct from the turgid, ghostwritten prose that fills out most of his two, often unreliable, memoirs. It helps to think of him, just a little, as one of the great Victorian inventors.'

The Victorian inventor analogy is lovely. There's something of the steampunk about Grace, the past and the future rolled into one. 'There was a prevailing idea that as long as a bowler was straight, the batsman could do nothing against him', he wrote. 'That idea I determined to test.'

And test it he did. When Fuller Pilch, the greatest batsman of his age, was taken to watch the man who had succeeded him he saw right away that Grace was attacking deliveries that the players of Pilch's era would try only to keep out. It was a psychological shift as much as a physical one, although Grace's supreme gifts made the physical easier for him. In his early years he was an athlete: the game-changing 224 at the Oval had been interrupted overnight by a trip to the Crystal Palace athletics track, where he won the quarter-mile hurdles in his pink running knickerbockers. Grace stood six feet two inches tall, an imposing specimen now, let alone in Victorian England. His height meant that he found it uncomfortable to crouch with his bat in the block-hole. Instead he held himself upright, hovering the bat above the ground, his reflexes fast enough to drop it down on the deadly shooters that were the bane of a batsman's life. He was unafraid to hit the ball in the air, to challenge the fielders. His brutal back cut, the bat dropped on the short ball from powerful shoulders, became his signature shot. A month after his 224, he returned to the Oval to play for the Gentlemen of the South against the Players, where, in poor light, he took apart two of the best bowlers in England, Ned Willsher and James Lillywhite Jr, hitting so fiercely he broke his favourite bat. It was stunning, futuristic batting that tore apart the status quo, that made cricket question itself.

That thread ran through his life, all the way to his final innings in July 1914 at Grove Park, when he was sixty-six years old and the captain of Eltham seconds. His beard grey, limping from injury or maybe just his years, he went in with the score at 31–5 and made 69 not out, beating his age by three runs, the magical timing, gimlet eye and fathomless hunger still there, even when so much else was gone. He left behind records that took generations to break, but more than that, he left a game that was transformed into the shape he had given it. The batsmen of the Golden Age, Fry, Ranji, Trumper, lived his philosophy, and the Doctor played long enough to see the debut of Jack Hobbs, the batsman who would break his record of centuries and runs.*

And yet ... If WG Grace had never picked up a bat, if he had not

---

* When Jack Hobbs was twenty-two years old and making his first-class debut for Surrey, Grace was in the opposing side. The Grand Old Man was fifty-eight and turning out for the Gentlemen of England: neither he nor Jack could know that here was the batsman who would go past Grace's towering record of 126 centuries, finishing with 199. It's a record that, given the structure of the modern game, will never be beaten. Hobbs also surpassed Grace's career total of 54,211 runs, finishing with 61,760, another unsurpassable total.

wasted a single brain cell on the art, he would still go down as one of the great bowlers of his or any other age. He lies tenth on the all-time list of first-class wicket takers. The numbers alone are astonishing: 870 matches, 124,831 deliveries, 2,809 wickets at 18.14, five wickets in an innings 240 times, ten wickets in a match 64 times, all of this so often a mere addendum to what he did with the bat.

The truth is that there was a deep synchronicity between the two. Grace the batsman arrived in 1864, just as overarm bowling became encoded in the Laws. He was the perfect player to combat this new form. But Grace the bowler was trapped by the same events, caught in amber like an unlucky fly. He learned his game in the roundarm era, and he would bowl roundarm for his whole career, becoming more and more anachronistic until he was – literally – a bowler from another century. The notice of his death published in *The Manchester Guardian* on 25 October 1915 read:

> As a bowler in his later years he looked rather ponderous; his lei-surely amble up to the wicket and slow round-arm delivery often excited merriment, but the simple-looking ball which he deliv-ered – a slow good-length one with a slight break, generally from the leg side – was by no means easy to judge. And perhaps his suc-cess was partly due to the fact that most of the batsmen felt that he knew a bit more than the best of them. He held to the old-fash-ioned theory that length and straightness were the secret of good bowling, and that one of the greatest mistakes a bowler could make was to try to 'break' too much.

Grace said that as a young player he 'did a great deal' to master bowl-ing, although conceded, 'perhaps not giving it the thoughtful attention I bestowed upon batting'. But as the *Guardian*'s paragraph implied, it was his deep understanding of the psychology of batting that offered him an edge. As he bestrode Victorian cricket, opponents knew that they weren't facing just any old bowler. This was Grace, the dominant, bullish king of the game, whom crowds flocked to see, who cowed umpires with a stare, who did pretty much as he pleased. It was the same cult that would come to surround Shane Warne, another master of the game's great depths (see page 178). 'Take stock of your enemy and attempt to outwit him', was Grace's advice, and Warne's too.

He had a good slower ball, and he exploited his apparent lack of threat. His bowling, unlike his batting, went under-reported, damned by faint praise. But there was another reason that Grace was keen to underplay his skill with the ball. Bowlers were the serfs of the game, often professionals engaged in a labourer's trade. Grace, the game's best-paid amateur, wanted to be seen as a batsman, the preserve of the gentleman, especially in his early years when he encountered the prejudice and snobbery of London's establishment.[*]

His skill with the ball magnified his greatness. He became the first man to do the 'double' of a thousand runs and a hundred wickets in a season. In 1875, a year that he regarded as a disappointment with the bat despite making his landmark fiftieth first-class hundred, he took 194 wickets at an average of 12.94. By then, his waistline was expanding as rapidly as his reputation, and his glory years as a bowler were coming to an end. He was not yet thirty, but his weight was approaching fifteen stone, and it would rise by at least another stone in the next decade. There was a certain darkness to this, underpinned by insecurity and fuelled by

---

[*] Grace had been the game's greatest star for several years before he was elected as a member of the MCC in the spring of 1869: it had been a saga of snobbishness and sniffy committees.

Bat, Ball and Field

his early angst over not being accepted. Officially unpaid, Grace was endlessly avaricious, driven by the urge to make money. He advised his schoolboy followers to eat in moderation while gorging himself. He was held up as a teetotaller, but often drank whiskey during the lunch break. Like lots of insecure men, Grace had a bluff, bullying streak.

His approach to the crease, never a fluent thing, became a piece of theatre. Grace would 'scuffle' up to the wicket, elbows jutting out, and his feet splayed, the left planted wide on the return crease to allow his belly room, his right arm swung level with his head, the ball lobbed out with some of what he called his 'leg tweak'. Allan Steel: '[The batsman] cannot believe that this baby-looking bowling is really the great man's.'

Grace knew enough to create as much noise as he could around his lobs. As they made their way down the wicket, doubt and fear came with them. The worst thing a batsman can do is to start thinking about the shot he was going to play, and he gave them the time to do just that. He set odd fields, often placing his brother EM directly in the batsman's eyeline. And there was the great sway of personality, having his way by sheer force of will (and the weight of his presence should not be underestimated – a batsman called James Southerton once hit a ball hard into the ground at the Oval and when Grace caught it on the first bounce, walked off and refused to return. The scorebook listed him as 'retired thinking he was out').

Though he slowly ate himself out of a job, the Doctor's roundarmers were an exercise in power, a lesson in the game's oddness and the many ways it could be played. Grace the cricketer was intimately at home in that terrain. He dominated cricket's landscape, and its mindscape, too.

WG Grace, the Leviathan
1864–1914
54,211 runs, 2,809 wickets

FIELDING POSITIONS

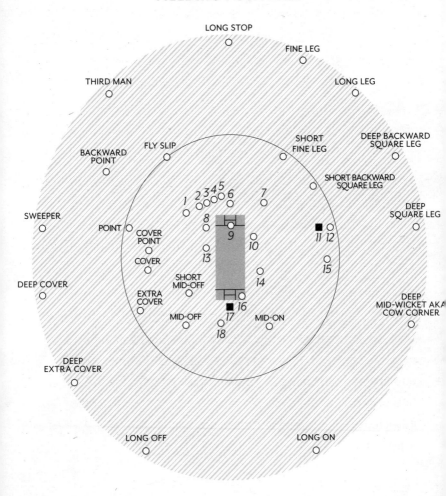

KEY					
1	GULLY	8	SILLY POINT	15	MID-WICKET
2	FOURTH SLIP	9	BATSMAN: STRIKER	16	BATSMAN: NON-STRIKER
3	THIRD SLIP	10	SHORT LEG	17	UMPIRE
4	SECOND SLIP	11	SQUARE LEG UMPIRE	18	BOWLER
5	FIRST SLIP	12	SQUARE LEG		
6	WICKETKEEPER	13	SILLY MID-OFF		
7	LEG SLIP	14	SILLY MID-ON		

On Hating Fielding

The twenty-fifth and in all likelihood the last batsman to score one hundred first-class centuries walked from the arena for the final time on 4 July 2012, taking one of the great landmarks of batsmanship into history with him.* Mark Ramprakash so loved the game that he'd played on until he was forty-two years old, but when someone asked him what he would miss the most about it all, he said, 'Well, it won't be the fielding ...'

---

* Grace was the first man to the mark. It took him 1,113 innings, a reflection of the wickets he played on. Bradman was quickest (of course) in 295 innings. Ramprakash did it in 676. The changing shape of the game, and the demands on players good enough, means that it's unlikely to be repeated. Sachin Tendulkar's feat of making 100 international centuries (51 Test, 49 ODI) is perhaps a modern equivalent, although an even greater feat. Virat Kohli has 27 Test and 43 ODI tons, so may have a shot.

There are lots of things that the amateur cricketer finds hard to conceive about the pro game, mostly the speed and power of it, its unrelenting, day-on-day nature, the rigour and discipline needed to produce the finest of motor skills on demand, but most of all, it's the fielding. Amateur cricket is over and done in an afternoon, a day at most, and with luck only half of that time will be spent in the field. The pro is regularly out there all day, three sessions of at least two hours each, often in hostile conditions, sometimes while up against it and occasionally when the wheels are coming off. The field is a factory floor, governed by a slow-moving clock, a place of constant labour.

Most of cricket is about failure. By the numbers, batsmen fail to make their average score two out of every three times they bat.* Bowlers have around a one in sixty chance of a wicket with their next delivery. Failure is commonplace, the usual outcome, and so it is accepted hundreds of times per day. But failure in the field is not, not in the professional game. The pro is expected to stop every ball, hold every catch. Assembling a decent slip cordon can be as complex as developing a batting order. The relationship between wicketkeeper and first slip needs some of the wordless understanding of a good marriage; the speed and feel of a ball deflected to third slip, usually dropping more quickly than one edged finer, is wildly different to a ball off the face of the bat that flies to gully, and yet the fielders are separated by no more than a few yards. Pros drill these things endlessly. Like boxers, who for every round in the ring fight ten in sparring, they take thousands upon thousands of catches every season in practice. When they don't, there's often a downward spiral, and how a team fields is a glimpse of its inner life.

---

* This is an odd statistic, and sounds like it can't be true, but it is. The bigger innings compensate for the failures.

Dropped catches can be sliding doors moments. England won one of the most extraordinary Test matches of the modern era by two runs at Edgbaston in 2005, the finish, with Australia's number eleven Mike Kasprowicz gloving a short ball from Steve Harmison to the keeper Geraint Jones, replayed endlessly. Yet it almost didn't happen. With Australia needing fifteen to win, Kasprowicz ramped a ball in the air to third man, which Simon Jones dropped. It was a hard catch but one Jones said he'd taken 'hundreds of times' in practice and other games. 'That,' he said, 'was the worst feeling I've ever had on a cricket field.' To compound matters, he was fielding in front of a section of Australian fans, who'd been swearing at him all morning.

'Cheers Jones', one shouted. 'That was fucking useless ...'

It seemed like a chance, *the* chance, to win the game. There is usually one but rarely two. There were lots of reasons to drop it. The tension was by that point overwhelming: had England lost, Australia would have taken a two-nil lead in the series, which was more than likely insurmountable given their greatness. England hadn't won the Ashes for eighteen years, so the weight of all of those was on that catch too. As Jones sprinted towards the ball, it dipped below the skyline, where it was easy to see, and against the stand opposite that was filled with people. He lost sight of it, and it didn't reappear until it was right in front of him. And like all of the players, he was feeling drained by the tension of the match and its significance.

But this was his chance and he should have caught it. It was forgotten when England won, and the narrowness of their victory set the series on its immortal path. But Simon Jones remembered nothing about those final minutes: all he could think of was that he had cost England the match.

For all of the advances in batting and bowling, nothing in the game has moved on like its fielding. Newsreel of Bradman is almost comical, with fielders trotting after the ball once it passed them. No wonder he scored so many. The commentator Henry Blofeld knew Bradman well, and I once had the chance to ask him about what fielding then was really like. 'It was better than it looks', he said. 'Players didn't dive, but they stopped the ball, they caught well. On the newsreels you only see the balls that go to the boundary, and so it seems odd. And Don was a master of placement, among many other things...'

But the culture has changed. In the World Cup final of 2019, with New Zealand needing two runs from the final ball of the Super Over to win the match, and under almost unthinkable pressure, Jason Roy, England's boundary rider, ran towards the ball, gathered cleanly, chose the right end to throw to. Seen live rather than on TV, that throw came in like a bullet, powered by fear and adrenaline. And Roy deliberately landed it a few yards short of the keeper Jos Buttler, who turned and broke the stumps with Martin Guptill short of his ground. Anything less than what Roy did, the slightest discrepancy in accuracy or power in the throw, and England's four years of planning to win the World Cup would have meant nothing. Amid the mayhem and ecstasy (for England at least), Roy's throw was hardly talked about. It was simply expected of him, that one perfect repetition drilled over hundreds of hours for those few short seconds.

Grace said that 'the best place to put a duffer is mid-on'. I have spent many thousands of overs there. It feels like my front room now, an angle on the game I'm so familiar with it sometimes feels odd to be anywhere else. Fielding in the pro game may be futuristically brilliant, but in the stiffs, the Don would feel right at home. For most of the years I have played, I hated fielding. It was simply the trade-off for the chance to bat. It was usually boring and tiring, but with an edge of terror, too, a fear and loathing of a mistake and how it will make you feel. The captain's gaze can burn you in those moments. You know

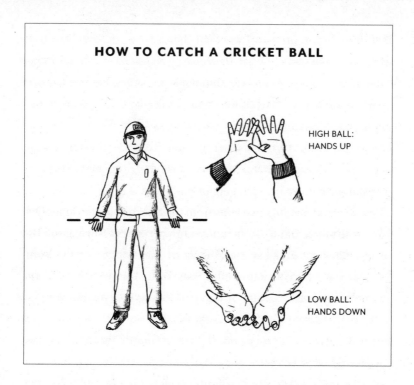

HOW TO CATCH A CRICKET BALL

HIGH BALL: HANDS UP

LOW BALL: HANDS DOWN

what they're thinking, and your mind starts to wander to the next selection meeting, what they will say ...

The biggest change in the game since I've been playing is how hard the ball is hit. It's absolutely smoked now, especially by younger players who have grown up on T20 and have no fear. They just want to smash it in the way they see it smashed on the TV, and they do. The first few weeks of the season, usually conducted in numbing April cold, can be nightmarish, your hands yet to toughen up, the ball slamming into chilled fingertips, trying to chuck it back while wearing three layers and praying no-one hits it in the air in your direction.

There's no feeling in cricket quite like dropping a catch. It's not like failure with the bat or the ball, which is more personal. It's a failure that directly and immediately affects the bowler and the captain. It feels like a hollowing out of the spirit. It weakens you psychically, sometimes physically. Success and failure in batting counterbalance – the satisfaction of playing well is great enough to offset the disappointment of missing out (two in three, remember). Unless it's a brilliant catch – unlikely in my case – the dominant emotion on holding one is simple relief. There's no fair exchange with the emotions of dropping one.

And yet cricket turns another face towards you as you get older. I hated fielding, and then, before I'd really noticed, the feeling had turned into something else – not love, exactly (let's not get carried away here), but an appreciation of all it offered. In his novel *Netherland*, Joseph O'Neill describes the rhythm of fielding, everyone walking in as the bowler runs up, as 'pulmonary'. It's an in-out with every ball, six times an over, again and again, through matches, through seasons, through decades. I have spent way longer fielding than I ever have batting, and now, on late sunlit afternoons on perfect grounds, I sometimes look around at the people I'm playing with, friends I've known for years, and feel a bond forged in shared experience, in walking in and out together for all of those overs, knowing something now that I didn't know back then: nothing, not even fielding, lasts forever.

Endless Summer

Maybe there's a word for the feeling of passing a cricket ground and sensing that you once played there, the almost-lost memory of it trapped beneath glass. I suppose it's a version of *saudade* – nostalgia for something that may once have existed. I've played cricket for most of my life, hundreds of games with thousands of people, and most of them exist in that place now, as fragments.

I once asked Mark Ramprakash about the two consecutive English seasons in which he averaged more than a hundred runs per innings, a streak of sustained excellence few have ever experienced, a long dream of endless summer. 'I can remember particular shots if I put my mind to it', he said. 'I remember down at Hampshire facing Powell, the West Indian, and hooking him ... I can remember bits ... Just the feeling of being pretty relaxed ...'

Those years had brought him a deep satisfaction. They were the high point of his professional life. He'd loved scoring all of those runs,

Bat, Ball and Field

and yet there were too many for the memory to hold and so they'd coalesced into feelings and sensations and might only come back clearly if he saw a video or went back to a certain ground or had his memory jogged by a teammate or a fan.

It seemed to be a common experience. At least pros had a framework for the games they played. There were scorebooks and websites, TV footage and books, ways of keeping the detail alive. But professional cricket was a fraction of all of the cricket that was played, and pros an even smaller fraction of the number of people who played it. The amateur game is vast and unmapped, cricket's real hinterland.

In *The Meaning of Cricket*, I wrote about a game I played for Basingstoke decades ago as an under-17. Our opening bowler Simon Lock had taken all ten wickets, a remarkable feat. I'd not seen Simon for many years, but when the book came out, he got in touch. He remembered the name of the team we'd played and several of the players on our side whom I'd forgotten. We had similar memories of the ground itself, surrounded by trees that stood almost at the boundary edge and with an old score box we'd had to unlock, but had no real idea of where it was or what it was called. The club we'd played had a website which listed several grounds they used, but it wasn't on there. Simon got in touch with them, but no-one playing now knew of it.

Did it exist? Of course it did – somewhere. Or at least it had done. We would never see it again. Maybe it was one of those cricket grounds that falls slowly out of use until people begin to forget that it was ever there. It was a marginal place now, ephemeral, not quite real. Like Mark Ramprakash's runs, and like so many games and places and people, it had been reduced to fragments.

But if I stumble on it one day, I'm sure I'll know it. I can see it now, feel what the weather was like, picture the old boundary markers that lots of grounds used to use, pieces of tin painted white, bent into a V-shape and dropped at intervals around the line.

It's the grounds themselves that trigger these memories. I grew up playing around Hampshire and Surrey on some of the oldest cricket fields in England, and they had similar characteristics: small, irregular, with swales and humps in the outfield that caught the light. They hold those long-off matches too. Going there brings them back again, and not just for me but for everyone who has played there, centuries of people: David Harris at Hartley Wintney. Silver Billy Beldham at Holt Pound. Beauclerk at Farnham. All of them at Hambledon, on Windmill Down and Broadhalfpenny Down by The Bat And Ball, where stout Richard Nyren served drinks and John Nyren listened as stories of long-ago matches were told.

It was like Dub Traynor said on his radio show (see page 216), that sadness gave the game its poetry. It was easy to get lost in the immediacy of it, the non-stop nature of modern cricket, but that was all transient noise. The past and time are its real subjects, its true measures, and they exist in the grounds where we all once stood.

Bat, Ball and Field

Postscript
Cricket as Metaphor

Samuel Beckett would sometimes tell actors playing Vladimir and Estragon in *Waiting for Godot* to imagine that they were batting at numbers five and six in a Test match, and the first wicket was yet to fall. Beckett remains the only Nobel prize winner to have appeared in Wisden: he played two first-class games for Dublin University, both against Northants, in 1925 and '26 as an all-rounder, opening the batting and sending down 23 overs of left-arm medium pace. Cricket offered him some shorthand for the existential angst of waiting around.

For a sport so ritualised and repetitious, one that resets itself after every single delivery, cricket has apparently endless uses as a representation of something else, its language standing in for much wider themes. In 1990, a few months before she was ousted as prime minister, Margaret Thatcher gave a speech welcoming a new Lord Mayor of London:

Since I first went into bat eleven years ago, the score at your end has ticked over nicely, you are the 663rd Lord Mayor. At the prime minister's end, we are stuck on 49. I am still at the crease, though the bowling has been pretty hostile of late. And in case anyone doubted it, can I assure you there will be no ducking the bouncers, no stonewalling, no playing for time. The bowling's going to get hit all round the ground. That's my style.

Nonetheless, she didn't quite make it to the close of play. It happens all the time in cricket. Thatcher's successor John Major, a true obsessive, went from Buckingham Palace, where he gave his resignation to the Queen, to the Oval to watch Surrey. Theresa May spent her first day out of office watching England play Ireland at Lord's.* In both cases, cricket wasn't just a consolation, but seemed to stand for something wider – a sense that life went on. Major wrote a very good history of early cricket, *More Than a Game*. May knighted two cricketers, Andrew Strauss and her childhood hero Geoffrey Boycott, in her resignation honours list. During May's travails, the leader of the opposition Jeremy Corbyn claimed that his 'big dream' was to open the batting for England, a nakedly obvious statement of his ambition for the top job, although his claim to be a fan of the game was somewhat undermined by a garbled description of a West Indies win over England and his subsequent meeting with Garry Sobers: 'The West Indies bowled England out for a very low total and then they won on the same innings. And I

---

* Along with annoying farmers by running through their wheat fields, May confessed that in her youth she'd had a poster of Geoffrey Boycott on her wall, the ultimate teenage rebellion.

Bat, Ball and Field

THE ARMY
ISN'T ALL WORK

said: "I thought Garry Sobers was absolutely fantastic" – and I met him the night before the great victory.'

Cricket has its political aspect, an almost Orwellian rendering of bowlers as servants and batsmen as masters (see WG Grace: Bowler page 230). The most famous line from the most famous book about the game, CLR James' *Beyond a Boundary*, 'what do they know of cricket, who only cricket know?' implies that another dimension is needed to fully understand the sport and its meanings. The line itself is a twist on Kipling's 'what do they know of England' and in conjunction with the title is saying that what happens inside the boundary can be interpreted and amplified outside. In his preface, James disqualifies the book right away as 'neither cricket reminiscences nor autobiography'. It does have both, though, and his portraits of players like Wilton St Hill, and the evocations of memory and place are superb. But *Beyond a Boundary* has come to be read as a history of colonialism and as a Marxist interpretation of the sport. That makes it sound cold and rigid, which it is not, but from the game James draws threads of race and class throughout the islands of the West Indies and in England and refracts them through the game, its Laws and its customs. 'Cricket,' he wrote, 'had plunged me into politics long before I was aware of it. When I did turn to politics, I did not have too much to learn.'

More often, though, the game is a gentle symbol used as a stand-in for a kind of eternal Englishness that the war poets yearned for. In the final episode of *Blackadder Goes Forth*, just before the men are due to go over the top, Captain Darling says to Blackadder: 'Rather hoped I'd get through the whole show. Go back to work at Pratt & Sons. Keep wicket for the Croydon Gentlemen. Marry Doris.' Cricket is perfect for sitcoms because they almost always involve class, and cricket very quickly allows social archetypes and class notions to appear. *Dad's*

Army has a cricket episode, and you don't need to watch it to know what sort of a player Mainwaring will be, or Pike, or Sergeant Wilson. *Ever Decreasing Circles* has a wonderful cricket episode. *Fawlty Towers* has the cricket-obsessed Major Gowan. English detective series love cricket episodes, too. *Inspector Morse* has a cricket mystery, 'Deceived by Flight', written by Anthony Minghella. *Midsomer Murders* has two. They arise in part from the game's sense of itself, created by the Victorians' cheesy rendering of it as Christian and moral, and the romanticised visions of its early, great writers. In that way, it's also inseparable from its settings, whether a sunlit Lord's or the idealised village green. They harbour its image.

In the summer of 2019, Steve Smith and David Warner returned to the Australian Test team after their bans for the sandpaper affair. Smith succeeded spectacularly, Warner failed almost comically badly. They were both booed, sometimes in panto fashion, sometimes more darkly, especially when Smith's relentlessness brought him milestone after milestone and comparisons with the Don. It seemed ridiculous, but there was a definite feeling that Warner was experiencing some kind of karmic retribution from the game, which was gleefully celebrated by the crowds. Smith had somehow escaped, and a section of fans felt cheated by that. 'We'll decide when to stop booing him', one told a journalist.

Here was another interpretation of the game's moral force – that it contained some kind of intelligent design that could reward and punish. This was impossible of course, an entirely false equivalence. Cricket, like every other sport, showed that some of its greatest players could, outside of the game, be made up of the paltriest human qualities. Like life, it wasn't based on a system of fairness.

It made me think about my own interpretation of the game, the meaning I laid on it. I think it is neither benign nor malignant, but genuinely impassive. It has its physical challenges but its real arena is its vast psychological depth. There, anyone can think anything they want to about it and find something that agrees with them. Cricket is complex, and that complexity lends itself to multiple ways of explaining it or using it as a metaphor.

In the autumn of 2019, at the end of a cricket tour of Corfu, I went to a talk by one of the players, the writer Anthony McGowan. It was held in late afternoon in a glade on the side of a mountain with sunlight pouring through the trees, and it was based around his book, *How To Teach Philosophy To Your Dog*. But instead of dogs – or maybe we were the dogs – he began to explain how each successive branch of philosophy would approach the moral dilemma of whether or not a batsman should walk when they'd edged the ball to the keeper. The stoics would go along with the umpire's decision whether they agreed with it or not; the epicureans, dedicated to pleasure, would stay if they were enjoying batting more than anything else; the Nietzschean *Übermensch* would do whatever they wanted to do at the time, regardless of the other players and the crowd; the utilitarians would consider which outcome offered the most benefits for the game as a whole. It was a brilliantly clever way of framing an introduction to the different strands of thought, but it illustrated just how big the game was, too, and how just one of its myriad happenings could contain an entire world within it.

A Note on Women's Cricket

The rise of the women's professional game over the last few years has been significant and meaningful for the future of cricket. That I haven't written much about it in this book is entirely my failing: I haven't seen enough, and don't know enough about it, to write on it with any confidence. I have had one encounter with England's great opening bowling pair, Katherine Brunt and Anya Shrubsole, in the nets at Loughborough. Brunt hit me on the head, and I played and missed like a novice, so it's fair to say that things very much went their way, and when Shrubsole bowled that extraordinary and decisive spell at a packed Lord's to win the World Cup final against India in 2017, I could at least empathise with India's batters – she had been way too good. That aside, I felt I'd be failing both the game and any potential readers if I tried to write any more about it. Instead, I highly recommend Rafaelle Nicholson's *Ladies and Lords: A History of Women's Cricket* in Britain as a literary way into women's cricket.

Acknowledgements

The essays in *Bat, Ball and Field* are new, but occasional parts of them sprung from other commissions. I'd like to acknowledge *Wisden Cricketers' Almanack* for the piece about groundsmen that allowed me to meet Gary Barwell at Edgbaston soon after Virat Kohli had made the hundred mentioned on page 126 and stand exactly where it happened, and Sky Sports for the visit with Shane Warne on page 178. I met Chris King at Gray-Nicolls, a trip mentioned on page 53, for a story on bat making for ESPNcricinfo. I can't remember why I was at the Middlesex press day mentioned in the essay about Phillip Hughes (page 63), but thanks to whoever sent me ... I worked with Simon Jones on his memoir *The Test*, and he told me about bowling to Brian Lara in Antigua (page 82) and about dropping the chance off Mike Kasprowicz at Edgbaston in 2005 (page 243). I'd also like to thank Alan Butcher for talking and later writing about Sylvester Clarke (page 216), and Arthur Conan Doyle's biographer Andrew Lycett for his help on Stonyhurst College (page 148) and Tom Spedegue (page 202). Thanks also to Jonathon Green, baron of slang, for the newspaper clipping about overarm bowling (page 176), Tom Holland, Mr Sport himself, for translating *In Certamen Pilae* (page 19) and Matt Thacker, who commissioned the piece about the nightwatchman (for *The Nightwatchman's* first issue) excerpted on page 110, and for setting up a memorable meeting with Mark Ramprakash, mentioned in the essay about hating fielding (page 241) and in 'Endless Summer' (page 247). Finally, Anthony McGowan for his talk on the philosophy of walking (page 256) and my old Basingstoke teammate Simon Lock (page 249). Maybe we will find that ground one day ...

Also the following books: Gideon Haigh, *On Warne* (Simon & Schuster) and *Mystery Spinner* (Aurum); Martin Amis, *Money* (Vintage) and *The Information* (Vintage); Sheehan Karunatilaka, *Chinaman* (Vintage); Richard Tomlinson, *Amazing Grace* (Abacus); Vic Marks *Original Spin* (Allen & Unwin); Chris Gayle *Six Machine* (Penguin); Mike Brearley *On Cricket* (Constable), and the websites ESPNCricinfo and Cricket Archive. Also, Andy Bull's piece for the *Guardian, Holding to Boycott: The Greatest Over Ever or Just the Most Memorable?* and Russell Jackson's story for the same newspaper, *Gray Nicolls Scoop, the Bat Every Kid Wanted, Turns 40.*

Thanks also to Hazel Eriksson and Myles Archibald at William Collins; Tom Killingbeck; my agent Lucy Luck; Charlie Campbell; Richard Beard; Dr Tim Beard and all of my teammates at Authors CC; and Yasmin Hounsell, Lily Hotten, Ruby Hotten, Maureen Hotten, Drew, Julie Simpson, Caroline Cope, James Bowyer.

Well batted George John Camden Hotten.

Index

Page references in *italics*
indicate images.

Accrington Cricket Club
   186
Adelaide Oval 39
Advisory County Cricket
   Committee 226*n*
Afghanistan (national
   cricket team) 10, *11, 25n*
Afridi, Shahid 22*n*, *101*
Agar, Ashton 71
age, player 22*n*
Agnew, Jonathan 107
Ajmal, Saeed 211, 214
Akhtar, Shoaib 122*n*, 159,
   220
Akram, Wasim 208, *226*
All England 68, 177, 231

Altham, Harry 125–6, 125*n*
Amis, Martin 179–80,
   180*n*, 182, 188, 199–200
   Money 182
   The Information 216–17,
   250
Anderson, Ian 7
Anderson, James 7, 62*n*,
   119, 129–30, 130*n*, 131–3
apartheid 221, 223
Archer, Jofra 159*n*
Arlott, John 16, 154*n*,
   203–4, 218, 219, 232–3
Arthur, Mickey 134
Arya Gurukul 68, 69
Ashes, The 71
   (1932–3) Bodyline series
   32n, 155
   (1974–5) 59

(1981) 31
(1986–7) 133*n*
(1993) 25*n*, 186–7
(1994–5) *36–7*
(2005) 82, 118–19, 133, 189,
   192–7, 200, 243
(2009) 63, 119, 133
(2010–11) 133*n*, 140
(2013) 71, 133–7
(2015) 49
(2019) 13–15, 51*n*, 119,
   136–7, 142*n*, 159
Asylum, Kingston 85–6, 87
Atherton, Mike 76–7, 114,
   116*n*, 157, 189
Athey, Bill 227
Attapatu, Marvan 107
Austin, Richard 'Danny
   Germs' 223

Australia (national cricket
     team)
  Ashes *see* Ashes, The
  Bradman and *see*
     Bradman, Don
  Brearley and 31
  'buddy' system 116
  Glenn McGrath and 36,
     66, 118, 118*n*, 122*n*, 130*n*,
     194–5, 196, 200
  Good Blokes and Shit
     Blokes 66–7
  greatest era of 66
  Hughes and *see* Hughes,
     Philip
  ICC membership status
     10, *11*
  Lara and 79, 83, 86–7
  sandpaper affair 137,
     137*n*, 255
  Steve Smith and 44, 46, 50,
     51*n*, 67, 133–43, 159, 255
  T20 internationals and
     96
  Warne and *see* Warne,
     Shane
Australian Academy 214
Australian Centre of
     Excellence 211
Australian Cricket Board
     198

bails 25
Bairstow, David 172*n*, 173
ball 144–237
  Ball of the Century
     185–8, *188*
  Bodyline and 155

bowling, evolution of
     220, *220*
bowling speeds 159
  condition of, changes in
     156–8
  cross seam 212
  doosra 175, 208–11, 214
  Dropper 202–7, 215, 218*n*
  duel between heroic
     batsman and demon
     bowler, notion of 154
  Duke ball 130, 151, 151*n*
  fastest deliveries
     recorded 159
  height of bowler 22*n*
  inswinger 213
  leg cutter 212
  lengths *146*
  lines *147*
  mystery spin 175
  off cutter 212
  origins of 150–9, *150*
  outswinger 213
  over 160–73
  overarm bowling 21, 90,
     126, 176–7, 220, *220*,
     231, 235, 260
  physical danger/
     psychological angst
     and 153–5
  protective equipment,
     grudging acceptance
     of 155
  reverse swing bowling
     156, 213, *213*
  roundarm bowling 21,
     90, 154, 177, 178, 206*n*,
     215, 220, *220*, 235, 237

sadness in cricket and
     216–29
  seam bowling 114, 146,
     156, 157, 212
  size and weight of 22
  sound of 152–3
  Spedegue's Dropper
     202–7, 215, 218*n*
  spin bowling 174, *174*
  Stonyhurst ball 148–51
  swing bowling 130, 131,
     132, 139, 156, 213, *213*
  Sylvester Clarke and
     222–9
  underarm bowling 21,
     90, 153, 220, *220*
  Warne and 178–201
  weight and hardness of
     152
  WG Grace as bowler
     230–7
Bancroft, Cameron 137*n*
Bangladesh (national
     cricket team) 10, *11*, 107,
     115, 122–3, 211
Barbados *81*, 160–1
Barker, Andy 186
Barrington, Ken 172
Barty-King, Hugh 150–1
Barwell, Gary 126–7, 129,
     156, 259
Basingstoke Cricket Club
     249
bat 28–143
  ages/evolution of 90, *91*
  bat names 88–90
  batsman as hero 30–52
  batsman height 22, 22*n*

batsmen having a bowl
113–23, 230–7

batting average,
Bradman's 44–52

batting averages,
calculating 40

batting averages,
comparing 46

batting averages, lowest
117

batting streaks, best 84

batting technique, early
evolution of 90

dismissal, modes of
106–7

earliest 90

Gayle and 92–109

groundsman 126–7,
136–7, 156

highest scores 68, 69

how to make/types of
58–62, 90

Hughes and 63–70

kit, batsman 43

Kohli and 126–33

Lara and 76–87

Martin and 113–23

most runs in all cricket
78

natural material of 22

nightwatchman 110–12

playing forward 32, 33

Ramp 97, 97

reverse sweeping 96, 96

rotary method 141–2

Scoop 57–9, 57n, 62, 90,
97, 97

sixes, most scored 101

Smith and 133–43

switch-hitting 96, 97, 97

wood material of 53–6

Beard, Alistair 39, 42

Beard, Dr Donald 39–40

Beard, Matthew 39, 42

Beauclerk, Lord Frederick
154–5, 155n, 250

Beckett, Samuel 251

Beldham, 'Silver' Billy 24,
34, 250

Bell, Ian 190–1, 194, 197

Benaud, Richie 47, 184, 193

Berkmann, Marcus: Rain
Men 217

Big Bash 103, 138, 159

Billings, Sam 60–2

Bird, Dickie 25n

birdsong 17–18

Birley, Derek: A Social
History of English
Cricket 25

Blackadder Goes Forth 254

Blofeld, Henry 45n, 244

Blundstone Arena 92, 102

Bodyline series 1932–3
32n, 155

Bonair-Agard, Roger 161

books, cricket 217

Booth, Lawrence 70

Bosanquet, Bernard 183n,
202

Bosey 183n

Botha, Johan 210, 211

Botham, Ian 31–2, 31n, 59,
106, 107, 154n, 173, 218,
221

Bowden, Billy 195, 196, 197

bowling. See ball and
individual bowler name

box 43

Boycott, Geoffrey 30–8,
33n, 78, 106, 160–73,
163n, 172n, 223, 227,
252, 252n

Bradley, Bill 203

Bradman, Don 35, 48n,
51n, 92, 120, 184, 190n,
231, 232, 241n, 243–4

batting average 27, 40,
44–52, 116

batting streaks 84

commercial and
business dealings 48n

fame 47, 48

Gayle and 98, 99

Hayden and 66

height 22n, 23

Hughes and 68, 72

innings that Bradman
regarded as his best 45

introvert, aloof and
remote from other
players 45, 47, 128n

Lara and 79, 87

records held by 44–5

retirement 47

rotary method 120, 141–2

Smith and 137, 139, 141,
142n, 143

Thomson and 42, 42n, 44

Bradman, John 48

Brand, Henry 26

Brathwaite, Kraigg 62, 62n

Brearley, Mike 30–3, 32n,
35, 59n, 218

On Cricket 30

Briant, Alexander 149

Brief Discors Contayning Certayn Reasons Why Catholiques Refuse To Go To Church, A 148-9

Broadhalfpenny Down 250

Brunt, Katherine 159, 258

'buddy' system 116, 116n

Bull, Andy 173

Bumrah, Jasprit 117, 120

Burdett, Les 39

Butcher, Alan 157, 223, 224, 225

Buttler, Jos 244

Butts, Clyde 42n

Campion, Edmund 148-149

Cardus, Neville 15, 24, 45, 128n, 218-19, 221

Carew, Dudley 218-19

catching 242-6, *245*
  credited to fielder 26
  dropped catches 19, 69, 130, 242-3, 245-6
  fatalities and 25-6
  how to catch a cricket ball *245*
  Stokes 14
  Tomlinson 61

chain 21-4, 26, 27, 152, 155

Champions Trophy 114

Chanderpaul, Shivnarine 93-4, 142

Chandrasekhar, Bhagwath 115n

Chappell, Greg 42n, 59, 59n, 209

Chappell, Ian 57-8, 59, 209

Chappell, Trevor 209

Chibhabha, Chamu 25n

chucking, aka throwing 211, 211n

Churchill, Winston 47

Clarke, Michael 67, 85, 134, 180, 197

Clarke, Sylvester 161, 222-9

Close, Brian 155, 162, 162n

Coles, Matt 61, 62

Collins, AEJ 67, 68n, 69, 70

Collins, Pedro 86, 222

Collymore, Corey 222

ComBat 59, 59n

Conan Doyle, Arthur 202-3, 259-60
  Memoirs and Adventures 206
  The Story of Spedegue's Dropper 202-15, 218n

Constantine, Leary 218

Cook, Alastair 22n, 114, 136

Cook, Jimmy 157

Corbyn, Jeremy 252-3

Cowan, Ed 134

Cowdrey, Colin 155

Cricinfo 27, 61

Cricket Australia 137n

Cricket Club 24

Cricket New South Wales 138

cricketers of the century 190, 190n

Croft, Colin 164, 168, 169, 219, 222

cross seam 212

Cummins, Anderson 80

Cummins, Pat 14, 15

Daniel, Wayne 161, 162, 164, 222, 226

Dark, James 151-2, 152n

Dark, Robert 151

Darwin, Bernard 232

Davidson, Alan 67

Davis, Charles 51

Decision Review System (DRS) 106

Dhanawade, Pranav 68, 69

Dhoni, MS 69, *101*, 114

Dicker, The 19

Dilshan, Tillakaratne 97, *97*

dismissal, modes of 106-7

diuretics 198-9, 198n, 200

doosra 175, 183n, 208-11, 214

Douglas-Home, Sir Alec 164

Dowlin, Travis 114

dropped catches 19, 130, 242-3

Dublin University 251

Duke ball 130, 151, 151n

Duleep Trophy 70

Durham County Cricket Club 80

Eager, Patrick 171

Edgbaston 44n, 45n, 79, 80, 87n, 126, 129, 131, 133, 136, 194, 243

Edwardes, Charlotte 103-4

Elizabeth I, Queen 15, 147–8
Elliott, Bruce 214
Engineer, Faroukh 226
England (national cricket team)
  Ashes *see* Ashes, The
  Brearley and *see* Brearley, Mike
  first Test match century 232
  Grace and *see* Grace, WG
  ICC membership status 10, *11*
  Kohli and 129, 130, 131–3
  Lara and 76–7, 79, 80, 82
  longest test match and 13
  politicians and 252–3
  unofficial tours 223
  Warne and 186–97, 200
  West Indies versus (14 March 1981) 160–73
  women's team 258
  World Cup final (2019) 244
Essex County Cricket Club 114, 157
European Court of Justice 226*n*
Evans, Godfrey 206
Excalibur 59

facial hair, gallery of *61*
failure, cricket and 242
Fairbrother, Neil 157
fastest deliveries recorded 159
fatalities 25–6
Faulkner, James 67

Fearnley, Duncan 59
Fernando, Vishwa 119
field 238–50
  catching 242–6, *245*
  fielding positions *240*
  hating fielding 241–6
  memory/nostalgia and 247–50
Fiennes, William 217
Fingleton, Jack 44*n*
Fitzpatrick, Cathryn 159
Fitzroy, Lady Anne 18
Fleming, Damian 103
Fletcher, Duncan 116, 116*n*, 195
Flintoff, Andrew 71, 115, 193–4
flipper 174, 184, 193
Foot, David 219
franchise cricket 95, 102, 104, 116, 130, 142*n*, 143, 214, 226*n*
franchise player 95
Fraser, Angus 63, 64, 77, 87, 116*n*
Fraser, Malcolm 47
Fry, CB 79, *84*, 234
Fuller-Eberle, Victor 69

Gambhir, Gautam *84*
Garner, Arthur 57
Garner, Joel 161, 164, 165, 168, 169, 226
Gatting, Mike 37, 96, 186–7, 187*n*, 223
Gavaskar, Sunil 126, 126*n*, 128–9, 128*n*, 132, 140, 163*n*

Gayle, Chris 22*n*, 41, 92–109, *101*
  Six Machine 99–100, 109
Gentlemen against the Players 154
Gentlemen of the South 234
George IV, King 151
Gibson, Alan 219
Gilchrist, Adam 13, 15, 66, 192, 195, 196
Gillespie, Jason 86–7
Glamorgan County Cricket Club 79, 157, 227
Goldwin, William: *In Certamen Pilae* (On a Ball Game) 19, 21, 24, 26
Gooch, Graham 25*n*, 37, 59, 74, 75, 75*n*, 78, 114, 157, 161, 166, 172, 222, 223
googly 132, 175, 183–4, 183*n*, 193
Goswami, Juhlan 159
Gower, David 57*n*, 74–6, 222
Grace, WG 22, 35, 76, 99, 241*n*, 244, 254
  batting technique 96, 105, 128, 215
  bowling 177, 230–7
  Conan Doyle and 202–3, 203*n*
  Gray-Nicolls and 56
  Hughes and 64*n*
  innings that created modern batting 68, 68*n*, 176

top batting streaks 84

Gray-Nicolls 56, 57, 57*n*, 59, 62

Greenidge, Gordon 161, 166, 171, 226

Greig, Ian 157*n*

Greig, Tony 157*n*, 162, 167, 210

Grimmett, Clarrie 184, 185*n*

groundsman 126–7, 136–7, 156

Grove Park 234

Gunter, Edmund 20, 21, 152

Guptill, Martin 244

Haddin, Brad 136

Hadlee, Richard 227

Haigh, Gideon 48, 188
  Mystery Spinner 209–10
  On Warne 182*n*, 192–3, 192*n*

Hair, Daryl 211*n*

Hambledon 153*n*, 250

Hamilton, Duncan 128*n*, 218

Hampshire County Cricket Club 61–2, 125*n*, 180–1, 225, 226, 226*n*, 247, 250

Handled the Ball 25*n*, 107

Haq, Majid 159

Harmison, Steve 243

Harris, David 153, 153*n*, 154, 220, 250

Harris, Paul 64

Harris Trophy 70

Harvey, Ian 66

Hayden, Matthew 66, 67, 82, 83, 195, 196

Haynes, Desmond 161, 165, 171

Hazlewood, Josh 67

Headingley 13, 119, 131

Headley, George 141–2

Hensher, Philip 200

Herstmonceux Castle 1, 18–19

Hick, Graeme 36, 78, 186–7

highest scores 68, 69, 80, 82, 99, 115, 123, 135

Hills, Tom 154

hitting the ball twice 107

hitting the wicket 107

Hobbs, Jack 75*n*, 78, 190*n*, 234, 234*n*

Holding, Michael 160–73, 223

Holland, Bob 184–5

Hollies, Eric 44, 44*n*, 52, 116

Holt Pound 250

homeworkgate 134

Hopps, David 219

Hossain, Shahadat 123

Howard, John 47

Howard, Mark 103

Hughes, Kim 31, 217

Hughes, Merv 25*n*

Hughes, Phillip 63–73, 64*n*, 134, 137*n*

Hughes, Simon: *A Lot of Hard Yakka* 156–7

hundreds
  Boycott and 38, 172

Bradman's most times scoring a hundred in a single session of play 45

Collins and 70

double-hundreds 70, 71, 80, 85–6, 108, 157, 157*n*

first hundred in international T20 cricket 98

Gayle and 98, 99, 108

Grace and 231, 232, 236

hundred first-class hundreds 221, 231, 232, 241

hundred on debut 70, 71

Kohli and 129, 142*n*

Lara and 79, 80, 85–6

Ramprakash and 221, 241, 247

Tendulkar and 70, 142*n*

Test cricket's fastest 121*n*

thousand runs and a hundred wickets in a season 236

three Australians score more Test hundreds than Bradman 66

three hundreds in first three innings as Test captain 129

triple-hundreds 157

youngest Indian to make Test hundred on debut 70

youngest player to score a hundred in each innings of a Test 64

Hundred, The 165*n*
Hurley, Elizabeth 179, 198

India (national cricket
    team) 42, 51*n*, 69, 98,
    114, 121*n*, 140, 177, 186,
    210
  ICC membership status
    and *10*, 11
  Kholi and 127, 128–31,
    130*n*, 131, 132
  Twenty20 World Cup
    and 94–5
  World Cup and 258
Indian Premier League
    (IPL) 92–5, 98, 99, 121*n*,
    130–1, 179
inswinger 131, 213
International Cricket
    Council (ICC) 11, 127,
    138, 211, 214
Ireland (national cricket
    team) *10*, 14, 252
Ironmonger, Bert *117*
Iverson, Jack 175, 209–10

Jackman, Robin 172*n*
Jacobs, John 124–5, 141
James, CLR 217–18
  Beyond a Boundary 254
Jardine, Douglas 32, 32*n*
Jayawardene, Mahela
    107
Jenner, Terry 140, 185,
    193, 211
Johnson, Brian 107
Jones, Allan 156
Jones, Geraint 243

Jones, Simon 82, 243
Jumbo 59

Kallicharran, Alvin 226,
    226*n*
Kallis, Jacques 84, 115
Karunatilaka, Shehan:
    Chinaman 205–6, 215,
    217, 218*n*
Kashmir willow 54
Kasparov, Garry 188
Kasprowicz, Mike 243
Katich, Simon 195, 197
KC Gandhi 68, 69
Keating, Frank 172
  *Another Bloody Day in
    Paradise* 172–3
Kensington Oval,
    Bridgetown, Barbados
    160–1, 169
Kent County Cricket Club
    19, 60–2, 202–3, 206,
    232*n*
Kent League 138
Kerrigan, Simon 133, 135,
    136
KFC Big Bash T20
    tournament (2008) 138
Khan, Imran 224, 226
Khan, Moin 210
Khan, Rashid 41
Khawaja, Usman 134
King, Chris 53, 54, 55, 56,
    60, 62, 259
King, Collis 161
kit, batsman *43*
Kitchen, Merv 219
Klinger, Michael 99

Kohli, Virat 44, 126–33, 140,
    142, 142*n*, 143, 241*n*, 259
Kolkata Knight Riders 92
Kolpak ruling 226*n*

Labuchagne, Marnus 159
Lancashire County
    Cricket Club 114, 133,
    157, 157*n*, 224–5, 226,
    227, 230
Lara, Brian 23, 35, 62,
    76–87, 84, 87*n*, 93–4,
    142, 163*n*, 259
laws of cricket
  dismissal, modes of
    106–7
  doosra and 211–12, 211*n*
  hitting the ball twice 107
  Law 17.1 164
  Law 21.2 220
  Law 41.3 213
  Obstructing the Field 25,
    25*n*, 107
  written down for the first
    time (1744) 24–6, 88
Lawson, Jermaine 222
Law, Stuart 66
Laxman, VVS 115
Leach, Jack 13–14, 119
Lee, Brett 122*n*, 159, 194
leg before wicket 106
leg cutter 212
leg spin 115*n*, 134, 138, 174,
    175, 183–6, 189, 209
Lehmann, Darren 134
Leicestershire County
    Cricket Club 79, 154,
    157, 222

length bowling 12, 90, *146*

length of a cricket pitch 20, 21–2

Lennard, Earl of Sussex, Thomas 18–19

Le Roux, Garth 226

Lewis, Chris 77

Lillee, Dennis 59, *59n*, 74, 155, 163–4, 169

Lillywhite Jr., James 233

Lillywhite, John 177

lines, bowling *147*

Liston, Sonny 222, 223, 228, 229

Lloyd, Clive 85, 160, 162, 167, 170, 224, 226, *226n*, 227–8

Lloyd, David *116n*, 155

Lock, Simon 249

Lord's Cricket Ground 7, 11, 14, 25, *25n*, 45, 62, 63, 64, 69, 71, 73, 79, 94, 151, 152, 154, 159, *164n*, 177, 194, 202–3, 205, 252, 255, 258

Lord, Thomas 24–5, *152n*

Lucas, Bunny 206, *206n*

MacGill, Stuart 211

Macksville RSL Cricket Club 65

MacLaren, Archie 80

Magnum 59

Magnus Effect 184, 186, 190

Mailey, Arthur 184

Major, John 252

More Than a Game 252

Malan, Dawid 132

Malik, Shoaib 210

Malinga, Lasith 120, 215

Mallett, Ashley 42, *42n*, 211

Mandela, Nelson 47

map of cricket *10–11*

Marks, Vic: *Original Spin* 219, 221

Marshall, Malcolm 74, 161, 164, 222–9

Martin, Chris 113–23, *117*, *121n*, 180

Martin, Ray 199–200

Marx, Groucho 7

Marylebone Cricket Club (MCC) 75, 90, 97, *125n*, 202–3, 220, *236n*

Coaching Manual 125

The MCC Cricket Coaching Book 125–6

May, Theresa 252, *252n*

McCrae, Donald 104

McCullum, Brendon 99, *101*, 121, *121n*

McGowan, Anthony: *How To Teach Philosophy To Your Dog* 256

McGrath Breast Cancer Foundation 118

McGrath, Glenn 36, 66, 118, *118n*, *122n*, *130n*, 194–5, 196, 200

McLaughlin, Mel 93, 102–4, 108–9

Melbourne Cricket Ground (MCG) 186, 201

Melbourne Renegades 92

memory, cricket and 247–50

Mendis, Kamindu 206–7

Merlyn bowling machine 189–91

metaphor, cricket as 251–6

Meyer, RJO 206

Mickelson, Phil 141

Middlesex County Cricket Club *32n*, 63–4, 70, 79, 116, 156, 187, 226, *226n*, 259

MIG club 70

Miles, Tony 188

Millfield School 206

Modi, Lalit 94–5

Moduretic 198

Mohammad, Hanif 80

Morris, Hugh 157

Morris, John 80

Muller, Scott 66–7

Mumbai Indians 95

Muralitharan, Muttiah 210–11, *211n*

Murray, David 161, 167, 223

Mushtaq, Saqlain 175, *183n*, 207

Mynn, Alfred 154, *154n*, 155, 220

mystery spin 175

Narine, Sunil 175, 214–15

Nash, Malcolm *226n*

Nason, David 48

NatWest Trophy 114

Nawaz, Sarfraz 226

Nel, Andre 70

Nemesis 60–2

Newbery, John 57, 59

Newbery, Len 57

New South Wales Cricket
    Club 65, 67–8, 72, 138,
    192, 192*n*
New Zealand (national
    cricket team) 10, *11*, 49,
    71, 94, 97, 101, 114, 117,
    118, 118*n*, 121, 121*n*, 130,
    159, 164, 244
nightwatchman 14, 86,
    110–12, 135
Nixon, Thomas 90
Noakes, Tim 141, 142*n*
non-stop nature of
    modern cricket 130–1
Noorbhai, Habib 141, 142*n*
Northamptonshire
    County Cricket Club
    226*n*, 232*n*, 251
notch 26–7, 155
Nottinghamshire County
    Cricket Club 226*n*
Nyren, John: *The
    Cricketers of My Time*
    27, 153, 153*n*, 154*n*, 250
Nyren, Richard 250

O'Brien, Iain 120, 122–3
Obstructing the Field 25,
    25*n*, 107
ODI (one-day
    international) cricket
    11, 23, 25*n*, 41, 71, 94,
    108, 131, 142*n*, 210, 241*n*
off cutter 131, 212
O'Keefe, Kerry 140
O'Neill, Joseph:
    Netherland 218*n*, 246
O'Reilly, Bill 184, 185*n*

Old Trafford 162, 164*n*, 194
Onions, Graham 119
origins of cricket 17–19,
    21–4
Orwell, George 254
Ostler, Dominic 80
outswinger 131, 213
Oval, The 14, 27, 44, 68, 70,
    116, 133, 135–6, 137, 140,
    157, 157*n*, 162, 164*n*, 176,
    177, 194, 195, 200, 224,
    231, 233, 234, 237, 252
over 160–73
overarm bowling 21, 90,
    126, 176–7, 220, *220*,
    231, 235, 260
overseas players 225–6,
    226*n*
Oxford University 157*n*

Packer, Kerry 167
Pakistan (national cricket
    team) 10, *11*, 22*n*, 66, 77,
    94, 101, 138, 159, 164, 167,
    183*n*, 193, 208, 208*n*,
    209, 210, 213, 217, 228
Pakistan Cup 208
Pakistan International
    Airlines 208*n*
Panesar, Monty 119
Parkin, Cecil 'Cec' 218
Pattinson, James 67
Penney, Trevor 87*n*
Perera, Kusal 119
Perry, Elise 159
Perry, Nehemiah 85
Persons, Robert 148–9
PIA 208, 208*n*

Pierce, Tommy 165
Pietersen, Kevin 22*n*, 97,
    136, 194, 200, 221
Pilch, Fuller 233
Piper, Keith 80
pitch *20*, 21–4
playing forward *32*, *33*
polishing the ball 213
Pollard, Keiron 99
Pollock, Graeme 49
Ponting, Ricky 35, 66, 94,
    95, 107, 115, 120, 140,
    194–5, 196, 197
popping crease 20, 25, 146
Pound, Dick 199
Powell, Darren 222
Powerspot 57*n*
Pratt, Gary 195
Previtera, Joe 67
Procter, Mike 79, *84*,
    226–7, 226*n*
Pryor, Henry 186
Pryor, Matthew 186–7
Pune Warriors 99
Pycroft, James: *The
    Cricket Field* 27

Rajasthan Royals 179
'Rally Round The West
    Indies' 85
Ramp, The 97, *97*
Ramprakash, Mark 221,
    231, 241, 241*n*, 247, 249,
    260
Ranji Trophy 70
Rashid, Adil 132–3
Redfearn, Tom 69
Redgate, Sam 154

rest days, test match 42n
retiring 107
reverse sweeping 96, *96*
reverse swing 156, 213, *213*
Rice, Clive 227
Richards, Barry 16, 59, 221, 226, *226n*
Richards, Jack 225
Richards, Robert 'Swan' 57–8
Richards, Viv 34–5, *35n*, 59, 76, 85, 136, 162, 190n, 221
Richardson, Vic 184, 209
Richmond, Charles Lennox, Duke of 24
Ring, Doug 185
Rizvi Springfield 70
Roberts, Andy 115, 159, 161, 162, 164, 168, 169, 222, 224, 226
Robertson-Glasgow, RC 47
Robertson, Stuart 94
Roebuck, Peter
  It Never Rains 219–20
  Tangled Up In White 219–20
Rogers, Chris 103, 134
Root, Joe 131, 134, 143
Ross, Alan 219
rotary method 141–2, 142n
roundarm bowling 21, 90, 154, 177, 178, 206n, 215, 220, *220*, 235, 237
Rowe, Lawrence 223
Roy, Jason 244

Royal Challengers Bangalore 92, 98, 99, 130–1
Royal Engineers 69
Rudder, David 85
run out 106
runs
  hundreds *see* hundreds
  most in all cricket 78
  most in a single day's play 45, 87n
  most in Test cricket 163
rural game 19
Ryan, Christian: *Golden Boy* 217

sadness, cricket and 216–29, 250
Samiuddin, Osman 217
Sandham, Andy 68
Satirist and Sporting Chronicle of Sydney 177
saudade (nostalgia for something that may once have existed) 247–50
Scoop 57–9, *57n*, 62, 90, 97, *97*
score card *36*–7
scoring system 26–7, *36*–7, *40*, *41*
Scott, Chris 80
seam bowling 114, 146, 156, 157, 212
Sehwag, Virender 94
Sevenoaks Vine 138
7/7 bombings 194
Shami, Mohammed 130n

Sharma, Anushka 127
Sharma, Ishant 114
Sharma, Rohit *23*, *101*
Shaw, Prithvi 70
Sheffield Shield 67, 192
Sherwin, Ralph 149
Shillinglaw, Tony 141
shortest test match 13
Siddle, Peter 135–6
Simpson, Bob 67
Singh, Harbhajan 210
sitcoms 254–5
sixes, most scored *101*
slider 193
Small, John 151
Smith, Graeme 115
Smith, Robin 188
Smith, Steve 44, 46, 50, 51n, 67, 133–43, 159, 255
Snow, John 224
Sobers, Garfield 76–7, 77n, 80, 82–3, 161, 163, 163n, 165, 190n, 226n, 227–8, 252, 254
Somerset County Cricket Club 14, 79, 92, 157, 162, 206, 219, 226
Sommers 118
South Africa (national cricket team) 10, *11*, 13, 14, 50–1, 63–4, 67, 71, 79, 85, 94, 119, 130, 137n, 164, 165
South Africa, rebel tour of (1983) 223
South Australia Cricket Association 39
South versus North 154

Southerton, James 237
spin bowling 13–14, 42*n*,
    64, 85, 108, 115*n*, 133,
    134, 135, 138, 139, 156,
    159, 174, *174*, 175, 183–4,
    186, 188, 193, 195, 206,
    208, 210, 212, 214, 215,
    219*n*, 226
Spooner, RH 'Reggie' 218
Sri Lanka (national
    cricket team) 10, *11*, 21,
    22*n*, 50, 71, 97, 130, 193,
    207, 215
statistics 26–7
Steel, Allan 230, 237
Stevens, Lumpy 24
Stewart, Alec 228
Stewart, Micky 224, *225*
St Hill, Winston 218
St John's Recreation
    Ground 76
Stoddart, AE 69
Stoinis, Marcus 67
Stokes, Ben 13–15, 119, 132
Stonyhurst College 149, 203
Stonyhurst Cricket 148–51
Storer, Bill 203*n*
Strauss, Andrew 63, 195–6,
    197, 252
strike rates 41, 99
stumped 106
stumps *20*, 25
Super Over 244
Surrey County Cricket
    Club 68, 70, 125*n*, 131,
    138, 157, 157*n*, 176,
    225–6, 226*n*, 227, 228,
    231, 232, 234*n*, 250, 252

Surridge, Stuart 59
Sussex County Cricket
    Club 226
Sutherland Cricket Club
    138
swing bowling 130, 131,
    132, 139, 156, 213, *213*
switch-hitting 96, 97, *97*
Sydney Cricket Ground 72
Sydney Thunder 92, 103

Tahir, Imran 226*n*
Tait, Shaun 93, 159, 196
Taunton Deane Cricket
    Club 14
Taylor, Mark 66
Tendulkar, Sachin 22*n*,
    23, 69, 70, 95, 114, 115,
    127, 128–9, 128*n*, 132,
    140, 142*n*, 163*n*, 226*n*,
    241*n*
test match cricket 108
    batting averages 40
    drawn game 108, 185
    ICC membership status
        and 11
    longest test match 13
    rest days 42
    shortest test match 13
    world-record Test match
        score 62
Test Match Special 45*n*,
    107, 207*n*
Thatcher, Margaret 251–2
The Meaning of Cricket 249
Thomson, Jeff 39, 42, 42*n*,
    44, 115, 155, 159, 163–4,
    167

Thorpe, Graham 83, 228
timed out 107
'Timeless' Test 42*n*
Tip-Ball 149
Tomlinson, James 61–2
Tomlinson, Richard:
    Amazing Grace: The
    Man Who was WG 233
Top Gear 178
top spinner 174, 184, 209
toss 26
Trap-Ball 149
Trent Bridge 114, 194, 227
Trescothick, Marcus 196
Trinidad 77
triple-century 108, 121,
    232
Trott, Jonathan 136
Tufnell, Phil 76–7, 116
Tuhuha, Lea 159
Twenty20 (T20) 11, 22*n*,
    40, 41, 60, 92, 94, 95, 96,
    98, 99, 100, 102, 105, 108,
    121*n*, 126, 127, 130–1,
    138–9, 142, 142*n*, 159*n*,
    215, 245
Twort, Thomas 151–2
Twose, Roger 79

underarm bowling 21, 90,
    153, 220, *220*
University of West Indies
    167
University of Western
    Australia 214

Vaughan, Michael 82, 114,
    196–7

vegan ball 151*n*

Villiers, AB de 115, 143

Villiers, Barbara 18–19

Vinall, Jasper 26, 107

Vogues, AC 46, 49–51

Waiting for Godot 251

Walker, Tom 153–4

Walsh, Courtney 85, 115*n*

Walter Lawrence Trophy 227

Warne, Shane 40, 67, 76, 118*n*, 120, 122*n*, 139, 140, 178–201, 211, 236

Warner, David 134, 134*n*, 137*n*, 255

Warwickshire County Cricket Club 44, 79, 80, 226*n*

Watson, Shane 66, 86, 116, 118, 118*n*, 134, 135, 222

Waugh, Mark 118*n*

Waugh, Steve 66, 116, 116*n*, 136, 222

Wendt, Jana 182, 182*n*, 199

West Indies (national cricket team) 51*n*, 214, 224, 227, 228, 252–3, 254

England versus (14 March 1981) 160–73

four-pronged attack of the 1980s 155

Gayle and 93–4, 114

ICC membership status 10, *11*

inter-island rivalries 65

Lara and 76, 79, 83, 85–7

nations and territories *81*

ODI World Cup (1983) 98, 176

relations between players and the board 98

Scoop and 62, 62*n*

shortest test match and 13

tour of Australia (2005) 99

unofficial tours and 222

Vogues and 49–50

Warne and 186

West Indies Cricket Board 93

Western Suburbs 67

Wheeler, Barrie 57

White Conduit Fields 24

white willow (*Salix alba*) 53–4

wicket, modern three-stump 25*n*

Willis, Bob 32, 114

Willsher, Edgar 177, 234

Winchilsea, George Finch, Earl of 24

Wisden Cricket Monthly 217

Wisden Cricketers' Almanack 27, 47, 70, 259

cricketers of the century 190, 190*n*

Wisden, John 27, 47, 70

Woakes, Chris 133

Woodhill, Trent 138, 139, 140, 143

Woods, Tiger 23*n*, 141

Woolley, Frank 75*n*, 78

Woolmer, Bob 141, 142*n*

World Anti-Doping Agency 199

World Cup, Cricket 14, 66, 67, 136, 140

(1983) 94, 176

(1987) 96

(2003) 198

(2007) 94–5, 98, 118*n*, 142*n*

(2015) 159

(2019) 14, 244

(2022) 11

World Cup, T20 127, 138

(2007) 98

(2016) 22*n*

World Series Cricket 167

Yadav, Umesh 132

Yorkshire County Cricket Club 34, 226, 226*n*, 227, 232*n*

Yousuf, Mohammad 84, 115

Zaltzman, Andy 207*n*

Zimbabwe (national cricket team) 10, *11*, 25*n*, 82, 97